THE SEVEN YEARS WAR
AND THE OLD REGIME IN FRANCE

T0329644

THE
SEVEN YEARS WAR
AND THE
OLD REGIME IN FRANCE

The Economic and Financial Toll

JAMES C. RILEY

M C M L X X X V I

PRINCETON UNIVERSITY PRESS

COPYRIGHT © 1986 BY PRINCETON UNIVERSITY PRESS
PUBLISHED BY PRINCETON UNIVERSITY PRESS
41 WILLIAM STREET, PRINCETON, NEW JERSEY 08540
IN THE UNITED KINGDOM: PRINCETON UNIVERSITY PRESS
GUILDFORD, SURREY

ISBN 0-691-05488-6

PUBLICATION OF THIS BOOK HAS BEEN AIDED BY
GRANTS FROM THE NATIONAL ENDOWMENT FOR THE HUMANITIES
AND THE IRA O. WADE FUND OF PRINCETON UNIVERSITY PRESS

THIS BOOK HAS BEEN COMPOSED IN LINOTRON BASKERVILLE

CLOTHBOUND EDITIONS OF PRINCETON UNIVERSITY PRESS BOOKS
ARE PRINTED ON ACID-FREE PAPER, AND BINDING MATERIALS
ARE CHOSEN FOR STRENGTH AND DURABILITY

PRINTED IN THE UNITED STATES OF AMERICA
BY PRINCETON UNIVERSITY PRESS
PRINCETON, NEW JERSEY

FOR ANDREW

CONTENTS

LIST OF TABLES

LIST OF TABLES

x

LIST OF CHARTS

Des notions vagues sont une boussole infidelle . . .

FORBONNAIS

S'il n'arrive point d'événemens militaires.[1]

To notice war in the old regime is to notice the commonplace. Between 1701 and 1815 France engaged in sixty years of major wars, not counting occasional diplomatic conflicts or comparatively minor struggles such as the War of Polish Succession. The preceding century was also an era of war, although the century that followed was not: from 1816 to 1914 there were only six years of major wars in Europe. To us living in the twentieth century the endemic quality of war in the old regime is fascinating both for its contrast to nineteenth- and twentieth-century experience taken as a whole and for its similarity to experience between 1914 and 1945.

There is, of course, a literature of war. One form—multi-volume works written largely in the nineteenth century—provides a narrative account of each conflict from the biased perspective of each belligerent. Reading these books we need to remind ourselves that it is the same war under discussion in each work. Another form—rarer and in smaller books—examines either the army, the navy, the administration, the town, or the countryside during war. This literature, and the very frequency with which we encounter war in the investigation of other phenomena, gives us the feeling that we know these wars and can explain their effects.

What, in truth, do we know about old regime wars? Did these wars sap vital economic resources, and were they therefore responsible for the puzzling failure of early modern economies to develop a pattern of sustained growth? Did these wars dominate economic life and its sequences and cycles? Did these wars, which cost so much and led to an accumulation of debts, contribute to the administrative and political development of states forced to build more efficient institutions in order to survive? And did these wars, which seem to have been the chief business of early modern states, finally undermine the old regime?

Opinions about the toll of old regime wars are divided. To some, the effects seem serious, even devastating. Jean-Claude Perrot be-

---

[1] Algemeen Rijksarchief, The Hague, Legatiearchief, Eerste Afdeling, Frankrijk, 786, p. 68.

lieves that old regime war "rompt les équilibres économiques et, par remous, plonge en vibration les phénomènes démographiques." Jean Imbert and Henri Legohérel detect grave financial stresses and economic dislocations. Paul Butel maintains that war was the "fait essentiel de l'histoire économique du XVIIIᵉ siècle." Christopher Friedrichs finds that wars of the seventeenth and earlier eighteenth centuries had profound financial, economic, and demographic consequences for German cities.[2] To others, however, these same wars seem remarkable for their limited effects. Phyllis Deane believes that old regime wars were less disturbing economically than were earlier or later wars. A. H. John maintains that for England the wars of 1700-1763 stimulated mining and metallurgy. And René Baehrel suggests that France was only mildly affected, except for the profits of a few.[3] William H. McNeill, reviving the controversy that separated John U. Nef from a narrow construction of the views of Werner Sombart, offers the most startling view of all, arguing that seventeenth- and eighteenth-century wars were actually profitable to the states fighting them.[4]

The division of opinion is more noticeable still when we single out one war—for instance, the Seven Years War of 1756-1763. Michel Morineau finds that this war was profoundly disturbing to French finances.[5] Steven Kaplan says the war was economically and socially "demoralizing and disorganizing." Ernest Labrousse holds that the war brought "un effondrement record du commerce colonial."

[2] Respectively, Jean-Claude Perrot, *Genèse d'une ville moderne: Caen au XVIIIᵉ siècle* (2 vols.; Paris, 1975), II, 719; Jean Imbert and Henri Legohérel, *Histoire économique, des origines à 1789* (3rd ed.; Paris, 1979), 334-35; Paul Butel, *Les négociants bordelais, l'Europe et les Iles au XVIIIᵉ siècle* (Paris, 1974), 382; and Christopher R. Friedrichs, *Urban Society in an Age of War: Nordlingen, 1580-1720* (Princeton, 1979), 28-34 and 44-45. Also Robert Forster, *Merchants, Landlords, Magistrates: The Depont Family in Eighteenth-Century France* (Baltimore, 1980), 12, believes both that French trade expanded dynamically and that the mid-eighteenth-century wars "had a permanent debilitating effect upon French overseas trade."

[3] Phyllis Deane, "War and Industrialisation," in J. M. Winter, ed., *War and Economic Development* (Cambridge, 1975), 91; A. H. John, "War and the English Economy, 1700-63," *Economic History Review*, 7, no. 3 (1955), esp. 330-31; and René Baehrel, *Une croissance: La Basse-Provence rurale (fin XVIᵉ siècle-1789)* (2 vols.; Paris, 1961), I, 500-504.

[4] William H. McNeill, *The Pursuit of Power: Technology, Armed Force, and Society since A.D. 1000* (Chicago, 1982), 144 and *passim*.

[5] Michel Morineau, "Budgets de l'état et gestion des finances royales en France au dix-huitième siècle," *Revue historique*, 264, no. 2, no. 536 (1980), 298.

Daniel Zolla called it "une guerre terrible dont les conséquences désastreuses ont pesé si longtemps sur la France."[6] Other scholars describe the war as having "battered the economies of France's maritime centers," or as exhausting, upsetting to business, exorbitantly costly because of waste in the army or in the administration.[7] But if J.K.J. Thomson believes that the war contributed to depression in industry and the economy at large, Nef argues that "this war, like the other inconclusive wars of the half century 1740-1789, hardly interfered with the remarkable increase in French industrial production."[8] And François Crouzet, who believes that the Seven Years War brought "une dépression très profonde" to Bordeaux's commerce, also believes that this and other wars "n'ont interrompu que temporairement l'élan vigoureux de la croissance."[9]

Discussing the effects of old regime war with fellow historians, I also met a curious dissonance between public and private opinion. The most widely held public belief is that old regime wars were extraordinarily costly in financial and economic terms; they are held to have sapped scarce resources and to have disrupted the patterns of lives and livelihoods. Historians respond differently in private, however, doubting that old regime wars had much of an impact. After all, there were so many of them. How could so commonplace an event have had a large historical effect, an effect felt in change

[6] Respectively, Steven L. Kaplan, *Bread, Politics and Political Economy in the Reign of Louis XV* (2 vols.; The Hague, 1976), I, 145; Ernest Labrousse, "Les ruptures périodiques de la prospérité: Les crises économiques du XVIIIᵉ siècle," in Fernand Braudel and Ernest Labrousse, eds., *Histoire économique et sociale de la France* (Paris, 1970), II, 556; and Daniel Zolla, "Les variations du revenu et du prix des terres en France au XVIIᵉ et du XVIIIᵉ siècle," *Annales de l'Ecole Libre des Sciences Politiques*, 9 (1894), 205.

[7] Respectively, John G. Clark, *La Rochelle and the Atlantic Economy during the Eighteenth Century* (Baltimore, 1981), 157; Orville T. Murphy, *Charles Gravier, comte de Vergennes: French Diplomacy in the Age of Revolution, 1719-1787* (Albany, N.Y., 1982), 211; David D. Bien, *The Calas Affair: Persecution, Toleration, and Heresy in Eighteenth-Century Toulouse* (Princeton, 1960), 13 and 72-73; Lee Kennett, *The French Armies in the Seven Years' War* (Durham, N.C., 1967), 98; and Pierre Léon, "Les nouvelles élites," in Braudel and Labrousse, eds., *Histoire économique*, II, 631.

[8] Respectively, J.K.J. Thomson, *Clermont-de-Lodève, 1633-1789: Fluctuations in the Prosperity of a Languedocian Cloth-Making Town* (Cambridge, 1982), 372-73; and John U. Nef, *War and Human Progress* (Cambridge, Mass., 1950), 302. Also Louis Bergeron, "Les réseaux de la finance internationale," in Pierre Léon, ed., *Histoire économique et sociale du monde* (Paris, 1978), III, 121-22.

[9] François Crouzet, "La conjuncture bordelaise," in François-Georges Pariset, ed., *Bordeaux au XVIIIᵉ siècle* (Bordeaux, 1968), respectively, 300 and 302.

rather than in sameness? In a generation of historians inclined to
see the old regime as *histoire immobile*, or history standing still, we are
unlikely to pause too long before this most banal of all collective activities, war.

My book is a study of the economic and financial toll of one old regime war on one country. For France the Seven Years War was significant in its territorial consequences—the loss of Canada to Britain
and the transfer, albeit temporary, of Louisiana to Spain—and significant in the blow it delivered to national confidence. It was commonplace in that it both followed and preceded a number of other
conflicts of more or less equivalent scale. Was this war a grave, even
devastating, event in economic and financial terms? How was the
French economy performing in the years before the war, and how
did the war affect that performance? How much did the Seven
Years War cost the monarchy, and in what areas were the costs felt?

These are specific questions I set out to answer. The result is at
once a book about the economic and financial aspects of old regime
war and about an important moment in the history of the old regime in France, although I cannot claim that French experience in
the Seven Years War will stand for old regime war in general. The
Seven Years War constituted another episode in a long and inconclusive struggle among European powers for hegemony and economic advantage in western and central Europe and at sea. Already
in the seventeenth century the belligerents had extended the fight
to North and South America. Nor did this struggle end in 1763.
Like other wars in the series, this one posed the customary problem.
The inclination within the competitive state system was to fight, so
that the participants are called warring states. But apprehension
about the political, financial, and economic costs of too vigorous a
conflict produced negotiations with a view to gaining allies, and negotiations tended to build alliance systems that balanced groups of
powers. On its own terms, insofar as those were the terms of dynastic ambition and vanity, war was a fruitless endeavor for these states.

As familiar as we are with the idea that wars have a profound impact upon civilian populations—a question brought to the center of
our curiosity by German experience in the Thirty Years War and by
the total wars of the twentieth century—we must notice that old re-

gime wars were not ordinarily fought on the territory of all the belligerents. One approach, that of Christopher Friedrichs and Myron Gutman, is to examine the consequences of wars in the region in which they were fought.[10] I have set out to study an area free from any but incidental conflicts (excepting only naval engagements in French waters). For Russia, Britain, France, Spain, and even Austria, this war was fought on foreign soil and mostly in distant waters. The issues, therefore, are not casualties from battle or disease, destruction and dislocation accompanying marauding forces or sieges, or any of the other ordinary influences upon the scene of war. They are instead the reallocation of resources—economic, financial, and human capital—toward war.

This book also discusses an important moment in the history of a regime that collapsed in 1789 because of an impending bankruptcy of the treasury and an economic recession aggravated by 1789 into crisis. Some scholars, most notably Keith Baker and Dale Van Kley, have called attention to long-term ideological causes of the Revolution,[11] suggesting something that will be affirmed here—that the discourse of the Revolution prospered long before 1789. In terms of ideas and rhetoric, France seems to have been ready for a revolution around 1760. But, of course, the Revolution did not begin then. Turning to economic and fiscal issues, we learn something about why it did not occur then and why it did occur later. The collapse of the old regime came about not because its critics devised a superior alternative, but because both critics and defenders wished to safeguard a burden that this regime could not bear in the long run—its debt. The Seven Years War returned France to the desperate financial position it had occupied at the death of Louis XIV, but in 1763 official and public opinion resolved to oppose a partial or complete bankruptcy, and also to reduce taxes.

This book brings some new sources to the attempt to deal with these issues. The most important consist of French financial memoirs and accounts found in archives outside France: in The Hague,

[10] Friedrichs, *Nordlingen*; and Myron P. Gutmann, *War and Rural Life in the Early Modern Low Countries* (Princeton, 1980).

[11] Keith Michael Baker, "On the Problem of the Ideological Origins of the French Revolution," in Dominick LaCapra and Steven L. Kaplan, eds., *Modern European Intellectual History* (Ithaca, 1982), 197-219; and Dale K. Van Kley, *The Damiens Affair and the Unraveling of the "Ancien Régime," 1750-1770* (Princeton, 1984).

Brussels, Vienna, London, Copenhagen, and Stockholm.[12] Foreign powers worried about France's financial capacity to make war, and they came into possession of copies of papers, which, in certain circles in France, were regarded as secret documents: prospective and preliminary retrospective accounts of revenues and expenditures, memoirs on taxation reform, accounts of the debt, inventories of naval and military resources, surveys of the private assets of the king and the church, and so on. Moreover, some powers spied on France, hiring agents to report the content of council of state deliberations and royal discussions and to gather information about French finances, the navy, and the army. Because the relevant French documents, especially the audited final accounts, were destroyed in archival fires, these foreign sources provide a way to reconstruct the year to year accounts, the development of the debt, and the insights available to French and foreign authorities attempting to understand the finances of the monarchy. Another new source of some importance is a price series for the French town of Tonnerre, on the Armançon River southeast of Paris. This series, joined with others for Paris, Pontoise, and Charleville, surrounds the zone from which troops, food, and forage were most heavily drawn for the war effort and therefore permits some steps toward an analysis of how mobilization and demobilization influenced prices.

For assistance in locating these sources, and for support that enabled me to research and write this book, I wish to thank several individuals and institutions. The financial documents came to my attention by chance. Doing research in Paris, reading the same documents that my predecessors for more than a century had also read, finding these papers on many occasions under the same call letters in the same archives, and remarking once again how much had been lost in French archival fires, I wondered whether foreign archives might contain some useful sources. On a free Saturday while in The Netherlands to attend a conference on the bicentennial of Dutch diplomatic recognition of the United States in 1782, I visited the Central State Archives in The Hague. The archivist there suggested a search through the inventories of the legation archives and the papers of the clerk of the States General, Hendrik Fagel. Both yielded copies of a number of accounts that I had not seen in

---

[12] These sources are discussed in more detail in my "French Finances, 1727-1768," forthcoming, *Journal of Modern History* (1987).

Paris, and of some I had seen, not at the Archives Nationales, but at the Bibliothèque Mazarine and the Bibliothèque de l'Arsenal. The search was on. For their cordial help I would like to thank the archivists at the institutions just mentioned, and those at the Bibliothèque Nationale, the Minutier Central des Notaires de Paris (at which citations supplied by John Bosher provided an introduction), the Haus-, Hof- und Staatsarchiv in Vienna, the Palæography Room of the University of London Library (who supplied material by mail), the Public Record Office, the Manuscript Department of the British Library, the Northamptonshire Record Office, the Kongelige Bibliotek and the Rigsarkiv in Copenhagen, the Riksarkiv and the Kungliga Bibliotek in Stockholm, Skoklosters Slott, and the Kabinet der Handschriften of the Koninklijke Bibliotheek in Brussels. I use the Flemish rather than the French name of this last library as an expression of appreciation to the faculty of the Katholieke Universiteit Leuven, who extended a fellowship during the spring term of 1983 that enabled me to begin writing and to search in Brussels for further documents. My colleagues and friends, Herman Van der Wee and Eddy Van Cauwenberghe, deserve special thanks. In Vienna Walter Winkelbauer and Anna Benna proved especially helpful in locating materials, and Karlheinz Mack extended every courtesy. In Copenhagen Palle Ringsted and Morten Westrup assisted in locating an important body of documents. Michel Morineau deserves thanks for providing information.

For financial assistance with several trips abroad to search for and examine manuscript sources, I wish also to thank the Committee on Research in Economic History for an Arthur H. Cole Grant-in-Aid, the American Philosophical Society for a Hays Fund Research Grant, and the American Council of Learned Societies for two grants-in-aid. Additional manuscript material came to light at the Huntington Library, at the Kress Library of Business and Economics, and in the Eleutherian Mills Historical Library, where also I encountered an excellent collection of pamphlets from the 1763 debate over financial reform. For kind assistance I wish to thank Martin Ridge, Virginia J. Renner, and Mary Wright at the Huntington; Ruth Rogers at the Kress; and B. Bright Low and Richmond D. Williams at Eleutherian Mills. Eleutherian Mills and the Huntington generously supported work in their collections. I wish also to thank Indiana University for financial assistance, in the form both of released time and grants to pay for microfilm and travel, and the National Endowment for the Humanities for a Summer Stipend.

The argument presented here has benefited from the critical appraisal of members of the Indiana University Economic History Workshop and the Shelby Cullom Davis Center for Historical Studies Seminar, from questions asked at a session of the Society for French Historical Studies, and from scrutiny by Keith M. Baker, Lee Kennett, James Pritchard, Gerald Strauss, and the readers consulted by the publisher.

August 1985   *James C. Riley*
                                                                  Bloomington

THE SEVEN YEARS WAR
AND THE OLD REGIME IN FRANCE

CHAPTER 1

ECONOMIC GROWTH AT RISK

"un tems de délices" [1]

*W*AR is a gamble. But for those in the old regime who decided whether or not to take this gamble—kings and oligarchs—the risk was attractive. Visible gains in territory, prestige, power, and economic advantage seemed to outweigh probable losses: war, along with marriage alliances, was the classical path toward state building. The ruler who went to war with the distressing frequency typical in the eighteenth century, however, knew much about probable costs. War meant the depletion of military and naval resources and supplies, vast and wasteful spending on campaigns, the accumulation of debts, and political tensions arising from higher taxation. Even so, these costs rested lightly on the minds of most rulers. France entered the Seven Years War unenthusiastically, but fought it nonetheless, and for goals no greater than these: to preserve French influence in Germany (but not with a realistic prospect of adding territory); to define the eastern boundary of possessions in North America; to retain Minorca, seized in 1756 before the declaration of war; and to protect French prestige. Some wars offered grander prospects. But the point is that the importance of these payoffs differed in the old regime from what may seem most plausible today. Small territorial gains and dynastic dignity bulked large, and were therefore worth what now seem to have been inordinate expenditures in resources.

War also involved certain other risks not always appreciated by those who engaged in it so freely. Beyond the visible risks to prestige and solvency (how tirelessly eighteenth-century statesmen and political commentators repeated the idea that finances are the sinews, *les nerfs*, of the state!) there were less obvious risks focusing on the economy. A theory of the political means of influencing economic issues was emerging in the middle decades of the eighteenth cen-

[1] Algemeen Rijksarchief, The Hague, Archief Fagel, 1567, p. 81.

tury. Rulers seem not to have stood in the forefront among readers of the literature on this theory, but discussions of policy options at Versailles reveal that economic issues were not ignored. The king and his ministers worried about colonial wealth. They worried also about the money stock and how war would affect the scarcity of money, a concern covering both the actual stock of specie in a nation and the cost of credit. But they worried less or not at all about how war would influence the allocation of economic resources and how it would affect forces favoring or impeding growth. These were the invisible risks.

The visible issues that fell under the scrutiny of rulers or political commentators provoked a search for information. If the data subsequently gathered are not always satisfactorily precise or altogether reliable, they provide at least so many sightings of a problem. The eighteenth-century estimates of France's money stock tend to range widely, but they also establish the parameters of an answer to the questions "how much?" and "what trend?" It is more difficult to find quantitative signposts for discussing the issues toward which people of the eighteenth century were inattentive or ambiguous. Nonetheless, to examine the costs of a war, we must look first at the scale of the resources at risk. The character of the investigation will be determined, and limited, by the kinds of evidence that are available.

BASIC DATA ON THE OLD REGIME ECONOMY

"Notre but essentiel était de dresser la statistique."[2] Thus Pierre Dardel explained the objective behind his study of shipping in the Norman ports of Rouen and Havre. It is a sentiment and goal characteristic of much recent French economic historiography: the works of Ruggiero Romano, Tihomir Markovitch, Jean Marczewski, François Crouzet, René Baehrel, and many others, which have recovered information compiled during the old regime and for the first time brought it together in coherent pictures of significant parts of the French economy. Only because of this patient accumulation of data is it now possible to frame questions about the long-run course of economic activity and the short-run effects of

---

[2] Pierre Dardel, *Navires et marchandises dans les ports de Rouen et du Havre au XVIIIe siècle* (Paris, 1963), 7.

events like war, with a reasonable expectation of arriving at satisfying answers. Of course, as Dardel warned, the answers will not depict matters as they actually were. A plethora of quantitative data about the old regime economy would not compensate for the inevitable imperfections of these statistics, or for the limits of statistical analysis, which can answer only certain questions. Even if the defects of the sources and methods require a degree of humility in the economic historian not called for in other historians, the data still permit the satisfaction of a compelling modern need to know the order and magnitude of things. The eighteenth-century ruler and his ministers felt the need to know order and magnitude, and therefore ordered the collection of data. But they did not often use those data to build quantitative and analytical portraits, which have become possible because we can combine the data collected then with theories and methodologies devised since.

Population

Population is the first measure of economic activity, because it is a measure of the number of participants. As a result of the use of family reconstitution techniques in analyzing the parish registers, the last three decades have provided rapidly improving information about the numbers of the French people, the trend of those numbers, and vital statistics. The reports, which appear in scores of local and regional studies, have been summarized by Jacques Dupâquier and appear in Table 1.1.[3] These figures revise sharply upward the

TABLE 1.1
French Population, 1700-1790

1700	21.5 million	1755	25.0
1710	22.5	1760	25.7
1720	23.2	1765	26.1
1730	24.2	1770	26.6
1735	24.4	1775	27.0
1740	24.6	1780	27.6
1745	24.6	1785	27.7
1750	24.5	1790	28.1

SOURCE: Jacques Dupâquier, *La population française aux XVIIe et XVIIIe siècles* (Paris, 1979), 34-35, 37, and 81. Dupâquier also suggests that the 1700 population may have been as high as 22 million.

[3] Jacques Dupâquier, *La population française aux XVIIe et XVIIIe siècles* (Paris, 1979).

size of the population believed to have been living during the eighteenth century within the present-day boundaries of France, an area not significantly larger than eighteenth-century France after the addition of Lorraine. Because the estimates for late in the century are higher than figures generally employed by scholars before 1979 when Dupâquier published these figures, previous adjustments of economic data into per capita figures now require correction. One consequence of this continuing process of maintaining a fit between economic and demographic data will show up in the discussion of output.

As Table 1.1 indicates, the eighteenth century was an era of population growth in France. But the scheme of growth there diverged from the experience of some neighboring states. French population growth exceeded the quite small growth experienced in the Dutch Republic, but it also peaked earlier than did growth in Britain. Dupâquier's estimates show an increase in numbers in each decade between 1700 and 1790, except for the 1740s, which opened with two years of serious grain shortages. The rate of growth was higher before 1740 than after, but the percentage growth before and after 1750 was approximately equal.

In 1700 France's population (including Lorraine, which did not formally become part of the monarchy until 1766) totalled 21.5 to 22 million. By 1790, following this process of unspectacular but persistent growth, it had reached a level of some 28.1 million. For these ninety years taken together, the growth rate was about 0.3 percent per annum, or three per thousand a year. To keep pace with population growth, economic output in real terms needed to grow at a comparable pace.

In 1735 France's rural population numbered some 20 million, and the urban population some 4.4 million, or about 18 percent of the total.[4] Among the largest cities were the major ports of Marseilles, Bordeaux, Nantes, and Rouen, but even together these cities fell short of matching the population of Paris. Although these ports were distributed among France's maritime frontiers, the heaviest concentration of population was in the northwest, from Nantes (including Brittany) to Lille. Between 1740 and 1806, when an urban

[4] *Ibid.*, 37.

census was conducted, there was little net change in the level of urbanization, which remained 18.8 percent at the latter date.[5]

Prices

The eighteenth century was also an age of inflation in France. The increase in prices was significant, distorting any measurements that fail to take it into account; and the course of inflation was irregular enough to undermine the use of rule-of-thumb estimates. French price history, like French employment, is skewed toward the agricultural sector. The most extensive sources are *mercuriales* from urban markets reporting wholesale prices of basic commodities—wheat, rye, barley, oats, and wine—and thus reporting on the supply of basic foodstuffs and the probability of food riots, a matter of ceaseless concern to public authorities. Whereas the kingdom was well supplied with important enough grain markets to warrant keeping such records, it lacked an entrepôt on the scale of Amsterdam. The course of prices for other goods remains obscure because no price currents listing the broad range of commodities in trade in the eighteenth century have come to light, and because historians have not found a way to exploit the records of institutions like asylums, *hôpitaux*, or prisons for substitute information. Thus the record is biased in a way that impedes an effort to detect shifts in the terms of trade between agricultural goods, for which data are plentiful, and non-agricultural goods and services, for which data are sparse. Did prices of other goods advance more or less rapidly than those of wheat and rye? What was the overall price trend?

To build a price index that will serve as a deflator to avoid money illusion—the comparison of sums across time without any adjustment for price change—requires information about a wide variety of goods in trade. As noted above, French price studies furnish the most important data set, the price of the basic grains, wheat and rye. These bulky commodities moved at greater expense than most goods in trade within France and between France and other countries. Therefore, grain prices in France are *less* likely to move in

[5] *Ibid.*, 91. Using a measure of urban marriages, Dupâquier suggests that urbanization expanded slightly during 1740-1773, then retreated to the level reported for 1806.

close association with grain prices elsewhere than are the prices of other goods—precious metals, wool, linen, spices, sugar, tobacco, potash, iron, and so forth—which were everyday objects of international and interregional trade, but which did not worry officials in the same way that grain prices did. From early in the eighteenth century, however, the wheat price series for the Amsterdam market, for which a broad spectrum of non-grain prices is also available, show a high degree of association with those for Paris.[6] For these two reasons—the close association between Paris and Amsterdam wheat prices and the likelihood of still closer associations for other goods cheaper to transport or more selectively available—prices recorded in the Amsterdam market for non-grain items may be used to estimate inflation among these items in French markets.

There is one large caveat. Although the Amsterdam grain market was closely associated with Paris, and grain markets in northern France with Paris, this association did not hold for the entire kingdom. Marseilles imported grain from the Levant, and wheat prices in that great port show no association with prices in Paris. Likewise, Toulouse stood at the center of an inland grain-growing area in the south, and its prices show periods of high association with Paris mixed with periods of low association. Except for coastal traffic, transportation costs between the northern market structure and the Garonne Valley around Toulouse were considerable, making the actual movement of grain feasible only in periods of exceptional price disparity. Thus France did not possess a national grain market, but rather one large and integrated market covering approximately the northern two-thirds of the country, and a southern tier of markets only partially integrated with the north in grains. There were associations between the two regions. The south provided seed-grain for the area of "la grande culture" in the north, and grain-growing regions made exchanges with viticultural areas.[7] But these associations were not yet strong enough to create a national market. Levels of integration among items less expensive to transport may have been greater than in wheat, but the data do not provide enough insight for a conclusion.

Under these circumstances, it follows that the grain price series

[6] See below, Chapter 3, where measurements of correlation are reported.

[7] Olwen Hufton, "Social Conflict and the Grain Supply in Eighteenth-Century France," *Journal of Interdisciplinary History*, 14, no. 2 (Autumn 1983), 305-309.

constructed for individual markets by a number of scholars, and for France as a whole from 1726 to 1789 by Ernest Labrousse, should be supplemented by other series. Table 1.2 reproduces Labrousse's multi-grain series, Micheline Baulant's wheat series for the Paris market, N. W. Posthumus' weighted series covering forty-four items traded on the Amsterdam market, the Frêches' wheat series for Toulouse, and René Baehrel's wheat series for Marseilles imports from the Levant.[8] Tests for integration compare variances in the

TABLE 1.2

Price Series in Index Numbers, 1700-1789

(1730-1734 = 100)

	Paris wheat	French grain	Amsterdam	Toulouse wheat	Marseilles wheat
1700	140	—	—	116	84
1701	101	—	—	108	86
1702	76	—	—	94	94
1703	80	—	—	93	84
1704	77	—	—	101	90
1700-1704	95	—	126	102	88
1705	74	—	—	83	88
1706	61	—	—	73	94
1707	53	—	—	65	122
1708	75	—	—	92	133
1709	260	—	—	187	137
1705-1709	105	—	118	100	115
1710	181	—	—	145	90
1711	115	—	—	94	103
1712	129	—	—	145	90
1713	175	—	—	160	95
1714	181	—	—	108	100
1710-1714	156	—	142	130	96
1715	102	—	—	80	111
1716	84	—	—	79	94
1717	68	—	—	71	122
1718	78	—	—	73	135
1719	96	—	—	115	140

[8] Data behind Labrousse's national grain index are presented in detail in C.-E. Labrousse, *Esquisse du mouvement des prix et des revenus en France au XVIIIe siècle* (2 vols.; Paris, 1933). N. W. Posthumus, *Inquiry into the History of Prices in Holland* (2 vols.; Leiden, 1946-1964), I, xcv, gives the weights used in constructing a general index and their changes from period to period. During 1700-1759 the four major grains, wheat, rye, barley, and oats, account for less than 11 percent of the total, which is intended to reflect price changes among Amsterdam trade flows rather than in a consumer's basket of goods.

TABLE 1.2 (*cont.*)

	Paris wheat	French grain	Amsterdam	Toulouse wheat	Marseilles wheat
1715-1719	86	—	107	84	120
1720	152	—	—	169	164
1721	94	—	—	89	137
1722	108	—	—	94	123
1723	165	—	—	121	129
1724	166	—	—	144	107
1720-1724	137	—	98	123	132
1725	181	—	—	137	101
1726	169	98	—	87	105
1727	121	93	—	81	102
1728	85	89	—	117	112
1729	105	95	—	131	112
1725-1729	132	94	107	111	106
1730	101	96	—	104	98
1731	124	100	—	88	82
1732	91	101	—	87	90
1733	75	94	—	106	107
1734	109	109	—	116	123
1730-1734	100	100	100	100	100
1735	81	100	—	112	101
1736	90	100	—	98	107
1737	94	104	—	125	112
1738	113	113	—	125	101
1739	129	110	—	121	101
1735-1739	101	105	99	116	104
1740	163	117	—	108	123
1741	235	133	—	116	101
1742	136	120	—	117	97
1743	81	110	—	95	95
1744	75	108	—	93	94
1740-1744	138	118	117	106	102
1745	77	111	—	90	101
1746	94	114	—	98	140
1747	99	122	—	163	168
1748	125	124	—	184	152
1749	118	121	—	153	120
1745-1749	103	118	112	138	136
1750	114	120	—	163	108
1751	125	118	—	158	120
1752	157	127	—	164	93
1753	128	121	—	107	97
1754	122	119	—	94	73
1750-1754	129	121	111	137	98
1755	94	109	—	95	84
1756	103	115	—	117	90
1757	140	124	—	127	107

TABLE 1.2 (cont.)

	Paris wheat	French grain	Amsterdam	Toulouse wheat	Marseilles wheat
1758	120	123	—	144	149
1759	127	129	—	179	155
1755-1759	117	120	117	132	117
1760	126	126	—	168	—
1761	101	118	—	139	—
1762	102	120	—	116	—
1763	101	124	—	130	—
1764	99	118	—	163	—
1760-1764	106	121	132	143	—
1765	116	124	—	159	—
1766	129	138	—	200	—
1767	140	145	—	187	—
1768	208	147	—	184	—
1769	206	152	—	196	—
1765-1769	160	141	141	157	—
1770	184	174	—	192	—
1771	212	181	—	210	—
1772	179	180	—	202	—
1773	187	171	—	225	—
1774	168	156	—	202	—
1770-1774	186	172	140	206	—
1775	187	166	—	179	—
1776	158	156	—	160	142
1777	147	165	—	186	139
1778	142	170	—	237	168
1779	129	159	—	168	—
1775-1779	153	163	149	186	150
1780	122	152	—	162	—
1781	132	165	—	186	—
1782	126	170	—	230	—
1783	128	175	—	212	—
1784	168	176	—	173	—
1780-1784	135	168	167	193	—
1785	158	186	—	186	—
1786	131	179	—	193	141
1787	140	169	—	183	148
1788	152	175	—	211	209
1789	—	205	—	253	219
1785-1789	145	183	173	205	179

SOURCES: Micheline Baulant, "Le prix des grains à Paris de 1431 à 1789," Annales E.S.C , 23, no. 3 (May-Jun 1968), 539-40; Ernest Labrousse, "Les 'bon prix' agricoles du XVIIIᶜ siècle," in Fernand Braudel and Ernest Labrousse, eds., Histoire économique et sociale de la France (Paris, 1970), II, 387; N. W. Posthumus, Inquiry into the History of Prices in Holland (2 vols.; Leiden, 1946-1964), I, ci, col. H; Georges and Geneviève Frêche, Les prix des grains, des vins et des légumes à Toulouse (1486-1868) (Paris, 1967), 88-90; and René Baehrel, Une croissance: La Basse-Provence rurale (fin XVIᵉ siècle-1789) (2 vols.; Paris, 1961), I, 545.

11

price movement between two markets, showing whether prices at the two sites fluctuated in harmony. Such tests establish strict standards that need not apply when the issue is the long-run trend. Chart 1.1 plots price changes among these markets. It reveals both the

Chart 1.1

Prices in France and Amsterdam, 1700-1789

(1730-1734=100)

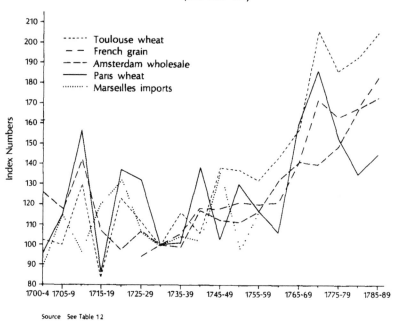

Source   See Table 12

universality of inflation in France and the similarity in the inflation curve among French markets and between French markets and Amsterdam. Prices in the south and the north of France did not vibrate together, but both were subject to the same pressures: population growth in a place and period of nearly stable agricultural technology and agricultural productivity, and growth in the money stock. To measure price change in French trade, heavily weighted, like Amsterdam's trade, toward textiles, wines, and colonial goods, it will be preferable to use the Posthumus series, which is weighted toward non-grain items. For other purposes, such as the measurement of price change in central government revenues, it will be preferable to use Labrousse's national grain index or the series of Paris wheat prices. No one series will perfectly capture price movement throughout France because these movements were not entirely harmonious. But deflation using the more appropriate of the two indexes will be superior to a rule-of-thumb approach, or to overlooking price change altogether.

National Output

The investigation of French national income toward the end of the eighteenth century, led by Jean Marczewski, has produced an estimate of the value of French agricultural and manufacturing output during the 1780s in current prices: 5.1 billion livres tournois (l.t.).[9] Other estimates, which are meant to include the value of services, government spending, investment, and net trade flows, produce a higher figure.[10] All of these attempts to reconstruct output may be compared with eighteenth-century estimates—those gathered by Marczewski, which are skewed toward the pessimistic views of the physiocrats, and others.[11] The more realistic mid-century estimates placed national income at 3 to 3.4 billion livres, depending on the population estimate preferred.[12] Asked to gauge the scale of transactions, including apparently secondhand sales and perhaps also barter exchanges, a group of *secrétaires d'état, intendants des finances, intendants du commerce*, and wholesale merchants suggested 5.8 billion for a period of eighteen months in 1751-1752, or an annual total of 3.9 billion.[13] The different sources cannot be expected to agree, since they are often discussing different issues: gross national product, national income, personal consumption, rural income, or all transactions (which is a significantly higher figure than GNP). But they are in accord in describing a pattern of growth during the eighteenth century. The issue of greatest significance is the scale of that growth.

[9] Jean Marczewski, *Introduction à l'histoire quantitative* (Geneva, 1965), 92.

[10] François Perroux, "Prise de vues sur la croissance de l'économie française, 1780-1950," *Income and Wealth*, ser. 5 (1955), 61: 6.1 billion l.t. Also Tihomir J. Markovitch, "L'industrie française de 1789 à 1964: Analyse des faits (suite)," *Cahiers de l'Institut de Science Economique Appliquée*, ser. AF, 6, no. 174 (Jun. 1966); and Paul Studenski, *The Income of Nations* (2 vols.; New York, 1961), I, *passim*.

[11] Jean Marczewski, "Some Aspects of the Economic Growth of France, 1660-1958," *Economic Development and Cultural Change*, 9 (Apr. 1961), 371.

[12] Anon., "Considérations sur les finances & le commerce de France," *Journal de commerce et d'agriculture* (Feb. 1761), 5, 13, 14, and 34.

[13] Algemeen Rijksarchief, Legatiearchief, Eerste Afdeling, Frankrijk, 793, pp. 267ff.

Two visions exist about the scale of growth. One, fashioned by Patrick O'Brien and Caglar Keyder, projects backward a growth rate of 1.0 percent per annum. Using Marczewski's figure for agricultural and manufacturing output during 1781-1790, O'Brien and Keyder imply that output during the first decade of the century totalled some 2.3 billion livres *in prices of the 1780s*.[14] This estimate refers to aggregate commodity output, and therefore sets forth a higher rate of growth than would be inferred from a calculation of per capita change. If the population totalled 21.5 million during 1701-1710, and averaged 27.6 million during 1781-1790, per capita output for these sectors would appear to have increased from some 107 l.t. to some 185 l.t. in constant prices. Or, since the rate of population growth was 0.3 percent a year, then the conversion from an aggregate to a per capita measure of change in output will deduct 0.3 percent. O'Brien and Keyder thus imply a per capita growth rate of 0.7 percent per annum, a figure that represents an upper limit among views on French economic performance.

Another vision emerges from Paul Bairoch's attempt to backcast European economic performance from the early nineteenth century. In Bairoch's view, high growth rates cannot plausibly be suggested for any sustained period before 1800 because high rates will leave the beginning-point economy without a reasonable level of output and consumption. For European per capita product in general, Bairoch suggests that a growth rate of 0.2 to 0.3 percent is the highest annual rate that can be backcast for 1800 to 1500.[15] In fact, these rates are excessive. Only if all the growth Bairoch projects for France during 1500-1800 is located in one century will the long-run rate reach even this modest level. What Bairoch does is underscore the dangers of exaggerating growth rates, for high rates necessarily imply low beginning point levels of output. Short- and medium-range rates may have been higher or lower than 0.3 percent. But in the long run even that rate may overstate actual performance in terms of per capita growth in constant prices.

All French growth between 1500 and 1800 was not located in the eighteenth century. But the beginning point, the first decade of the

[14] Patrick O'Brien and Caglar Keyder, *Economic Growth in Britain and France, 1780-1914* (London, 1978), 57.

[15] Paul Bairoch, "Europe's Gross National Product: 1800-1975," *Journal of European Economic History*, 5, no. 2 (Fall 1976), 277.

century, was a decade of extraordinarily weak performance in an economy savaged by war, monetary instability, and harvest failure. For this reason, growth in the French economy may, from Bairoch's point of view, have reached as high a figure as 0.3 percent a year in the eighteenth century. Since recent historians agree on the fact of growth but disagree about its scale, the O'Brien/Keyder and Bairoch estimates serve as ceiling and floor for estimating French performance.

There is a vast difference between the two rates. The lower, 0.3 percent a year, fits expectations for a traditional economy temporarily enjoying conditions favorable to growth within a longer period in which contrary conditions will also appear. The higher, 0.7 percent a year, implies something else altogether. It suggests a departure from the conditions regulating economic performance in the preindustrial economy: the limits on resource use, capital goods and human capital formation, and technology that held growth back. Even growth at 0.3 percent sustained for as long a period as 1701-1710 to 1781-1790 implies a decisive step away from the traditional limits to growth. But the higher rate, in a society that did not experience conspicuous industrial modernization, suggests an important if surreptitious growth. Establishing where within these boundaries French growth may lie is trebly difficult: 1) scholars disagree about the distribution of economic activity across sectors; 2) controversies persist about the performance of individual sectors; and 3) the absence of a leading sector, such as cotton textiles, spreads the search across the entire economy.

One estimate of the distribution of economic activity is provided by Marczewski. In 1781-1790 agriculture is held to have accounted for 42 percent of output, manufacturing (including handicrafts) for 27 percent, trade for 13 percent, and other (services) for 18 percent.[16] Of agriculture and manufacturing alone, agriculture would then have accounted for 61 percent and manufacturing 39 percent. After reflection, Marczewski elected to reduce slightly the share assigned to agriculture (to 57 percent) and increase that assigned to manufacturing (to 43 percent).[17] Another source, François Per-

---

[16] Paul Bairoch, *Révolution industrielle et sous-développement* (2nd ed.; Paris, 1964), 347, drawing on J[ean] Marczewski, "Y a-t-il eu un 'take off' en France?" *Cahiers de l'Institut de Science Economique Appliquée*, suppl. 111, ser. AD, no. 1 (Mar. 1961), p. 72.

[17] Marczewski, *Introduction*, 92.

roux, prefers this distribution: agriculture, 49 percent; manufacturing, 18 percent; trade, 12 percent; other, 20 percent.[18] For Perroux, between agriculture and manufacturing alone, agriculture is held to have made up 73 percent. The primacy of agriculture is not in dispute. What is uncertain is its scale. Differences as large as these do not help establish where within the parameters the growth path may lie.

Which sectors experienced growth? The generous estimate of French agricultural performance provided in 1961 by J.-C. Toutain has come under attack from Michel Morineau and, most recently, Emmanuel Le Roy Ladurie and Joseph Goy.[19] Toutain suggested that grain output expanded from 826 million francs (i.e., livres tournois) in 1701-1710 to 1,179 million in 1771-1780, and to 1,369 million in 1781-1790. Other commodities—wine, wood, fruit, vegetables, and animal products—shared this growth. Aggregate agricultural product, deducting seeds and animal consumption, expanded from 1,388 million l.t. in 1751-1760 to 2,601 million in 1781-1790.[20] These are current prices. They include inflation, and they also include population growth. Deflated by means of Labrousse's national grain index, and stated in per capita terms using the higher late century estimates provided by Dupâquier, Toutain's picture changes sharply. Rather than the agricultural revolution that these figures seemed at first to imply, per capita output between the 1750s and the 1780s increased only from 56 to 63 l.t. in constant prices—a growth rate of 0.4 percent per annum. The illusion of rapid economic progress lies in price change and population growth.

It is this picture of slow growth that other authorities have concluded most faithfully describes changes in agricultural output. The central problem of French agriculture, as Morineau has pointed out, was a deficiency of fertilizer, and that problem, although rec-

---

[18] Perroux, "Prise de vues," 61.

[19] J.-C. Toutain, "Le produit de l'agriculture française de 1700 à 1958: II. La croissance," *Cahiers de l'Institut de Science Economique Appliquée*, suppl. 115, ser. AF, no. 2 (Jul. 1961), pp. 6-7 and *passim*; Michel Morineau, *Les faux-semblants d'un démarrage économique: agriculture et démographie en France au XVIIIᵉ siècle* (Paris, 1971); and Emmanuel Le Roy Ladurie and Joseph Goy, *Tithe and Agrarian History from the Fourteenth to the Nineteenth Centuries*, trans. by Susan Burke (Cambridge, 1982), esp. 154 and 175.

[20] Toutain, "Le produit de l'agriculture," 64 and 91.

ognized by agronomists, remained unsolved. Some new plants were introduced. Potato and corn (maize) cultivation spread, the latter especially in the southwest. But overall levels of consumption did not rise, and may have fallen in the last years before the Revolution.[21] Clearance and drainage brought some new land into cultivation and may have substantially diminished exposure to such disease vectors as mosquitoes. But Labrousse believes that land cleared between 1766 and 1789, when the effort was most vigorous, added only 2.5 percent to the arable area within the monarchy.[22] Nor can grounds be found for a more generous view of productivity growth in sporadic reductions in the area given over to fallow.

Le Roy Ladurie and Goy, revising an earlier estimate, suggest that even a growth rate in grain or agricultural output of 0.4 percent per annum may be excessive. They believe that agricultural output increased by about 20 percent between 1700 and 1789, and therefore fell short even of the population growth rate (0.2 percent a year versus 0.3 percent.)[23] Subsistence crises—the coincidence of harvest shortfalls, high agricultural prices, and mortality spasms—disappeared in the eighteenth century, but this they relate to improvements in distribution rather than gains in output. In their view, based on evidence from records on tithe payments to the church, no long-run per capita growth can be detected.

This view introduces its own complications. If aggregate output grew less than the population, or only as much, if transportation improvements eliminated major distribution problems, and if France remained except in years of harvest shortfall a small-scale participant in the international grain trade, then grain prices would be expected to have increased in tandem with the French money stock. But the money stock grew more rapidly than did prices. Using the Paris wheat series, French prices expanded at an annual rate of 0.5 percent, whereas the specie stock grew by 1.5 percent a year.[24] Thus

[21] Morineau, *Les faux-semblants*, esp. 68-72. Also Georges Frêche, *Toulouse et la région midi-pyrénées au siècle des lumières (vers 1670-1789)* (n.p., [1974]), 311; and André J. Bourde, *Agronomie et agronomes en France au XVIIIᵉ siècle* (3 vols.; Paris, 1967), esp. I, 21-22.

[22] Ernest Labrousse, "L'expansion agricole: La montée de la production," in Fernand Braudel and Ernest Labrousse, eds., *Histoire économique et sociale de la France* (Paris, 1970), II, 429.

[23] Le Roy Ladurie and Goy, *Tithe*, 175 and 177.

[24] Using prices from Micheline Baulant, "Le prix des grains à Paris de 1431 à

this latest estimate from Le Roy Ladurie and Goy may understate
gains in grain output, at least before 1765, after which the price data
clearly indicate that demand grew more rapidly than the supply of
grain (Chart 1.1). Nevertheless, the agricultural sector seems to
have grown toward the Bairoch rather than the O'Brien/Keyder
end of the scale.

Research of the last three decades has dramatically revised ideas
about French manufacturing performance in the eighteenth century. This revision may be attributed in the first place to a recognition that output in industries using traditional technologies expanded during much of the century, and in the second place to a
realization that expansion was sustained in the latter decades of the
century where newer technologies were introduced. In the judgment of the leading student of the wool industry, "la France était
au XVIIe-XVIIIe siècle la première puissance industrielle du
monde."[25]

Such a portrayal looks, of course, at aggregate rather than per
capita performance, and compares French output and its estimated
rate of growth with British output. Among the most important and
best studied segments of French manufacturing is the woollen industry. At the end of the century wool accounted for some 20 percent of France's industrial product.[26] Concentrated in Normandy,
Picardy, and Champagne, the woollen industry produced for export as well as domestic use. Aggregate output increased, according
to Markovitch's estimates, from 1,111,470 to 1,551,530 pieces from
the beginning to the end of the century, or at a rate of 0.48 percent
per annum. If measured in square ells, the increase was more rapid
still.[27] Also Pierre Léon has estimated a growth in woollen production from 1703/1708 to 1789 of 61 percent, or an annual rate of 0.57

1789," *Annales E.S.C.*, 23, no. 3 (May-Jun. 1968), 539-40; and money stock estimates
from James C. Riley and John J. McCusker, "Money Supply, Economic Growth, and
the Quantity Theory of Money: France, 1650-1788," *Explorations in Economic History*,
20 (1983), 277. The comparison is from money stock in 1700 at the silver equivalent
of 7.27 grams to the livre to the stock in 1788 at the silver equivalent of 4.45 grams,
and from prices of 1700-1704 to 1785-1789.

[25] Tihomir J. Markovitch, *Histoire des industries françaises: Les industries lainières de
Colbert à la Révolution* (Geneva, 1976), 457.

[26] Tihomir J. Markovitch, "Statistiques industrielles et systèmes politiques," in *Pour
une histoire de la statistique* ([Paris], [1977]), 324n5.

[27] Markovitch, *Les industries lainières*, 458. These estimates omit production for autoconsumption and report on output in about half of overall production.

percent.[28] In Markovitch's adjustments, per capita production expanded by 0.18 percent for pieces, and 0.50 percent for square ells. But the low growth population estimates used by Markovitch lead to the appearance of considerably faster growth than do the more recent high growth estimates from Dupâquier. Using these latter figures, it appears that per capita production in pieces grew only negligibly, whereas that by measure increased more, but at a rate of some 0.33 percent per annum rather than 0.5 percent. Throughout, France is believed to have imported a slightly increasing portion of woollen goods.[29]

Of other industries, more is known of detail than of the trend of aggregate output.[30] Nevertheless, in the scholarly literature a conviction has arisen both that Markovitch's judgment about France's aggregate industrial prowess is justified, and that the high rates of current value growth suggested by Marczewski's estimate for increase in French industrial product at the end of the century—1.6 to 1.9 percent—may faithfully depict the eighteenth-century path of growth.[31] Both Crouzet and Léon claim that French industrial growth during the eighteenth century more or less matched that achieved in Britain according to the estimates of Deane and Cole, a comparison drawn also by Markovitch.[32] Since Deane and Cole believe that British industrial output grew in real values at a rate of 1.2 percent between 1700 and 1790, this claim means that French industrial ouput increased as much.[33] Indeed, Léon suggests that the

[28] Pierre Léon, "L'élan industriel et commercial," in Braudel and Labrousse, eds., *Histoire économique*, 517.

[29] Markovitch, *Les industries lainières*, 484.

[30] E.g., Léon, "L'élan industriel," 514-21; and Michel Morineau and Charles Carrière, "Draps du Languedoc et commerce du Levant au XVIIIᶜ siècle," *Revue d'histoire économique et sociale*, 46, no. 1 (1968), 109-111.

[31] Calculated from Jean Marczewski, "Le produit physique de l'économie française de 1789 à 1913 (comparaison avec la Grande-Bretagne)," *Cahiers de l'Institut de Science Economique Appliquée*, ser. AF, 4, no. 163 (Jul. 1965), pp. xiii and xx.

[32] François Crouzet, "Angleterre et France au XVIIIᶜ siècle: Essai d'analyse comparée de deux croissances économiques," *Annales E.S.C.*, 21, no. 2 (Mar.-Apr. 1966), 266; Pierre Léon, "Structures du commerce extérieur et évolution industrielle de la France à la fin du XVIIIᶜ siècle," in *Conjoncture économique, structures sociales: Hommage à Ernest Labrousse* (Paris, 1974), 407; and Markovitch, "Statistiques industrielles," 324n5.

[33] Phyllis Deane and W. A. Cole, *British Economic Growth, 1688-1959* (2nd ed.; Cambridge, 1969), 78: 1.2 percent in aggregation, and 0.8 percent in per capita terms. Newer studies, e.g., C. Knick Harley, "British Industrialization before 1841: Evi-

overall rate of growth will have fallen between 1.5 and 1.9 percent per annum, which means that other industries must have outperformed woollens by very substantial margins.[34]

Yet these judgments conflict with more impressionistic knowledge about French industry supplied in many cases by the same authorities. Léon detects a "net freinage" of textile production within a "rupture structurelle" in the second half of the century between industry using old and new techniques.[35] Textiles and other industries were only slowly transformed in France. Clearly there was no export-led industrial modernization. Thus there is sharp conflict between the high estimates of growth rates and descriptive evidence showing unevenness in French industry. To some degree, the generous impression of French industrial growth is the result of estimating progress without adjusting for price change, which Deane and Cole do. No series of prices of French manufactured goods is available, but both piecemeal evidence and data from other countries indicate that prices of manufactured goods were rising, if more slowly than agricultural prices. The manufacturing sector needs further investigation. Pending that, the conclusion best warranted by what we know now is that, overall, both agriculture and manufacturing contributed to an increased national product, but that their contributions suggest rates of growth toward the lower, or Bairoch, end of the scale.

It is important to notice that the vision of French economic performance so far developed relates only agricultural and manufacturing growth. These two largest sectors of the economy were less dynamic than foreign trade. Official trade statistics report "une progression régulière et importante,"[36] but they report only on acknowledged maritime exchanges through French ports. Thus they omit smuggling and overland trade. Crouzet estimates that French trade grew from 215 million l.t. during 1716-1720 to 1,062 million during 1784-1788. Using an index of agricultural prices, he suggests further that prices rose in the same period by 60 percent.[37] Thus trade seems to have expanded at a rate of 1.7 percent per an-

dence of Slower Growth during the Industrial Revolution," *Journal of Economic History*, 42 (Jun. 1982), 267-89, revise these rates downward.

[34] Léon, "L'élan industriel," 521.
[35] Léon, "Structures du commerce extérieur," 418-20.
[36] Dardel, *Navires et marchandises*, 49.
[37] Crouzet, "Angleterre et France," 261.

num in constant values, a performance that establishes for it the designation of most dynamic sector of the economy. An even higher rate of growth (1.9 percent a year in aggregate terms) prevails when the Posthumus composite price index, one including many non-grain items, is used.[38]

How much did trade contribute to national product? During 1726-1730 France imported and exported goods to a (constant) value of 8.2 l.t. per capita; by 1766-1770 that figure had nearly doubled, to 15.9 l.t. Rapid expansion, yet on a small scale. The customary means of measuring the contribution of trade to national income is to compare exports to national product. In 1770-1774 exports averaged 320.6 million l.t., and around 1780 commodity output came to some 5.1 billion[39] and national product to a higher figure. Exports equalled about 6 percent of combined agricultural and manufacturing product, and less than 6 percent of national income. Earlier export ratios may have been higher, according to one estimate peaking at some 12 percent of output around the middle of the century.[40] Nevertheless, these figures reveal the severely limited capacity of trade to impel growth within the economy at large.[41]

Trade values and the proportion of exports to national product do not speak adequately about the value of commercial services, much less all services within the economy. In expanding, trade drew in its train a number of allied activities: shipbuilding and outfitting, maritime employment, insurance, credit, and merchant expertise. Even if the direct contribution of trade to output was modest, the indirect contributions may have been quite substantial. But evidence about these linkages is only beginning to appear on the scale necessary to understand French performance in the service sector.[42]

To sum up, French agricultural growth was not much greater than population growth at 0.3 percent a year. Manufacturing output ex-

[38] See Chapter 4.

[39] Exports are averaged for these years because they represent a peacetime era in which war was not expected. See Chapter 4 for a discussion of trade flows in years in which war was expected.

[40] Marczewski, "Some Aspects," 372.

[41] Also Patrick O'Brien, "European Economic Development: The Contribution of the Periphery," *Economic History Review*, 2nd ser., 35, no. 1 (Feb. 1982), 1-18, esp. 4.

[42] E.g., T.J.A. Le Goff and Jean Meyer, "Les constructions navales en France pendant la seconde moitié du XVIIIe siècle," *Annales E.S.C.*, 26, no. 1 (Jan.-Feb. 1971), 173-85.

panded more rapidly, but the rate of growth is difficult to estimate because we know little about some industries and about output for autoconsumption. The rate of change in industrial performance seems to be situated (in constant per capita values) between the low rate achieved by wool, about 0.3 percent a year, and some higher figure intended to draw in all other industries. Overall performance probably occurred at a rate close to the 0.3 percent growth of wool output. In trade there was more dynamic growth, in excess of 1.0 percent a year, and perhaps as high as 1.7 percent. But trade played a much smaller direct role in output than agriculture or manufacturing.

Considering the three sectors, which Marczewski estimates to have accounted for 82 percent of all output, and the long-run performance of the economy from 1701-1710 to 1781-1790, we confront an economy weighed down by the failure of agriculture to break away from traditional rates of productivity change. Industrial and trade performance ran counter to agricultural performance, but not by substantial enough margins to leave the impression of large overall growth. In the end, therefore, the evidence lends more credence to the image given by Bairoch, an image of slow growth, than that given by O'Brien and Keyder or Marczewski. The O'Brien/Keyder estimate implies a 1701-1710 output of some 2.3 billion l.t. (in 1781-1790 prices). At the other extreme, Bairoch's growth path of 0.3 percent implies a 1701-1710 agricultural and manufacturing output close to 4 billion l.t. (also in 1781-1790 prices). It is this latter figure that is more plausible, and thus it is this latter figure that needs to be converted into 1701-1710 prices for purposes of later comparisons. That conversion is made difficult by the instability of the money of account, the livre tournois, in silver and gold during 1700-1726. Using the Paris wheat series, which reports prices in current livres and thus makes no adjustment for changes in the silver or gold equivalence of the money of account, the conversion produces a ceiling output estimate for 1701-1710 of 2.7 billion l.t. in current prices, about 125 l.t. per capita.[43]

What is especially significant is the mere presence of growth—that agriculture kept pace with population growth, and that industry and trade also expanded, if somewhat less than is usually said be-

[43] Comparing a truncated thirteen-year average centered on 1705 with the 1781-1788 average from price data in Baulant, "Le prix des grains," 539-40.

cause these issues are usually discussed in terms of current rather than constant values. This is significant because even an overall growth rate of only 0.3 percent sustained through the eighteenth century is a considerable achievement when compared to prior economic performance. It suggests that the French economy was breaking with the past, deviating from the long-run immobility that had for so long been characteristic. It is this backdrop, together with the specific data introduced here, that allow the economic effects of war to be investigated.

THE CONJUNCTURE IN 1755

Although kings and their advisers did not carefully investigate the capacity of the economy to pay for war before beginning a conflict, this is nevertheless an issue of some importance. Modern and traditional economies alike seem to be prey to long, intermediate, and short-run cyclical movements of expansion and shrinkage. Some conflicts will be begun, haphazardly in these terms, when the economy possesses a large measure of discretionary resources, and when people sense that there are surplus resources to be allotted to war. Others will be begun at less auspicious times, in the decline phase of a cycle, or in that still unhappier setting in which two or more of these cyclical patterns combine in regression. How did France stand on the eve of the Seven Years War? Were the economic signs auspicious? Could France afford to begin another conflict only eight years after having concluded the War of Austrian Succession?

Economic cycles usually chart output fluctuations, but the only way to deal with French output in the eighteenth century—interpolations between point estimates (e.g., between 1701-1710 and 1781-1790)—cannot bring any cycles to light. Recognizing this problem, French historians have turned to price data, constructing series and estimating the chronology of economic cycles on the basis of grain prices that are intended to stand for overall economic performance, often with a lag recognizing the tendency of price change to lead adaptations in output.[44] Using a framework suggested by

---

[44] Many economists are uncomfortable with the use of prices to infer output cycles and with the proposition that rising prices, identified especially with periods in which population growth causes demand to outpace supply, are a sign of growth in output. This difference of opinion between historians and economists appears to emerge be-

François Simiand, it has become customary to designate long cyclical eras of rising prices as *A* phases, and long cyclical eras of declining prices as *B* phases. One of the objectives of this branch of investigation has been to establish the long-run trend of economic performance, applying the assumption that secular price increase is advantageous to producers, bringing profits and expansion, and therefore signals growth in output. On the basis of these assumptions, historians recognize the period from about 1650 to 1690 as an era of contraction, from about 1690 to 1730 as an era of confusion (both in the sources, which are difficult to interpret because of frequent monetary adjustments, and in performance), and the era from about 1730 on as a period of expansion.[45] This conceptualization shows up briefly in the 49-year moving average provided in Chart 1.2, which, using Paris wheat prices, locates the 1750s within a period of sustained price increase.

If the presence of long-run cycles, often referred to as Kondratieffs, is often conceded, there is some skepticism about the robustness of intermediate cycles. The price data can be made to depict cyclical movements, such as show up in Chart 1.2 in the curves of 13- and 25-year moving averages. Do these movements coincide with regularly reappearing cycles? Opinion is divided. Crouzet and Charles Carrière find one well-defined business cycle in two ports, Bordeaux and Marseilles, for 1768-1775, and suppose that other cycles existed but that they are left obscure by war effects.[46] But

---

cause of different beliefs about the mechanism behind rising prices. The economist's view seems to be that population growth will increase the demand for cash balances but that economies of scale should increase the size of the monetized sector of the economy. "Other things equal, the effect of population growth is deflationary." Joel Mokyr, "Discussion" [of Jack A. Goldstone, "The Origins of the English Revolution: A Demographic Approach"], *Journal of Economic History*, 45 (Jun. 1985), 473. Aside from being a generalization from observing that, in the short run, prices rise when demand outruns supply, the historian's view seems to be that this assumption about the behavior of monetary forces should not be made until more is known of the old regime monetary system. That is, it has not been demonstrated that inflationary episodes produce more rather than less monetary efficiency in an economy such as that of the old regime, in which the authorities could not supply specie at low cost and in which many people felt keenly anxious over having enough money to pay bills, and already held large cash balances. These differences of opinion are part of a larger, and completely unresolved, debate over how old regime markets operated.

[45] For example, J[acques] Dupâquier, M[arcel] Lachiver, and J[ean] Meuvret, *Mercuriales du pays de France et du vexin français (1640-1792)* (Paris, 1968), 233-34 and chart 1.

[46] François Crouzet, "La conjuncture bordelaise," in François-Georges Pariset, ed.,

Chart 1.2

Price Cycles on the Eve of War

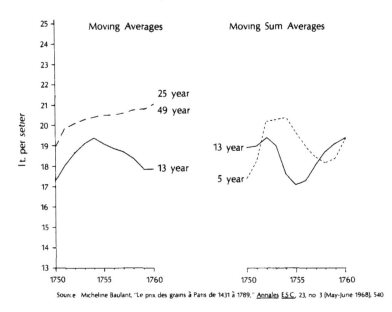

Source Micheline Baulant, "Le prix des grains à Paris de 1431 à 1789," *Annales E.S.C.* 23, no 3 (May-June 1968), 540

Morineau argues that even Kondratieffs should be construed as *séquences* rather than long cycles, sequences structured by war and the effects of war on government spending, purchasing power, the public debt, and interest rates.[47] Thus eighteenth-century wars are said to have had the capacity to distort or obscure economic cycles. The intermediate course of prices pictured in Chart 1.2 in the 13- and 25-year curves give conflicting testimony. According to one, the war began in the downward slope of a cycle; and according to the other, in the upward slope. The customary confusion of pattern, noticed by Braudel and Spooner,[48] is evident once again. But it is also apparent that these price cycles do not show any war effect. All

---

Bordeaux au XVIIIe siècle (Bordeaux, 1968), 302-303; and Charles Carrière, *Négociants marseillais au XVIIIe siècle* (2 vols.; n.p., n.d.), I, 379 and 396.

[47] Michel Morineau, "Pour une reconsidération des mouvements de longue durée et, notamment, des mouvements dits de Kondratieff," unpublished manuscript, p. 5, which the author has kindly permitted me to cite.

[48] F[ernand] P. Braudel and F[rank] Spooner, "Prices in Europe from 1450 to 1750," in *Cambridge Economic History of Europe*, ed. by E. E. Rich and C. H. Wilson (Cambridge, 1967), IV, 430-42.

three cycles had established a trend by 1755-1756, and that trend continued despite the beginning of conflict at sea in 1755 and in Europe in 1756.

The Seven Years War began in the middle of a long cycle of economic expansion, and in that sense came at a point when resources that might be shifted to war were becoming more plentiful. The intermediate-run picture is confused, perhaps because of the difficulty of finding appropriate data to reveal regular rather than random price cycles, perhaps because of the absence of such cycles in eighteenth-century France, and perhaps because of the imperfections of using price data to infer economic performance. In any event, the war began at a time of low grain prices, which show up forcefully in Labrousse's national grain index (Table 1.2). For consumers, the prewar years were years of cheap grain within a longer cycle of inflation and economic growth.

How consumers and producers saw these price trends is difficult to determine. Few series exist for French wages and salaries, and those that do depict wages for one or a few occupations that may not be representative. They are also silent about shifts in time worked, so that we learn from them the wage rate but not necessarily the compensation received. Unlike prices, wages tended to change slowly. In periods of inflation this stickiness is usually said to have left wage earners with contracting real incomes. With these things in mind, it is worthwhile to look at approximate figures based on fragmentary data assembled by Ernest Labrousse for wages of *professionnels des campagnes*:[49]

1726-1733	.75 francs (i.e., livres tournois)
1734-1761	.80
1762-1769	.85
1770-1774	.90
1775-1784	.95
1785-1788	1.00

Thus prices, which (using Labrousse's index) increased by 21 percent between 1726-1733 and 1751-1755, rose more rapidly by far than did wages in this series, which increased very modestly indeed during that period. Still, the putative gap between rising prices and

---

[49] Jean Fourastié, *L'évolution des prix à long terme* (Paris, 1969), xxii, drawing on Labrousse, *Esquisse*, II, 447ff.

sluggish wages widened more rather than less rapidly after 1761 than before. Thus the decades of the 1730s, 1740s, and 1750s appear as a period advantageous to agricultural producers (whose revenues rose more rapidly than labor costs) but not, in comparison to coming times, seriously disadvantageous to wage earners. And in the immediate prewar years, 1754-1756, when harvests were abundant and the price trend temporarily favorable to consumers, wage earners enjoyed good times.

The idea that the eve of the Seven Years War was a period of relative good times is easy to accept from the statistical evidence, but more difficult to accept from prevailing views on popular welfare and from impressionistic judgments ventured at the time. The economic and social historians of old regime France stand at odds. Among the first, it is believed that the eighteenth-century trend was rising prosperity, a movement that may have been cut off in the 1770s and 1780s. Among the second, in contrast, the striking fact seems to be immiseration and pauperization, conditions easier to generate in periods of economic contraction than in periods of growth. Social historians—Hufton, Gutton, Frêche, Fairchilds, Jones, Forrest, and others—believe, in Jones' words, that "the gap between population rise and economic growth probably increased as the century wore on," which "led remorselessly towards mass pauperization."[50] Forrest believes that poverty was the customary condition of about one-third of the French populace, and that below this category may be distinguished yet another, the destitutes.[51]

There is more appearance than reality in this confrontation. It is a question of timing. The evidence from economic history distributes growth throughout the century, but points to the considerably more rapid rise of prices after 1765 than before. After that point

---

[50] Colin Jones, *Charity and "Bienfaisance": The Treatment of the Poor in the Montpellier Region, 1740-1815* (Cambridge, 1982), 30. Also Olwen H. Hufton, *The Poor of Eighteenth-Century France, 1750-1789* (Oxford, 1974); id., "Social Conflict and the Grain Supply in Eighteenth-Century France"; J.-P. Gutton, *La société et les pauvres: L'exemple de la généralité de Lyon, 1534-1789* (Paris, 1970); Cissie Fairchilds, *Poverty and Charity in Aix-en-Provence, 1640-1789* (Baltimore, 1976); Frêche, *Toulouse*; and the sources cited in the note that follows.

[51] Alan Forrest, "The Condition of the Poor in Revolutionary Bordeaux," *Past & Present*, no. 59 (May 1973), 147: poverty was "the customary state of perhaps one-third of French families in the eighteenth century"; and id., *The French Revolution and the Poor* (New York, 1981).

much of the growth disappears when the money illusion is noticed. And it is especially in the later decades of the century, the era that Labrousse styled the *malaise prérévolutionnaire*, that pauperization and destitution show up—although not perhaps on the scale asserted by Forrest. Thus around 1770 the A phase changed character. Growth continued, but its effects in income and material goods were distributed more unevenly, so that the poor became more numerous and perhaps also poorer, while modal or average economic well-being changed slowly.

Hindsight gives a large advantage in distinguishing secular trends in national income and its distribution. Eighteenth-century observers had more trouble detecting a trend, tending to see economic issues in the several shades of popular misery. This is evident in the investigation of François Damiens, who attempted on January 5, 1757, to assassinate Louis XV, or, in his own terms, to get the king's attention.[52] Damiens argued that he had acted on behalf of one side in a complex theological and political dispute between the archbishop of Paris, seconded by the king, and the parlement of Paris, in which the former was the party of orthodoxy and the latter the party of Jansenism, Gallicanism, and the defense of constitutional responsibilities claimed by the parlement. Formerly a servant in the employ of different members of the parlementary nobility, but more recently a thief, and mad, Damiens claimed the comparatively lofty motive of wishing the king to oblige the archbishop to rescind a restriction on giving confession to those *religieux* lacking sufficient orthodoxy. The men who investigated the case, parlementaires, doubted that Damiens would have acted from such lofty motives, and probably also feared that an inquiry into his motives might reveal the degree to which his action expressed views consistent with the parlementaires' own outlook. The investigators preferred to suspect selfish motives, and looked into Damiens' recollections of hard times—an ironic tack in light of Damiens' large theft, which had left him in the months before his attack on the king quite well off by the standards of domestic servants.

This event reveals something about the popular conception of public welfare. The investigation discovered that "concern over misery, taxes, and the high price of grain was common in 1756-

[52] Dale K. Van Kley, *The Damiens Affair and the Unraveling of the "Ancien Régime,"* *1750-1770* (Princeton, 1984).

1757."[53] Both in the remonstrances of the parlement, aimed at the king, and in Damiens' confessions, popular misery was a prominent motif.[54] As we see, however, grain prices were not high on the eve of the war, a localized shortage on the Channel coast notwithstanding. Nor, as we shall discover later, had taxes yet risen significantly. Beyond doubt there was misery amidst plenty in old regime France, but it is especially difficult to find forces that might have contributed to any unusual hardship in the early 1750s—quite the contrary.

Another way to seek evidence about economic expectations is to look at prices in another manner. The moving average used to this point implies a retrospective view, for it lumps forward and backward values together to smooth an inevitably uneven movement, thereby to uncover trend. The same information can be used to calculate moving sum averages, which include only values for years past. This procedure more successfully captures the long-run, intermediate, and short-run conception that people living in the mid-1750s will have had of the price trend, which will of course have been a conception recalling only prior experience rather than one of past and future prices. This eighteenth-century notion of price change was informed not by specific estimates of price experience or explicit projections of future price movement, but by intuition from experience. Historians who have considered mathematical skills in the seventeenth and eighteenth centuries find a surprising ability to predict the outcome of problems with which that society had had considerable experience but for which the appropriate mathematical procedures and values had not yet been devised, or were not yet widely known. For example, French investors in life annuity loans and tontines, who included a broad segment of the populace, are known to have made fine distinctions in assessing the value of contracts offered by the government on nominees of different ages, this before either knowing the procedures of mathematical expectation or possessing the data necessary to put those procedures into operation.[55]

Thus seemingly vague and qualitative expressions about inflation, which are all we encounter in the literature of that day, may

[53] *Ibid.*, 42.
[54] *Ibid.*, 43.
[55] George Alter and James C. Riley, "How to Bet on Lives: A Guide to Life Contingent Contracts in Early Modern Europe," forthcoming, *Research in Economic History* (1986).

nevertheless have supported conclusions more or less as exact as those arrived at today by sophisticated quantitative techniques. Discussion of prices in eighteenth-century sources reveals awareness of inflation, but the awareness is stated in language that leaves us with little sense of how the quantity of prior or future inflation may have been perceived.[56] The key problem lies in deciding what period the awareness covers, what length of memory may have been brought to this intuitive grasp of inflation. The moving sum averages in Chart 1.2, calculated for 5- and 13-year periods, are intended to depict prior price experience for people with two memory lengths, one recent and one covering a longer period.

From this it is apparent why, to people living before the war or at any point in the 1750s, prices did not seem to be inflating as rapidly as they are portrayed by the historian's artifact of moving averages, which combine future and historical price information (and in this case combine rapidly rising future prices with slowly rising or declining past prices). The years just before the war were years of deflation. Using Paris wheat prices, average year-to-year price change over the five years 1749-1750 to 1753-1754 amounted to −0.4 percent, and over the thirteen years 1741-1742 to 1753-1754, to −8.7 percent. Recent price experience pointed toward deflation, or at the very least, toward future rates of inflation much lower than those actually to be experienced.

This simple insight helps explain the otherwise puzzling French attitude toward interest rates in the earlier part of the period of rising prices beginning about 1730. Legal and official policy dictated that interest should not be charged in most of old regime France. But lenders were allowed to be compensated in the form of a *rente*, a regular payment for the term of the loan, usually left unspecified.[57] This *rente* could not exceed the ceiling fixed by law in each province. During the seventeenth century declining prices had brought declining nominal interest rates in their train. Thus in Burgundy the *taux de l'ordonnance* fell from 6.25 percent during 1602-

---

[56] E.g., [Mathon de la Cour], *Collection de comptes-rendus* . . . (Lausanne, 1788), 225 and 226.

[57] The most common form of loan contracts was the *rente constituée* in which specified assets were mortgaged but no term was set for repayment, leaving to the borrower the option of deciding when to retire the loan by repaying the principal. Some authorities maintain that this *rente* should not be considered interest, but that argument seems to rest on a legalistic interpretation.

1673 to 5 percent during 1673-1687.[58] In those decades price deflation tended to be greater than experience suggested it would be. During the eighteenth century, in contrast, inflation did not bring adjustments to the *taux de l'ordonnance*, which in most of France remained fixed at 5 percent until 1789, when the National Assembly declared interest legal, and eliminated the need for ceilings to be fixed. Actual inflation regularly exceeded expected inflation (which can be estimated on the basis of an assumption about the operative memory length and year-to-year price changes within that time). Presumably because people consistently expected less inflation than they got, the pressures that had lowered legal ceilings in the seventeenth century did not raise them in the eighteenth.

For borrowers, the eighteenth century opened with two unusually favorable periods. During the first years of the century and again during the late 1710s, public authorities sharply increased the French money stock, with the result that prices soared. *Rentes constituées*—private loan contracts—were fixed in nominal money of account terms, so that inflation gave borrowers the option of retiring loans at considerable advantage. Lenders reacted by lowering interest rates in an effort to induce borrowers not to redeem their contracts.[59] The period of concern for us began with interest rates below the legal ceiling. In the 1730s and 1740s, according to data from one sample, those already low nominal rates declined further (Table 1.3).[60] Thus, in a period of rising prices, real interest rates

TABLE 1.3
Nominal Interest Rates in One Sample

1720s	3.6 percent	1760s	4.3
1730s	3.5	1770s	4.1
1740s	3.2	1780s	3.9
1750s	3.0		

SOURCE: Emmanuel Le Roy Ladurie, *Les paysans de Languedoc* (2 vols., Paris, 1966), II, 1,024-25, inferred from a chart.

[58] P[ierre] de Saint Jacob, *Les paysans de la Bourgogne du Nord au dernier siècle de l'ancien régime* (Paris, 1960), 162. See also Mohamed El Kordi, *Bayeux aux XVII*e* et XVIII*e* siècles* (Paris, 1970), 252; Pierre Goubert, *Beauvais et le Beauvaisis de 1600 à 1730* (2 vols.; Paris, 1960), I, 538-40; and Frêche, *Toulouse*, 569-70.

[59] Saint Jacob, *Les paysans de la Bourgogne*, 226; Emmanuel Le Roy Ladurie, *Les paysans de Languedoc* (2 vols.; Paris, 1966), I, 599.

[60] Since other series are unavailable, it cannot be said whether this sample is rep-

were lower still, and the unusually favorable position of the borrower was preserved beyond the era of monetary instability, which ended in 1726. During the 1750s the *rente* charged in this sample of contracts remained 3 percent, but then rose sharply to a plateau of approximately 4 percent that was sustained until the Revolution.

The low rate of 3 percent responded to temporary price deflation: the average year-to-year price change from 1749-1750 to 1755-1756 was −0.7 percent,[61] so that the real interest rate was higher than 3 percent. Nevertheless, the eve of the Seven Years War was an exceptionally good time to borrow money. Both entrepreneurs intending capital investments and the government stood to benefit from the low cost of credit, and from subsequent price trends that would quickly erode the value of debts contracted during the 1750s.

Another way to approach the economic conjuncture on the eve of this war is to look for signs of instability. Preindustrial economies are known to have been crisis prone, subject especially to unpredictable and often violent changes in the production of basic foods, and food production is known to have strongly influenced the health of other sectors of the economy. A shortage of food meant that people allotted more income toward food, and reduced purchases of wine, textiles, and other manufactured goods.[62] In 1741 and 1770-1772 agricultural prices rose sharply, suggesting that one might expect to find that output in other sectors contracted because of harvest failures. But the period between 1741 and 1770 is notable for the absence of serious harvest failures that struck broad regions. In some years, 1749 and 1752, wheat prices peaked, and food riots occurred.[63] In general, however, these were years of mild harvest reverberations.

As a result, these were good years for French industries using traditional technologies. Amiens drapery production peaked in 1750

---

resentative of national trends. Evidence from neighboring countries, where interest rates were low and declining at mid-century, implies that these rates agree with regional trends. See James C. Riley, *International Government Finance and the Amsterdam Capital Market, 1740-1815* (Cambridge, 1980), 47-48, 111, and *passim*.

[61] Calculated from Labrousse's index numbers (see Table 1.2).

[62] Georges Durand, *Vin, vigne, et vignerons en Lyonnais et Beaujolais* (Paris, 1979), 74-76; and Markovitch, *Les industries lainières*, 489-91.

[63] Louise A. Tilly, "The Food Riot as a Form of Political Conflict in France," *Journal of Interdisciplinary History*, 2, no. 1 (Summer 1971), 24.

after a long era of rising output, held steady at a high level until 1765, then declined gradually until the mid-1780s.[64] Languedoc cloth output for the Levant trade doubled between the second half of the 1720s and the first half of the 1750s, and continued to grow until 1776.[65] French wool production, an important item in export trade, climbed between 1726-1728 and 1748-1751 before entering a period of decline.[66] For other centers in general, output seems to have continued to expand.[67] The "rupture structurelle" which Léon detects between the traditional and the modern sectors of manufacturing became evident only later in the century.[68] Up to about 1780 France and England marched "d'un même pas vers la grande industrie de l'avenir. . . ."[69] In some industries the rate of increase in output during the middle decades of the century was phenomenally high. For the century in general, Léon believes that silk output grew by 2 percent per annum, cast iron by 2.1 percent, Rouen cotton production by 3.9 percent, coal in Anzin and Littry by 4.1 and in Rive-de-Gier by 4.8 percent.[70] These measures are all undeflated. But, clearly, adjustments to constant prices and per capita measures would not much diminish these rates during the years of slow growth in prices and population of the 1740s and 1750s.

Population growth occurred especially before 1740 and after 1755 (Table 1.1). Between these years Dupâquier's estimates indicate an expansion of no more than 400,000 people, and a rate of growth (0.11 percent) about one-third the level of the longer period from 1700 to the Revolution. If these were indeed the years of most rapid growth in manufacturing output, as the evidence gathered by Léon and Markovitch suggests, then these were also the years of the most rapid growth in per capita output.

What is true for manufacturing is true also for trade. In the quarter-century from 1726-1730 to 1751-1755 French imports and

---

[64] Pierre Deyon, "Le mouvement de la production textile à Amiens au XVIIIᵉ siècle," *Revue du Nord*, 44, no. 174 (Apr.-Jun. 1962), 205-206.

[65] Morineau and Carrière, "Draps du Languedoc," 109-110. Also J.K.J. Thomson, *Clermont-de-Lodève, 1633-1789: Fluctuations in the Prosperity of a Languedocian Cloth-Making Town* (Cambridge, 1982), 306 and 375, on output in Clermont-de-Lodève.

[66] Markovitch, *Les industries lainières*, 486.

[67] Léon, "L'élan industriel," 514-21.

[68] Léon, "Structures de commerce extérieur," 420.

[69] *Ibid.*, 407.

[70] Léon, "L'élan industriel," 519-21.

exports increased, in constant prices,[71] at a rate no less than 3.4 percent a year (Table 1.4). That startling figure, which reflects substantial and important development, is also diminished very little by shifting to a calculation of per capita performance. And since exports of industrial goods did not grow during the century in comparison to overall trade,[72] it follows that most of the additional output was consumed in France.

TABLE 1.4
French Imports and Exports, 1726-1755
(millions of constant livres tournois)

1726	190	1736	259	1746	269
1727	189	1737	249	1747	290
1728	207	1738	275	1748	295
1729	212	1739	309	1749	435
1730	212	1740	348	1750	428
1731	223	1741	351	1751	425
1732	231	1742	326	1752	492
1733	222	1743	353	1753	477
1734	209	1744	262	1754	484
1735	235	1745	284	1755	448

SOURCES. Ruggiero Romano, "Documenti e prime considerazioni intorno alla 'Balance du commerce' della Francia dal 1716 al 1780," in *Studi in onore di Armando Sapori* (2 vols.; Milan, 1957), 1,274; and n. 71 in the text of the present volume

These were also years in which France's money stock expanded. The pace of growth indicated by eighteenth-century estimates, themselves usually based on mint output data, show that the specie stock alone grew more rapidly than did prices.[73] If the money stock is construed more broadly to include commercial paper and IOUs, the rate of growth was higher still.[74] Even if we use only the specie stock estimates to gauge growth, the money supply expanded at a pace of 0.9 percent a year between 1700 and 1754. This increase in the money stock greater than in prices should be expected to show up in either or both an expansion of output or a rise in cash balances

[71] See below, Table 4.1, for the price adjustment technique.
[72] Léon, "Structures de commerce extérieur," 411-12, 414, and 423-32.
[73] Riley and McCusker, "Money Supply," 277 and 286-89.
[74] Ernest Labrousse, "Les 'bon prix' agricoles du XVIIIᵉ siècle," in Braudel and Labrousse, eds., *Histoire économique*, II, 394.

held by the public. Other evidence surveyed here indicates that output expanded, but does not rule out the possibility that cash balances also increased.

CONCLUSION

To bring together in this way what constitutes the best informed opinion about the scale and trend of eighteenth-century French economic activity is disheartening. After so many years of inquiry, we still know distressingly little about fundamental matters. Behind the quantities discussed here stand scores of detailed studies of individual businesses and sectors of the economy. Behind the impressions, some of which are expressed as quantities, stand the wisdom and judgment of several generations of historians who have lived with the problem of reconstructing economic activity. The question has been approached directly, examining output measures and estimates. And it has been approached indirectly, examining monetary and social signs.

If all this effort has not produced precise figures about the scale or the trend of economic activity, it has nevertheless produced a consensus that growth prevailed, at least in the middle decades of the century. The problem is to estimate the rate of growth in circumstances in which the boundaries, an average between 0.3 and 0.7 percent a year in constant values and per capita growth, represent very different things. The truth seems to lie closer to a 0.3 percent rate of growth.

This is, in itself, an important conclusion, for it indicates that in the years before the Seven Years War, France enjoyed rude economic health. A profound transformation had begun. In manufacturing, trade, and the money stock, France was experiencing unusually high growth rates. Other sectors failed to match this uncommon pace of expansion, but grew nevertheless. Sporadic estimates of national output do not bring to light periods of especially intensive growth. But this survey of trends identifies the years from about 1715 to 1765 as the period during which a substantial part of the entire growth estimated for the eighteenth century was concentrated.

In Labrousse's view the postwar period, 1763-1770, was "l'apogée économique de l'ancien régime," an extraordinary "flambée de prospérité."[75] This interpretation is based on the price trend and the putative beneficiaries of inflation, in his view especially agriculturalists who leased land.[76] The apogee is therefore to be located in the last phase of inflation, which benefited the lease-holder because lease contracts, struck ordinarily for nine years, still underestimated future price trends, and in the underestimation delivered profits to the lease-taker rather than to the lease-giver. This is a narrow definition of prosperity even for an agricultural economy like that in France, for it finds prosperity in the claim that agricultural lease-takers are not only the largest occupational group, which may be true, but also that circumstances benefiting them benefited the entire economy. Furthermore, most of the eighteenth century was not, in Labrousse's terms, as advantageous to the lease-taker as to the lease-giver, because inflation did not, within the nine-year periods common in agricultural leases, amount to much until the decade after 1763 (Table 1.2). In those years, however, only lease-takers who negotiated contracts within a very short period, from about 1763 to 1765, benefited much from the price peak of 1770-1771. This is so because those who negotiated nine-year contracts earlier had first to suffer the losses from deflation during 1761-1763 before enjoying gains from inflation, and those who negotiated contracts after 1765 had to balance the inflationary gains of 1766-1771 against deflationary losses after 1771. Thus it will be more persuasive to shift the location of this apogee back in time, to the years during or just before the Seven Years War.

In economic resources, France was better prepared to go to war in 1756 than it had been at any point since at least the 1680s. Part of this economic preparedness was owing to good luck—the absence of catastrophes that devastated the harvest. Part of it was owing to long-run growth of the economy, which brought France to an apogee of prosperity between 1755 and 1765. And part of it was owing to low expected rates of inflation, which left interest rates at their lowest levels since the 1720s. Whether the greater income was spread over all of France or concentrated in some regions, and whether it was dispersed widely among the populace or seized by a

[75] C.-E. Labrousse, *Crise de l'économie française à la fin de l'ancien régime et au début de la Révolution* (Paris, 1944), xxxii.

[76] *Ibid.*, 535 and *passim*.

few, the additional wealth underscores France's economic preparedness to fight. Insofar as an economy can ever absorb the costs of
war, France's economy was prepared to absorb the costs of a new
conflict. But the populace apparently did not sense this. Spokesmen
such as the parlementaires of Paris complained of economic misery
whenever they wished to resist the king's will, which is to say in good
times and bad. To them, France's position behind only the Dutch
Republic and Britain as the European leader in per capita resources
and income seemed less important than the misery of the poor, or
the political and rhetorical advantages of lamenting popular misery.

Behind the visible risks of going to war stood the invisible risk of
jeopardizing a tentative departure from the characteristic long-run
immobility of incomes in the old regime. The French economy had
not yet achieved income levels prevailing in the Dutch Republic.[77]
But it had begun to break from the past, to embark on a peculiarly
French scheme of simultaneous growth across sectors, to shift toward growth at a rate surpassing customary performance in the traditional economy. The Seven Years War put this departure at risk.

[77] James C. Riley, "The Dutch Economy after 1650: Decline or Growth?" *Journal of European Economic History*, 13, no. 3 (Winter 1984), 521-69.

FRENCH FINANCES ON THE EVE OF WAR

Le Royaume qui gémit sous le poids des Impôts.[1]

*I*N the eighteenth century in Europe one power possessed more aggregate financial and economic resources than any other, enough more to create the idea of dominance but not enough more to bring this idea into reality. "La France est sans contredit de tous les Royaumes celui qui peut le plus contribuer à la richesse du Prince et des Peuples. . . ."[2] If France could better afford to fight wars, it still could not afford to fight as often or as vigorously as it did. This is so not because the people and the economy were oppressed by taxes, but because they believed they were, because they believed that theirs was "le Royaume qui gémit sous le poids des Impôts." The first and most important feature of French finances on the eve of the Seven Years War and at every other point in the eighteenth century is this: the French detested the tax. When levies were heavy and when they were light, the French felt toward them an "hostilité violente et constante."[3] (Even the French historians are handicapped by this aversion.[4])

The French claimed that they were overtaxed and that the excess caused economic misery. By tradition such laments are taken seriously, which they should be, and straightforwardly, which they should not be. Marion relates a situation in which up to 600 l.t. was

---

[1] Bibliothèque Nationale, Paris, Joly de Fleury, 1432, folio 168r.

[2] Bibliothèque Mazarine, Paris, 2767, by Dufort de LaGraulet, folio 2r.

[3] François Hincker, *Les Français devant l'impôt sous l'ancien régime* (Paris, 1971), 11. Also Jean Meyer, *La noblesse bretonne au XVIII' siècle* (2 vols.; Paris, 1966), II, 1084: "La peur de l'impôt domine toutes les réactions nobiliaires." For an eighteenth-century source developing this theme, see [Claude Jacques Herbert], *Essai sur la police générale des grains* . . . (Berlin, 1755), 416ff.

[4] Pierre Goubert, *L'ancien régime: Les pouvoirs* (Paris, 1973), 134-35.

spent to contest assessments of 5 l.t. or less.[5] The laments are not, as Marion and many other authorities have suggested, evidence of misery, for after all, they were made by articulate and well-placed people who did not know misery themselves and who, for the most part, had little sincere sympathy for the downtrodden. The laments are rather evidence of the susceptibility of the system to manipulation, of the prevalence of the feeling that the tax laws—this "espèce de labyrinte [sic]"—could be adjusted to serve the usually selfish ends of the lamenter.[6] They partake also of the rhetoric of reform, which is sometimes based on principle.

It is the aversion that explains the structure of French taxation, the inadequacy of royal revenues, and some elements of the aversion itself. The French loathed their tax system in the first place with a great primeval loathing. As recently as the seventeenth century they had believed that the king's authority to tax was a usurpation.[7] They loathed it in the second place for its malleability, which existed at least in part because the French despised taxes, and because they insisted on pursuing an eternal quest for personal advantage in the tax system. Such behavior was rational, for the tax system offered many payoffs for those who would manipulate it. The French loathed their tax system in the third place because they believed that those who collected the taxes drained off the people's wealth and the king's revenues.[8] And they loathed it finally because they vastly exaggerated the taxes they did pay. One form of this exaggeration held that the people paid one-third of their revenues in royal, provincial, and municipal taxes.[9] We must keep this loathing in mind as we explore the financial structure in the eighteenth century and on

[5] Marcel Marion, *Histoire financière de la France depuis 1715* (5 vols.; Paris, 1927-1928), I, 8.

[6] Anon., "Considérations sur les finances & le commerce de France," *Journal de commerce et d'agriculture* (Brussels) (Jan. 1761), 8.

[7] Jean Meuvret, "Comment les Français du XVIIᵉ siècle voyaient l'impôt," *Dix-septième siècle*, no. 25-26 (1955), 60.

[8] These sentiments are found in nearly every commentary, e.g., Bibliothèque de l'Arsenal, Paris, 4489, including a manuscript on the taxes dating from 1711; and in the pamphlets discussed in Chapter 7.

[9] Algemeen Rijksarchief, The Hague, Legatiearchief, Eerste Afdeling, Frankrijk, 786, p. 124, from "une personne bien au fait des affaires des finances"; and Bibliothèque Nationale, Joly de Fleury, 1432, folios 170r-170v, in a memoir from the parlement of Bordeaux to the king.

the eve of war, and as we look into the capacity of the French monarchy to augment taxation to pay for war.

A FINANCIAL LABYRINTH

Within the last two decades historians have come to agree with eighteenth-century observers that France was a rich land. This was not always so. When the history of the royal fisc was first written in the modern style of scholarship, by Clamageran (1867-1876), Stourm (1885), and Marion (1891-1931), this economy was portrayed as a scene of misery and bitterness, and the French tax system was held responsible.[10] Marion, the fiscal conservative condemning waste and deficits in French finances in his day, wrote because he wanted to expose "les détestables pratiques financières de l'ancien régime, ses fautes multipliées."[11] But we now know that eighteenth-century France was one of the wealthiest countries in the world in both aggregate and per capita measures of income.

If France was so rich, why was it also so poor in financial resources? This is a central question to ask because it has such a large bearing on the development of the old regime and its collapse beginning in 1787 in a financial crisis, and because the answers to this question shed light on what is apparently an unending problem of civilization: governments tend to spend more than they take in. Marion, like Clamageran, answered this question by pointing to the effects of privilege, claiming that the people were exhausted by the taxes they paid and that the privileged elite refused to bear its fair share. The resulting financial plight built slowly but inescapably into the collapse of 1787.[12] Other scholars have followed Marion's lead and his preference for an administrative history rather than Clamageran's history of the financial accounts. They have examined the elements of the system of privilege without clarifying what its actual costs were. The literature is replete with iterations of Marion's

[10] J[ean]-J[ules] Clamageran, *Histoire de l'impôt en France* (3 vols.; Paris, 1867-1876); René Stourm, *Les finances de l'ancien régime et de la Révolution* (2 vols.; Paris, 1885); Marion, *Histoire financière*; Marcel Marion, *L'impôt sur le revenu au dix-huitième siècle principalement en Guyenne* (Toulouse, 1901); and id., *Les impôts directs sous l'ancien régime* (Paris, 1910).

[11] Marion, *Histoire financière*, I, v. Also Clamageran, *Histoire de l'impôt*, III, vi-viii and xv-xvi, to the same effect.

[12] Marion, *Histoire financière*, I, vi.

judgment, which was not novel in 1927. But the hypothesis has never been tested, and the costs of privilége have never been established. This approach is inadequate, because it relies upon a misreading of the level of prosperity in France, because it oversimplifies the causes of financial distress, and because it fails to detect significant fluctuations in the trend of financial healthiness during the eighteenth century.

The failures of old regime royal finance are usually divided into two parts. First, the French paid more in taxes than the king received. It is usually alleged that the difference was taken out by tax collectors, and especially by a fortunate few individuals who held some part of the collection apparatus as venal officers or tax farmers, holding a lease on a public trust. This is the defect of an excessively expensive overhead. It can be identified with the criticisms made by Jacques Necker, who had charge of royal finances during 1777-1781 and 1788-1790, with earlier controllers general such as Sully and Colbert, with critics such as Mirabeau and the physiocrats, and with the historians who have judged this the principal defect, especially Bosher.[13]

Second, not all of the French paid all of the taxes, and in general wealthier people and communities escaped more taxation than did the poor. Thus exemptions from taxation—one aspect of a complex structure of privilege—cost the treasury out of proportion to their social or political benefits. This is the defect of tax avoidance and, because privilege was not always fixed in law or custom in an incontestable manner,[14] and because some people defied the law, it encompasses the defect of tax evasion. It can be identified with criticisms made by Calonne, who had charge of the finances during 1783-1787, with previous controllers general such as Machault, with reform theorists such as Roussel de la Tour, and with the historians Clamageran and Lüthy.[15]

[13] John F. Bosher, *French Finances, 1770-1795* (Cambridge, 1970). Also id., "The French Government's Motives in the *Affaire du Canada, 1761-1763*," *English Historical Review,* 96, no. 378 (Jan. 1981), 59-78, esp. 66, on corruption in the French administration.

[14] Guy Chaussinand Nogaret, "Le fisc et les privilégiés sous l'ancien régime," in *La fiscalité et ses implications sociales en Italie et en France aux XVIIᵉ et XVIIIᵉ siècles* (Rome, 1980), 191-206, esp. 193, for the discussion of the concept of privilege.

[15] Clamageran, *Histoire de l'impôt*; and Herbert Lüthy, *La banque protestante en France de la révocation de l'édit de Nantes à la Révolution* (2 vols.; Paris, 1959-1961). Also Gabriel Ardant, *Histoire de l'impôt* (2 vols.; n.p., 1971-1972), II, 90.

Both perspectives contain much truth, and both are misleading. It is true that the people paid more in taxes than the king collected. But the difference did not all go into the pockets of tax agents, whether royal officials or tax farmers. Much of it went to pay the costs of local and regional government, especially in the areas more recently added to the realm, the *pays d'état* and the *pays conquis*, and to meet central government responsibilities paid at the local level.[16] This legitimate seepage of revenues, which sometimes escaped the attention of eighteenth-century critics, has escaped the notice of many historians. Nevertheless, the archives of Paris and the provinces are rich in information on this point.[17]

It is also true that people avoided and evaded taxes. Two features of this problem need to be distinguished. Some tax avoidance is legal; it is allowed by the laws in force at the time. Some avoidance is illegal—let us call this "evasion." One of the historian's tasks is to examine the scale of avoidance and evasion. But it is not the historian's responsibility to judge avoidance. Ideas about taxes have undergone some fundamental shifts since the eighteenth century, and some historians have been too eager to apply later standards to judge earlier behavior. Since the old regime, ideas about tax equity have changed. One change is that exclusions from taxation are no longer given on social grounds. They continue to exist, and indeed remain plentiful. Even American scholars who have fellowship income enjoy a tax exclusion. A later age may judge our exclusions ill, in the same way that we are tempted to condemn eighteenth-century France for granting exclusions to some classes but withholding them from others.

Furthermore, the monarchy campaigned nearly continuously against certain forms of avoidance and evasion. In the seventeenth century many abuses were ended.[18] Seemingly all of articulate France was alive to the king's putative interest in this, for the ar-

[16] Algemeen Rijksarchief, Archief Fagel, 1571, pp. 23-24: "Ces Revenus Royaux et part.ers pour ce qui ne revient point directement au Roy, sont employés en Dépenses que S. M. Seroit obligée de faire si Elle recevoit directement ces Sortes de Revenus. . . ." For example, at the middle of the century the king split one category of taxes producing 18 million a year with certain municipalities. The towns also collected their own revenues.

[17] Bibliothèque de l'Arsenal, 4489, folios 75-80; and Archives Nationales, Paris, esp. the P series.

[18] Meuvret, "Comment," 71.

chives are full of memoirs explaining how to curtail abuses, and at certain times large numbers of tracts were published on this theme. No idea, however wise or foolish, is absent from this discussion; even what is today called the Laffer curve—the idea that higher taxes may actually diminish revenues and correspondingly that reducing taxes will augment revenues through economic growth—was articulated. But the reforms were always piecemeal, for the state, which lived on its revenues, could not afford the hiatus in revenues that most reform proposals required. Moreover, some tax advantages, such as those which distinguished the *pays d'état* and the *pays conquis* from the *pays d'élection* and the clergy from the laity, were embedded in law. Changes in them raised issues basic to the continuation of the monarchy.[19]

The existence and the implications of the system of privilege are, like French hostility toward royal taxes, central to an understanding of the fiscal system. Properly interpreted, this system will be recognized both as a way of distinguishing social orders and as a path of mobility. The desire to acquire privileges, or more privileges, activated social behavior in eighteenth-century France. To be sustained as a system, it had to be used: privileges had to be granted. They were the most useful designations of status, because they both reminded one's neighbors of status and provided economic benefits. Upholding this system, which monarchs used to their own advantage, meant that the proceeds of any tax would tend to stagnate or even diminish over time, as privileges were granted and acquired. Thus new taxes would have to be added to compensate the treasury for rising expenses or even for a stable quantity of expenses. As long as the population was growing, as it was in the eighteenth century, the redistribution necessitated by new grants and privileges tended to bring not higher per capita taxes for those lacking privileges, but about the same current value levy. Thus, in an era of inflation, this system provided declining revenues for the government when revenues are measured in livres tournois of constant value. Hence the government was compelled to introduce new or to enlarge old taxes, and thereby repeatedly possessed opportunities to take back with one hand the privileges it had granted with the other. To inter-

[19] This issue is discussed in many sources. See, for example, Koninklijke Bibliotheek, Brussels, Manuscript Department, 3132, for an historical view; and Bibliothèque de l' Arsenal, 4062.

pret the effects of privilege on taxation requires a constant attentiveness to changes in the mixture of tax laws and in the benefits available to privilege.

This system met with the approval of the king and the realistically ambitious segments of this society (excluding, therefore, the inarticulate poor, who had no reasonable prospect of obtaining privileges, and the highest ranks of the nobility, who already enjoyed all the privileges to which they could aspire and who wanted to tighten access). For the king, it was a way to augment approval and support, one he could manipulate at will by cheapening the value of privileges already granted or by introducing new taxes that compensated the treasury for privileges previously granted. For the upwardly mobile, the system was a motor of advancement, a motor powered by real economic benefits rather than only by honors. For the king, it was part of a deception in which privileges were made reversible, and in which the privileged obtained less than appearances suggest.

Another major shift since the old regime in ideas about tax equity lies in the realm of distribution. There is alive in every age a doctrine of fairness, a prevailing sense about what constitutes equity in the distribution of taxes. In the eighteenth century opinion was in flux. Some theorists adhered to the established view, according to which taxability took two forms: "Celui qui contribuë le plus de sa personne doit le moins contribuer de ses Biens: c'est de ce principe que dérivent toutes les exemptions légitimes."[20] This version of the doctrine of fairness held that, all else being equal, contributions should be proportional to wealth. Since the privileges conveying legitimate tax exemptions—these contributions "de sa personne"—clustered toward the top of the income scale, this view is one way of saying that cash taxability will be inversely related to income. The privileged shall pay less in cash because they pay more in service, and the unprivileged shall pay more in cash because they give so little service.[21] But many of the unprivileged were rich, so that it would not be just to argue that taxation fell only upon the poor rather than the rich.[22] Even reformers recognized the doctrine of

[20] Bibliothèque Nationale, Joly de Fleury, 1432, folio 168v.

[21] Nevertheless, this memoir recognized some unjust distribution of the taxes, admitting (folio 169r) that the rich were exempt from the *taille* and the poor were overburdened.

[22] Goubert, *Les pouvoirs*, 148-49, makes this point.

privilege. Thus Claude Jacques Herbert, who anticipated some of the ideas of the physiocrats, wrote: "On devoit payer de sa personne ou en argent, chacun suivant son Domaine, ou ses facultés."[23] Herbert objected to specific exemptions, such as operated in the *taille*, but not to the foundation of the system, which was payment in "service."

Some thinkers took another view, holding that taxation should be neutral, which is to say that everyone who had to pay taxes should pay them on the same footing. People who took this view, such as the controller general Machault, heir to a rich tradition of progressive thinkers which included Vauban and Saint-Pierre, often favored, in principle, taxes on consumables, which they judged the most equal and the least noticeable, but which they recognized to possess the disadvantage of costliness in collection.[24] They did not trouble themselves with what to a later age would be seen as the regressive effect of taxing necessities, probably because they realized that the excises fell more heavily on the bourgeoisie and the urban poor, who bought most of what they consumed, than upon peasants, who supplied much of their own consumables.[25]

The decrees of August 4, 1789, which abolished the seigneurial system of extra-rental income for some landowners and the church's chief source of revenues, the tithe, also proclaimed the principle of equality before the tax law. Before that time the legal system both tolerated and sanctioned inequality before the tax law, if inequality of one sort only. The idea of taxing the rich more heavily than others does not figure prominently in the old regime discussion, Rousseau's argument in the *Encyclopédie* notwithstanding. Very few people asserted that the proportion of income or wealth paid in taxes should rise with income and wealth.[26] Discussion cen-

[23] [Herbert], *Essai*, 395.

[24] Bibliothèque Nationale, Joly de Fleury, 1432, folio 168r, the views of the parlement of Bordeaux expressed in 1764.

[25] Meuvret, "Comment," 76, about the seventeenth century.

[26] Historians have been no more successful than present-day fiscal authorities in deciding how taxes may be shifted from intended and primary payers to final payers. See the unresolved discussions between Betty Behrens, "Nobles, Privileges and Taxes in France at the End of the *Ancien Régime*," *Economic History Review*, 2nd ser., 15, no. 3 (1963), 451-75; id., "A Revision Defended: Nobles, Privileges, and Taxes in France," *French Historical Studies*, 9, no. 3 (Spring 1976), 521-27; and G. J. Cavanaugh, "Nobles, Privileges, and Taxes in France: A Revision Reviewed," *French Histor-*

tered instead on the elimination of unreasonable privileges, which each writer defined in his own way, and on the discovery of a tax system that allowed fewer opportunities for unreasonable profits.

For two reasons—costly overhead and tax avoidance—a rich land is held to have become poor in financial resources. The ways in which this interpretation is valid will emerge from a discussion of French taxes, revenues and expenditures, overhead, and debt management. The same discussion will reveal that, on the eve of the Seven Years War, France was not in fiscal ill health despite the war just past. Tax revenues were expanding, the debt remained manageable, the peacetime deficit was small, and financial authorities[27] were watching the situation closely.

The Taxes

The taxes in force in France on the eve of the Seven Years War had grown by accretion during more than three centuries. Some taxes previously collected had disappeared, but more frequently authorities added new taxes and extended old.[28] It is customary to observe that the French tax system was complex. But it was also quite simple. Its complexities lay in the variety of forms applied in different regions, in the contrast between theory and practice, in the multiplicity of designated taxes, and in the problem of seeing eighteenth-

---

ical Studies, 8, no. 4 (Fall 1974), 681-92; id., "Reply to Behrens," *French Historical Studies*, 9, no. 3 (Spring 1976), 528-31; and among Peter Mathias and Patrick O'Brien, "Taxation in Britain and France, 1715-1810: A Comparison of the Social and Economic Incidence of Taxes Collected for the Central Governments," *Journal of European Economic History*, 5, no. 3 (Winter 1976), 601-650; id., "The Incidence of Taxes and the Burden of Proof," *Journal of European Economic History*, 7, no. 1 (Spring 1978), 211-13; and Donald N. McCloskey, "A Mismeasurement of the Incidence of Taxation in Britain and France, 1715-1810," *Journal of European Economic History*, 7, no. 1 (Spring 1978), 209-210. Also, for an eighteenth-century version of this discussion, *Journal de commerce et d'agriculture*, Sept. 1761 and Jan. 1762.

[27] Michel Antoine, *Le conseil du roi sous le règne de Louis XV* (Geneva, 1970), 403, defines "la finance" as "l'organisation collégiale qui, autour des Conseils royaux des Finances et du Commerce, groupait le contrôleur général, les intendants des finances et du commerce et leurs nombreux services." Here this term is used to set this group off from "la finance" of the tax farmers, bankers, and lenders.

[28] Algemeen Rijksarchief, Archief Fagel, 1566: "Depuis près de trois siècles, on a augmenté en France les revenus du Roi, par nouvelles taxes et augmentation de celles créés." Bibliothèque de l'Arsenal, 4062, gives an introduction to each type of tax and its history.

century usages in twentieth-century terms and concepts.[29] Its simplicity lay in the tendency of tax collectors, whether government officials or private entrepreneurs, to adapt taxes to circumstances. By 1755 the taxes assessed in France had come to resemble certain basic types. Thus the *capitation*, initially a hearth or head tax, had been transformed into a levy indistinguishable from the *taille*, a tax on property.

The *taille* and the *capitation* are usually called direct taxes; that designation will be preserved here, and the direct taxes will be introduced first. But the distinction between taxes levied directly on the intended taxpayer and those levied indirectly, on an intermediary who is expected to pass them along (e.g., a merchant), is not well suited to the eighteenth century.[30] Many French levies were assessed on intermediaries. Tax farmers, purchasers of temporary alienation rights, government officials, and private subjects selected by their peers all were objects of such assessment, and attempted to shift their liability.[31] Perhaps this explains why historians have arrived at such radically different judgments about the level and trend of direct and indirect taxes in France.[32] Moreover, in modern theory one purpose behind distinguishing between direct and indirect levies is to introduce a proxy for measuring the progressivity of a tax system. If direct taxes exceed indirect taxes, then the tax incidence is likely to be progressive, since direct taxes are often believed to be paid by the groups intended to be taxed (whereas it is difficult

[29] Another complexity shows up in a dual system of accounts, one based on geography and the other on specific taxes. Here *états* of the latter kind will be used because they clarify the issue of overheads. Bibliothèque de l'Arsenal, 4062, 153-316, gives an example of accounts of the geographical type.

[30] In modern literature the distinction between direct and indirect taxes remains unfixed, and this is only one form of it. The other leading form defines indirect taxes as those levied on objects, or at least not on income. Richard A. Musgrave, *Fiscal Systems* (New Haven, 1969), 173; and David N. Hyman, *Public Finance* (Chicago, 1983), 369-70.

[31] Consider the laments of collectors of the *taille* about *non-valeurs*, which they had to make good and attempted to recover with a surcharge in the following year. Algemeen Rijksarchief, Legatie, 786.

[32] E.g., Clamageran, *Histoire de l'impôt*, III, 120-21n6, versus Marion, *Histoire financière*, I, 40. Also Ardant, *Histoire de l'impôt*, II, 32, 44, and 87; Jean-Claude Perrot, *Genèse d'une ville moderne: Caen au XVIIIe siècle* (2 vols.; Paris, 1975), esp. I, 342-46; Peter Claus Hartmann, ed., *Das Steuersystem der europäischen Staaten am Ende des Ancien Régime* (Munich, 1979), 329-35; and Roland Mousnier, "L'évolution des finances publiques en France et en Angleterre pendant les guerres de la Ligue d'Augsbourg et de la Succession d'Espagne," *Revue historique*, 205, no. 1 (Jan.-Jun. 1951), 4.

to identify the ultimate payer of an indirect tax). Such a distinction is of little use for the old regime, for the proxy assumption does not hold: taxation was intended to be neutral.

Direct taxes were assessed on both wealth and income. Each year the monarchy established an amount of *taille* revenues needed for the forthcoming year and issued a *brevet* stating that sum. This amount was then distributed among subdivisions of the land in two regions, the *pays de taille réelle* (chiefly the *pays d'état*) and the *pays de taille personnelle* (about two-thirds of France).[33] In the region of the *taille réelle* eligible taxpayers provided declarations of their revenues, which made up a basis for assessments. In the larger region, the *pays de taille personnelle*, assessors selected by the local community divided the community's contribution among those liable to pay according to their own or to a general sense of ability to pay. Proceeds were remitted to the *receveurs des tailles*, who paid wages, *rentes*, and other *charges* settled on these receipts and sent the balance to the receiver general, who paid *charges* assigned at that higher level (e.g., certain military expenses) and sent the rest to the royal treasury. An *état* specified to whom these various payments were to be made and thus constituted a budget within a budget.[34]

The old regime designated this levy also as the *taille arbitraire*, and historians have taken over this apparently pejorative usage. But the word "arbitraire" had two meanings in eighteenth-century French, as it has two meanings in twentieth-century English: one suggests capricious or despotic action, and the other an act depending on choice or discretion. To call the *taille personnelle* a *taille arbitraire* was to acknowledge that the amount a given individual paid was left to the discretion of the locally selected assessors. Undoubtedly, the assessors were sometimes capricious and despotic in the eyes of their enemies, and fair-minded in the eyes of their kith and kin. In any event, the *taille* was assessed with an eye to previous payments, and taxpayers could (and did) protest levies they deemed excessive. It did provoke local contentions, but Jean-Pierre Gutton has noticed

[33] Jean-Pierre Gutton, *Villages du Lyonnais sous la monarchie (XVIᵉ-XVIIIᵉ)* (Lyons, 1978), 33-40, discusses how this operated at the local level in a de facto area of *taille personnelle*.

[34] Bibliothèque Nationale, ms. fr. 11162, folios 15ff., discusses the administrative network.

that in the Lyonnais disputes intensified after each reform effort, in 1765 and 1787.[35] At other times the community was reconciled to the *taille*.

In theory the *taille* was a levy on the wealth or income of the greatest part of the populace, but if practice had closely resembled theory then the proceeds of this tax would have been greater. It is appropriate to notice that even in villages people acquired exemptions from the *taille*. For the *taille réelle* exemptions were attached to property rather than to persons so that anyone who could buy such land could acquire this tax benefit, which was presumably reflected in the price. (This putative two-tier price structure—a higher price for tax-free than for taxable land—should help explain broad resistance to the elimination of such privileges. Anyone, noble or non-noble, who had paid a premium for tax-free land would be especially loath to face both a decline in its value and the payment of taxes on it.) Nobles paid taxes on non-exempt land, but not otherwise. These exemptions were lawful, and as has already been observed, they were an important means and sign of social mobility. That some people were *non-taillable* is usually taken as evidence that those people who remained *taillable* were abused and paid too much.[36] This conclusion does not rest on a study of the distribution of the *taille*, but on complaints about it. Marion's is an administrative history, and his sources are preeminently the papers generated in administrative disputes.[37] Thus his view minimizes the vast gap between what the *taille* should have produced, and what it actually did produce, and neglects the importance of privileges in tax law as a motive force in the society and therefore as an economic stimulus. It also neglects the capacity of a growing population and income to absorb the burden of exemptions. The relevant question therefore is whether population growth exceeded, in aggregate terms, growth in the number of *non-taillables*, which it most certainly did. No one would suggest that the numbers of the privileged grew by 6.6 million between 1700 and 1790, or by 3.5 million between 1700 and 1755 (Table 1.1).

[35] Gutton, *Villages*, 35. Gutton speculates (pp. 40-41) that the disappearance of marked resistance to the *taille* after the mid-seventeenth-century Fronde may have been the result of a decline in community cohesion.

[36] Marion, *Histoire financière*, I, 5; and Marion, *Les impôts directs*, 3 and *passim*.

[37] Marion, *Histoire financière*, I, xi-xii, and the notes, *passim*.

As all authorities recognize,[38] this scheme of assessment encouraged people to hide their wealth and income and to delay paying over an assessment as long as possible. But the *taille* was an old tax, so that long before 1755 everyone understood how the game of assessment and payment should be played. The government shared this insight, and encouraged it by fixing the annual amount of the *taille* at a level that did *not* increase in proportion to the depreciation of the livre tournois or population growth. In the eighteenth century the *brevet* of the *taille* called for a lesser sum in nominal value than it had under Mazarin in the middle of the seventeenth century and less in terms of silver content than the level generally collected under Louis XIV.[39] Between 1730 and 1745 and again after 1760 the inflation of prices and incomes significantly reduced the real cost of this basic old regime tax, and its real yield. In short, this tax, into which tax avoidance through privilege was most openly built, diminished in importance in the eighteenth century because it remained stagnant while incomes and wealth grew.

Certain other direct levies, such as the *taillon*, were included in the first *brevet* of the *taille*; a second *brevet*, assessed on the *taille* roles, added the *quartier d'hiver* and other levies intended to support troops and militia. *Brevet* amounts had been established earlier in the century and were little changed during the eighteenth century except on occasions when the king granted extraordinary remissions for hardship or local public works projects. Thus in 1740 when the harvest was bad the remission on the *tailles* totaled 14 million, and in 1751 the *pays d'élection* and the *pays conquis* each received a remission of 1.5 million l.t.[40] Remissions were a regular feature of old regime taxes, and they diminished, by a small amount, the sums actually collected.[41]

[38] *Ibid.*, I, 2-10; Hinkler, *Les Français devant l'impôt*, 20-21.

[39] Marcel Marion, *Dictionnaire des institutions de la France aux XVIIᵉ et XVIIIᵉ siècles* (Paris, 1923), 526; Marion, *L'impôt sur le revenu*, esp. 3n1; Clamageran, *Histoire de l'impôt*, III, 8, 245-46, 248, 299, and 315, for the amounts; and Micheline Baulant and Jean Meuvret, *Prix des céréales extraits de la mercuriale de Paris (1520-1698)* (2 vols.; Paris, 1960), I, 249, for the silver equivalents of the livre tournois before 1700. After 1726 the silver equivalent was 4.45 grams to the livre.

[40] Algemeen Rijksarchief, Legatie, 786 and 789.

[41] E.g., Bibliothèque Nationale, ms. fr. 11162, folios 46v and 47r, for information on the size of remissions in the early 1760s. In 1760 all remissions on the first *vingtième* came to about 3 percent. Bibliothèque Nationale, Joly de Fleury, 577, folios 173-76, gives an example at the parish level.

Another direct tax, the *capitation*, had been introduced in 1695 as an independent levy to be assessed in twenty-two classes according to *état*. But in the *pays de taille personnelle* the *capitation* had become another supplement to the *taille*, although one assessed, in theory more often than in practice, without exemptions. Proceeds of the *capitation* grew slowly during the eighteenth century, in part because of supplements added during the Seven Years War. Together, the *taille* and its supplements along with the *capitation* formed the category of revenues labelled the *recettes générales*. They were assessed each year in October and from 1749 to 1754 brought a stable sum between 72 and 78 million, with much of the difference accounted for by reductions granted by the king after the War of Austrian Succession.[42]

If in the case both of the *taille* and the *capitation* there was some confusion about whether the object of taxation was wealth or income, the other principal direct taxes were, in principle, straightforward assessments on income. The *dixième*, begun in 1710, let lapse in 1717, reestablished during 1733-1737 and 1741-1749, was superseded in 1750 by the *vingtième*. From 1756 there were two *vingtièmes* in force, and from 1760 to 1763, three. Supplements took another form also: from 1746 an addition of two sols per livre, or 10 percent, was added to the *dixième*, making it a levy of 11 percent.[43] These were intended to raise a tenth or a twentieth of the income of individuals and businesses without exception. In practice they brought in considerbly less, because the monarchy sold or granted exemptions and the people liable to pay these taxes understated their incomes, and because in practice chiefly landed incomes paid. The law itself created an ambiguity about the kinds of income liable to assessment.[44] Clamageran describes the modification of the *vingtième* as a consequence of the play of two contrary forces, the king's reluctance to violate the secrecy of household affairs, which constituted a basic liberty of the French, versus the king's desire to collect

[42] Algemeen Rijksarchief, Legatie, 779, 784, and 787-789; and Archief Fagel, 1566. Bibliothèque de l'Arsenal, 4489, also gives some information on 1751, but in a different form. These issues are sorted out and a general table of central government revenues provided in James C. Riley, "French Finances, 1727-1768," forthcoming, *Journal of Modern History* (1987).

[43] Anon., *Epoques de l'établissement des dixièmes* . . . (Chalon, 1762).

[44] Haus-, Hof- und Staatsarchiv, Vienna, Böhm-Supplement, Frankreich, Böhm 960-W922, 210; and Clamageran, *Histoire de l'impôt*, III, 327-28.

revenues. The result was a compromise: evaluations submitted by taxpayers were not subject to verification; when the king needed more revenues he added *vingtièmes* or supplements.

Like Clamageran, Marion judged the *vingtièmes* "le plus correct et le moins mauvais" of old regime taxes.[45] Their yield also was stable for each assessment in effect. After the 1750 financial year, during part of which the *dixième* was in force and part the *vingtième*, this tax yielded 22 to 25 million,[46] an amount that did not increase thereafter. In 1789 a single *vingtième* was expected to raise 23.7 million.[47] Thus these levies also did not rise with inflation, population, and income.

That the *vingtième* yield failed to grow from the beginning to the end of the century[48] reveals that it was not in truth a levy on income, but another undifferentiated tax. The *dixièmes* and *vingtièmes* also resembled the *taille*, for they were assessed in a way that compounded and confused income and wealth. If formal exemptions could not always be acquired (even the clergy was liable for the *vingtième*), still the growing difference between what this levy should have raised and what it did raise uncovers the latitude for evasion. At the beginning of the century a 5 percent levy on income, using the output figure estimated in Chapter 1 of 2.7 billion and the theory of a levy on all income, might have returned as much as 135 million l.t.; in the 1780s it might have returned some 255 million. Instead it brought in only some 23 million. Since *vingtièmes* were assessed more frequently as the eighteenth century wore on, it follows that the role of privilege in the direct taxes was shrinking. More and more, legally sanctioned tax avoidance was giving way to tax evasion. Perhaps the beneficiaries were the same in both cases—people of authority able to browbeat the assessors and collectors. But that is speculation; the evidence remains to be collected.

Marion distinguished between the *taille* and *capitation*, on the one hand, and the *dixième* and *vingtième*, on the other hand. As we now see, the only significant difference between the two categories lies in

---

[45] Marion, *Dictionnaire*, 556; and Clamageran, *Histoire de l'impôt*, III, ix.

[46] These figures refer only to the *dixième*, after 1750 the *vingtième* on property and industry. The sources are Algemeen Rijksarchief, Legatie, 779, 784, and 789; and Bibliothèque de l'Arsenal, 4489. The manner of stating the proceeds of this levy differs from document to document.

[47] Marion, *Dictionnaire*, 559.

[48] Dividing out from data in *ibid.*, and sources cited in n. 46 above.

the manner of assessment: in most of France the *taille* and *capitation* were levied according to an assessor's judgment, and the *dixième* and *vingtième* according to declarations by taxpayers. Neither produced a yield approaching what would be expected on the basis of property values and income amounts. One type, the *taille-capitation*, produced many complaints in Marion's administrative sources about unfair assessments. The other did not, because it was left to the individual taxpayer to set the level of his or her responsibility. From the perspective of litigation, which is Marion's point of view, one tax type was inferior to the other. Is more evasion likely in a system using assessors or in a system relying on the honesty of the taxpayer who is known to feel contempt for royal taxes? What can be concluded is that both types of taxes were pragmatic. They acknowledged the absence of any means to check on the value of assets or income, and allowed evasion to sort itself out at the local and individual level.

Because resistance to taxation was so general and intense, the monarchy prospered best when using a variety of assessments, including taxes usually designated as indirect. The leading indirect levy was the *gabelle*, a state salt monopoly in which the price was fixed at different levels in six regions of the royalty.[49] Detested for this feature and because the state set compulsory minima of salt to be purchased according to its needs for revenue, the *gabelle* was in some areas virtually a direct tax. Also important in terms of proceeds, and nearly as contentious, were other levies collected by the General Farm: customs; excises; the *domaines de France* (as distinct from the domains of the king), which included the duty on notarial acts; and the royal monopoly on tobacco. In these areas too financial authorities sought to fix the amount of revenues, but during the first half of the century the amounts involved in these levies increased far more substantially than did the taxes deemed direct. The scale of proceeds from the principal indirect taxes, taking 1750 as a representative year, is depicted in Table 2.1.[50] The General Farm lease rose from 80 million during 1726-1732, when it was said to be exceptionally profitable to its holders, to 152 million during

[49] On the *gabelle*, see especially Jacob M. Price, *France and the Chesapeake: A History of the French Tobacco Monopoly* . . . (2 vols.; Ann Arbor, 1973).

[50] Gross proceeds totalled 104.6 million, and net proceeds, deducting some expenditures made directly by the Farm, 101.6 million.

TABLE 2.1
Major Indirect Tax Revenues in 1750
(millions of l.t.)

gabelles	28.2
5 Great Farms (mostly customs)	10.8
aydes and *droits* (mostly excises)	38.6
domaines de France	12.6
domaines d'occident (Canada and New France)	1.8
tabac	12.6
TOTAL	104.6

SOURCE: Algemeen Rijksarchief, The Hague, Legatiearchief, Eerste Afdeling, Frankrijk, 789.

1774-1780.[51] This increase can be explained by the growth of public spending on items subject to taxation, by the monarchy's efforts to prevent tax farmers from profiting too much from their activities, and by the assessment of additional taxes and the transfer of old taxes to the Farm.

These are the major taxes levied in France. An exhaustive list is unnecessary here, for anyone seeking that information may refer to one of the treatises on the taxes.[52] By the early 1750s the so-called direct taxes, the *taille, capitation,* and *vingtième,* produced a relatively stable yield of about 100 million a year. Revenues were rising, and the portion of these taxes in the total was contracting. Only the so-called indirect taxes, chiefly those under the General Farm, which also brought in about 100 million a year, continued to increase in nominal and real terms, and as a proportion of revenues. Thus the king used two methods to augment revenues: he laid on additional *vingtièmes,* and he encouraged the General Farm to keep pace with the rising consumption of goods subject to its taxes while also forcing a higher consumption of salt under the monopoly. In the eighteenth century the king continued to grant privileges. But the proportion of revenues lost to privilege declined as more of the tax burden was shifted to the kind of levies raised by the Farm, which presented fewer opportunities for tax avoidance, and as the direct

[51] Clamageran, *Histoire de l'impôt,* III, 254 and 442; and Bibliothèque de l'Arsenal, 4062, p. 6.
[52] Such as [Jean Louis Moreau de Beaumont], *Mémoires concernant les impositions et droits* (2nd ed., 5 vols.; Paris, 1787-1789), vols. 2-5.

taxes emphasized the *vingtième* over the *taille*. Thus the importance of privilege was shrinking both to the extent that population was growing faster than the privileged classes and because the relative scale of real benefits to privilege was declining with the relative weight of taxes open to privilege. Whether or not the portion of income paid in taxes grew, the opportunities for legal tax avoidance diminished. The social motor of the old regime—privilege—was losing its value.

Revenues and Expenditures

In the eighteenth century a distinction was drawn between taxes collected without any limit on their duration, which were called ordinary, and taxes that were of limited duration, which were called extraordinary.[53] In peacetime most revenues were ordinary and consisted of income from taxes collected every year. In wartime, however, the king often acquired a temporary right to assess new taxes or to augment old levies. War also required loans, assessments, new or enlarged security bonds extracted from *officiers*, and other non-tax revenue sources grouped with extraordinary revenues and affairs. Thus wartime financial accounts are decidedly more intricate than peacetime accounts, which themselves are not simple.[54] Table 2.2 provides some basic data about revenues and expenditures on the eve of the Seven Years War.[55]

To illustrate the principal issues involved, let us consider the case of 1752.[56] Ordinary revenues—principally from the royal domains, the *taille* and *capitation*, the General Farm and some lesser farms, and grants (*dons gratuits*) from the *pays d'état*—totalled 233.7 million,

[53] This was an old distinction, and the list of revenues deemed ordinary had expanded over time. See Koninklijke Bibliotheek, Brussels, 3132.

[54] One source, dealing at unusual length with a year of peace, claims to condense twelve volumes on expenditures, themselves a condensed version of the more than one hundred volumes needed to detail the royal revenues and expenditures in one year. Algemeen Rijksarchief, Legatie, 784.

[55] The 1751 and 1754 figures are projected estimates. The *vingtième* surcharges allotted for service of the royal lottery, 6.2 million, are excluded here. For 1753 and 1754 the *vingtième* on Jews (960,000 l.t.) is shifted from the ordinary revenues column to the *vingtième* column. For 1749, no figure for ordinary expenditures is given. Expenditures totalled 374.1 million, and ordinary and extraordinary revenues 373.8 million.

[56] Algemeen Rijksarchief, Legatie, 784.

TABLE 2.2
Ordinary Revenues and Expenditures, 1749-1754
(in millions of l.t.)

	ordinary revenues	dixième- vingtième revenues	total revenues	expendi- tures	deficit/ surplus
1749	245.0	42.0	287.0	—	—
1750	236.2	27.1	263.3	263.4	− 0.1
1751	(234.3)	(28.4)	(262.7)	(269.1)	−(6.4)
1752	233.7	28.7	262.4	273.8	−11.4
1753	232.5	24.0	256.5	—	—
1754	(232.8)	(24.0)	(256.8)	—	—

SOURCES: Algemeen Rijksarchief, The Hague, Legatiearchief, Eerste Afdeling, Frankrijk, 779, 783-84, 787-89; and id., Archief Fagel, 1566.

as appears in Table 2.2. Extraordinary revenues—the *vingtièmes* and their surcharge—added 28.7 million, for a sum of 262.4 million. The same document, entitled "Affaires Générales et Secrèttes des Finances du Roy," provides some detail about both collection costs and the sum of revenues spent before reaching the royal treasury. We can recognize in this accounting structure a threefold division. One sum, the sum to which most attention was given, represented ordinary revenues, an income available to the royal treasury year in and year out. A second sum—which I designate "total revenues"—combines ordinary and extraordinary income; in this instance the only addition is the income from the *vingtième*. A third total—which does not appear in Table 2.2 and which I designate "aggregate revenues"—provides the most fascinating revelation of all. If the data in this document are reliable—with the destruction of so many financial documents, the issue of reliability is difficult to settle—then they provide a figure for all the revenues extracted from the populace under the authority of the king: 424.8 million l.t. According to this source, the taxpayers paid 162.4 million in 1752 that did not reach the king. Even the aggregate tax figure was considerably below what many people believed, for "l'opinion vulgaire" held that the taxes totalled 600 million (and therefore that some 338 million did not reach the king).[57]

In 1752 ordinary expenditures, dominated by military allocations, debt service, and foreign affairs (and excluding expenditures

[57] *Ibid.*, 146-48, quote from 148.

on *vingtième* proceeds), totalled 243.6 million, leaving a deficit that was carried to the next year's budget.[58] The king's subjects were alive to the problem of deficits. Between 1744 and 1748 they had submitted some 200 proposals for financial improvements.[59] These were years also of retrenchment. By 1750 some 10 million had been cut from ordinary spending, and both the military and the large item of subsidies to foreign governments had been reduced sharply from wartime levels. Major savings were difficult because the central government did not spend lavishly on items on which retrenchment was feasible, as can be seen by examining the leading directions of spending. From the ordinary revenues spending in 1752 fell into the following categories:

the court	28.2 million
army and navy	102.0
ministry appointments	3.4
royal pensions	9.9
justice	1.7
administrative salaries	10.0
public works	5.4
debt service	51.6
indemnities	8.2
foreign affairs	19.1
other	4.1
TOTAL	243.6 million

Spending on the extraordinary revenues was divided in this manner:

the royal lottery	6.2 million
deficits of 1749-1751	3.6
remissions for hardship	2.4
reimbursement of perpetual annuities	2.0
annual grant to the Compagnie des Indes	2.0
rentes héréditaires	8.0
reimbursement to the Paris hôtel de ville	6.0
TOTAL	30.2

Beyond this total, 273.8 million, and the overhead, 40.2 million, this

[58] The monarchy often dealt with comparatively small deficits in this manner.
[59] *Ibid.*, 786, 107.

document identifies 122.2 million in revenues spent without being passed through the royal treasury, in the form of some municipal and provincial revenues collected under the king's authority, taxes assigned to specific institutions such as the Ecole Militaire and the Hôtel Royal des Invalides, fees charged by the judicial courts, public works projects funded by tax surcharges, and revenues alienated (including domains and tax rights) for a limited time or in perpetuity.

The largest expenditures under the king's immediate control were on items on which economies meant reducing the military readiness of the kingdom or cutting debt service. Only the king, who lived well on tax revenues and on additional private income,[60] and who spent nearly as much on pensions as on administrative salaries, might have saved a significant amount. But Louis XV was already spending a smaller share of the budget than had his great grandfather, Louis XIV. Moreover, the king was supposed to live lavishly. Finally, only a very large retrenchment indeed, fully a third of spending on the court and royal pensions in 1752, would have economized enough to cover even the small deficit of that year.

Machault d'Arnouville, controller general from 1745 until 1754, saw the possibility of economies, but did not believe they could be large enough to tackle the leading problem, the debt. He suggested a one-time increase in revenues by obliging tax farmers and *taille* collectors to buy non-hereditary offices.[61] Royal authorities preferred to continue the *dixième*, scheduled to expire at the end of the War of Austrian Succession, at half its former level, as a *vingtième*, with proceeds used to fund debt retirements. Machault thus directed a significant increase in tax revenues, in the form of a continuation into peace of the *vingtième* and *vingtième* surcharge of about 25 million a year and sharply increased proceeds from the General Farm lease (from 80 million a year during 1732-1738 to net proceeds of more than 101 million during 1750-1756). Taxation measured in nominal values rose sharply up to mid-century. But when adjustments for price change are made, it emerges that these increases merely kept pace with inflation. By 1752 the constant value burden of the taxes was very little greater than in 1733.[62]

---

[60] Algemeen Rijksarchief, Archief Fagel, 1572.
[61] *Ibid.*, 1565, Dec. 1752.
[62] See Riley, "French Finances, 1727-1768."

The taxes had many faults, but they were delivering a stable quantity of real revenues to the treasury. Potential revenues were diminished on a vast scale by tax evasion, which shows up not so much in smuggling as it does in the gap between what the *taille*, the *capitation*, and the *dixième/vingtième* might have produced and what they did produce in revenues. But the scale of evasion was so vast that we cannot conclude that the king ever seriously intended that his subjects should pay 10 or even 5 percent of their income, or otherwise meet the formal terms of these taxes. Even seventeenth- and eighteenth-century estimates of national income,[63] which often underestimate, revealed that the *dixième* gathered a mere fraction of 10 percent of income. Financial authorities understood these realities, and devised a variegated tax system that compensated for the French loathing of taxes. Did they, however, create a system that was too cumbersome and too costly?

Overhead

In France the eighteenth century was an age of capitalism. Many royal and public functions were entrusted to private entrepreneurs, and some people argued, well before Adam Smith, that "l'intérêt particulier" would surpass public management of resources.[64] Even the church often farmed the collection of the tithe.[65] But private entrepreneurship in the public interest also had its critics, who were numerous. People who condemned this system condemned it not for its mixture of private enterprise with public charge but for the reputedly excessive costs of the mixture. These critics believed that private enterprise introduced not more but less efficiency. We can recognize at least three camps. Private entrepreneurs like the farm-

[63] Collected by J[e]an Marczewski, "Some Aspects of the Economic Growth of France, 1660-1958," *Economic Development and Cultural Change*, 9, no. 3 (Apr. 1961), 371.

[64] An anonymous memoir in Bibliothèque Nationale, ms. fr. 11162, folios 69r and ff. Also Yves Durand, *Les fermiers généraux au XVIII' siècle* (Paris, 1971), 5; and the case made by Claude Dupin, a tax receiver and farmer general, in his economic and fiscal musings, *Œconomiques* (3 vols.; Paris, 1745; reprinted Paris, 1913). Even Montesquieu considered private entrepreneurship, represented by the General Farm, superior in certain circumstances.

[65] P. Gagnol, *La dîme ecclésiastique en France au XVIII' siècle* (Geneva, 1974 reprint), 118ff.

ers general pointed to inefficiencies in the existing form of public service, which was dominated by venality in office. For example, they underscored the threat of bankruptcies among venal officers holding the king's money.[66] Public servants, who owned their offices, accused the tax farmers of greed. And reformers often condemned both groups, calling for a low- or no-cost collection apparatus but seldom attempting to explain how that might be achieved.

Do the documents sustain the charge of critics of capitalism in public functions? Where the documents speak of the *frais de recouvrement*, they provide evidence of a comparatively efficient and inexpensive system of collecting taxes, and sometimes they provide evidence about the exploitation of office holders by the royal government. But the sources do not often speak of additional charges that critics claimed were levied. This is an issue that cannot be settled, for even the historian with apparently comprehensive records from the tax farmers might suspect them of having kept yet another set of books.[67] Let us see what the records say, and acknowledge that the truth of the matter may lie elsewhere.

In 1752 the acknowledged overhead on royal taxes totalled 40.2 million, of which the bulk falls into three categories: *taille* and *capitation*, 7.8 million; grants from the *pays d'état*, 4.0 million; and the General Farm, 19.0 million, together 30.8 million.[68] On the portion

[66] E.g., Bibliothèque Nationale, ms. fr. 11162, folios 69r and ff.

[67] Marion, *Les impôts directs*, 120-21, refused to estimate the collection overhead but believed this was the central defect in the old regime financial apparatus. Also George T. Matthews, *The Royal General Farms in Eighteenth-Century France* (New York, 1958), 262-63 and 266ff.

[68] Algemeen Rijksarchief, Legatie, 784. See also, on the issue of overhead in the 1760s, Bibliothèque Nationale, ms. fr. 11162, folios 50ff., and ms. fr. 14101. The latter, however, includes a sleight of hand trick. Administrative costs are presented (p. iv) as collection costs. Its estimates of General Farm profits are unusually high and are based on flimsy techniques.

These figures do not include collection costs on taxes established during the War of Austrian Succession and sold for payments in advance. It is difficult to estimate these. For example, in 1744 the king decreed a tax on wood and charcoal traded in Paris, for a period of fifteen years, and alienated this levy for payments of 15 million in 1744, 9 million in 1745 and 1746, and 12 million in 1747—a total of 45 million. Algemeen Rijksarchief, Legatie, 787 and 789. In 1750 this levy was projected to yield 5.2 million a year to its collectors, or 78 million over fifteen years. To calculate the overhead, it is necessary to take the discounted present value of both the sale price and the income stream of proceeds at the rate of interest that prevailed in 1744, which is not known. At 5 percent, the discounted present value of the proceeds to the king was 42.1 million, and of the proceeds to the buyers (assuming an annual yield

of revenues deemed ordinary, these costs totalled 37.8 million, so that if these revenues had been levied without cost, they would have amounted to 270 million. Using that figure, collection costs on this portion of revenues come to 14 percent.[69] On the extraordinary revenues alone, excluding lottery loan service charged against the *vingtièmes*, costs totalled only a little more than 7 percent. Here is a document full of scorn for the existing system of finances, for royal monopolies and *friponneries*, a celebrated document that circulated among many people of consideration,[70] a document that reveals the scale of spending on the court and on royal pensions. But it does not suggest that the costs of collection were higher than these figures allow.

Moreover, some of the entries included in these costs represent charges of another sort than overhead. The *pays d'état* were authorized to raise 12 million under royal authority. Of that, 8 million was forwarded to the treasury, and 4 million went to support the provincial assemblies and other costs of provincial administration. This item represents a loss in royal revenues, but it is not one associated in a significant way with collection costs. Even the overall figure of 14 percent is therefore excessive, and would be reduced to about 13 percent by a proper allocation of *pays d'état* charges. For comparison, the overhead of the British revenue system has been estimated at 10 percent toward the end of the century.[71] Although Britain is almost universally held to have possessed a more efficient and less costly fiscal apparatus, the French taxes do not seem to have cost significantly more to collect, especially when the size of the monarchy and the aversion of the king's subjects to taxation are taken into account.

---

of 5.2 million) 54.0 million. The overhead may have come to about 6 percent a year.

[69] Compare with [Jean-Baptiste Naveau], *Le financier citoyen* ([Paris], 1757), II, 76-77, estimating the revenues at 300 million, of which the royal treasury received 250 million and the collectors, administrators, and farmers, 50 million, or 17 percent. Naveau, a Breton tax farmer, seems to have been unusually well informed. A harsh critic, the anonymous author of a January 1761 essay in the *Journal de commerce et d'agriculture* (Brussels), argued that an army of over 100,000 tax agents and other elements of enforcement cost at least 60 million a year (p. 30). In the February number this figure for tax agents is reduced to 25,000, but the cost estimate is preserved (pp. 1-2).

[70] As asserted in a memoir on secret events, dated Paris, Dec. 1, 1753, in Algemeen Rijksarchief, Archief Fagel, 1566.

[71] Peter Mathias, "Taxation and Industrialization in Britain, 1700-1870," in *The*

Critics identified the costliest portion of the French system as the assortment of taxes under the General Farm, "a piece of royal property comprising a series of tax rights."[72] They were correct, for these cost some 16 percent of their proceeds, as opposed to 13 percent for all revenues, and 7 percent for the *vingtièmes*. Certainly, the Company of General Farmers holding the current lease charged more than the king allotted the collectors of the *taille* (10.8 percent) and the *capitation* (10 percent).[73] But it also employed an "army of agents" to collect the multitude of levies in its lease; according to one source 10,000 agents operated in 1750 (yet could not prevent the activities of an organized *compagnie des contrebandiers* reputed to involve thirty French and English smugglers).[74]

What troubled critics was the suspicion that the General Farm concealed profits, and thereby levied more in taxes than estimated by official sources. A memorandum of 1750, discussing how to augment revenues, reveals that the farmers were found to be making "un bénéfice secret" of about 10 million a year.[75] The amount of the lease could be increased from its level during 1744-1750: 92 million in peacetime. And it was increased, to 101.1 million for 1750-1756.[76] What is more interesting about this memorandum is what it reveals of gifts paid by the farmers general to the king's circle for the right to continue the lease:

princesse de Conti	2.0 million
madame de Pompadour	2.4
controller general	.3
other costs and gifts	.4
TOTAL	5.1 million

Transformation of England (London, 1979), 120, discussing the period after 1788; and Mathias and O'Brien, "Taxation in Britain and France," 642.

[72] Matthews, *Royal General Farms*, 16.

[73] The receivers and collectors were also allowed 4 percent in salary on the value of their office, called the *finance*.

[74] Algemeen Rijksarchief, Archief Fagel, 1565.

[75] Algemeen Rijksarchief, Legatie, 786. Machault believed the gain to average 9 million a year. Marcel Marion, *Machault d'Arnouville. Etude sur l'histoire du contrôle général des finances de 1749 à 1754* (Paris, 1891), 373.

[76] Bibliothèque de l'Arsenal, 4489; Clamageran, *Histoire de l'impôt*, III, 293 and 314.

This specification appears to list individual sums within the "present à la protection" and other costs, set at 12 million by another memorandum, which the Farm paid at the extension of the lease in 1750.[77]

Another memorandum, acquired by the Austrian statesman Karl von Zinzendorf in 1767, suggested that at that time the *frais de perception* of the farm totalled only 13.3 percent (or 17.6 million out of 132 million), but that the farmers lined their pockets with up to 20 million more. Thus the overhead might have amounted to as much as 22 percent (38 million of up to 170 million collected).[78] Undoubtedly, the profitability of the Farm did not remain constant, so it is difficult to extract from the many estimates a reliable sense of what the average of these secret benefits may have been.

The evidence shows that the General Farm made more than official figures suggest, but in a manner that was officially tolerated. The royal court worked in collusion with the farmers general to allow them to collect more than they paid for the lease, and to augment their officially authorized collections from year to year. It was a symbiotic relationship in which the court received gifts, the farmers general extra profits, and the royal treasury larger tax revenues (since subsequent leases increased in yield to the treasury). The court also protected the farmers. In 1752 General Farm revenues declined by a million because of newly imposed import restrictions, and the king granted an indemnity of 800,000 in addition to 2 million in new and increased excises. The latter compensated the Farm for a large 8 million shortfall in wine taxes, the proceeds of which had fallen off as wine prices rose and consumption declined.[79]

Nevertheless, there is a dissonance between the apparent scale of the deception, which amounted to a few million a year, and the severity of the scorn poured upon the farmers general for their *friponnerie* and their alleged profits. In the 1750-1756 lease, the forty farmers were believed to have collected some 122 million a year, distributed as follows:

[77] Algemeen Rijksarchief, Archief Fagel, 1566, dated Dec. 1753, no pagination, given as part of a gratuitous addition to the 1750 memo in Legatie, 786.

[78] Haus-, Hof- und Staatsarchiv, Böhm 960-W922, pp. 220-22. Also Bibliothèque Nationale, Joly de Fleury, 1432, folio 182v, on the lease of 1724.

[79] Algemeen Rijksarchief, Archief Fagel, 1565. The taxes added for lost wine revenues presumably compensated for 1746-1748 and 1750. In 1752 wine prices were

101.6 million	to the royal treasury
3.0	to royal expenditures made directly by the Farm
3.6	for the *frais de régie*
12.0	profits to the farmers and sub farmers
<u>2.0</u>	hidden charges allowed in compensation for the costs of obtaining the lease
122.2 million	TOTAL

Thus the farmers and subfarmers divided 12 million a year.[80] The farmers also received from the king a 5 percent return on the security bond of 20 million put up in 1750 (in practice an advance), and another 5 percent from the General Farm itself. These payments consist of interest charges, for the farmers lent the treasury money in anticipation of tax collections. Thus this portion of the yield should be considered separately from what the sources suggest about the profitability of the Farm.

The Company of Farmers General pocketed generous earnings, but what is not known is the cost of capitalizing the Farm. The documents admit only that the farmers, who up to 1750 paid 300,000 for each *place* plus 500,000 toward a security bond, had to sustain their network; they do not discuss the erection of this impressive national system for levying taxes or the human capital endowment which in practice made up the Farm. Upon what investment was the return paid?

I suspect that this dissonance between the scale of the deception and the scorn of the critics points up at once the unusual profitability of the Farm, an inattentiveness to some costs encountered by the farmers, a reaction against the ruthlessness of the Farm, and a curious intolerance. In a society in which public capitalism took the form of venality, guardians of public morality, even pragmatic guardians, condemned the farmers general for their excesses. Why? It is not because the farmers general profited from their public charges, for many people did that, including some of the critics. It is also not because the farmers charged the king for the anticipation of revenues, for so did the venal receivers general. What galled

---

quite modest. C.-E. Labrousse, *Esquisse du mouvement des prix et des revenus en France au XVIIIᵉ siècle* (2 vols.; Paris, 1933), I, 275.

[80] Algemeen Rijksarchief, Archief Fagel, 1566.

critics was the favoritism shown tax farmers, who profited more than their counterparts in the judiciary or even in other parts of the financial structure. The holders of venal offices had undergone a difficult half-century. They had been called on to make large sacrifices for the state, among them a reduction in *gages*—sometimes salary and sometimes simply interest—in 1714 from 5 to 4 percent, and for many of them the price of an office was so high that its proceeds amounted to only 3, even 2, percent.[81] What is more, their opportunities for profiting from their offices were more carefully restricted than was the case with the farmers. This is because of the nature of venality. Officeholders with real duties paid a lump sum for this asset and were allotted either a salary or the right to collect fees at a certain level. Thus the *trésoriers de la marine* received a net yield of 7 to 8 percent on their investment,[82] a generous return if construed exclusively as interest, but far from generous when compared to a business venture in which the entrepreneur expects a return from both his investment and his commitment of time and expertise. The active venal officers, those who performed serious and time-consuming functions, received less for their services to the state than did the tax farmers, and resented this discrimination in a way similar to that in which the nobility of the sword in an earlier day had resented the usurpations of the nobility of office.

Other officers had simply lent the state money in the form of the purchase of an office, upon which they expected a yield as any other creditor would. But the yield they got was often below that paid in ordinary public loans.[83] In short, what galled the critics was the contrast between an open-handed approach to the Farm and a tight-fisted approach to venal offices.

More generally the articulate public loathed the farmers, I suspect, because the Farm collected a significantly larger share of the revenues due the king than did the king's venal officers or the locally appointed assessors. Of course, who can say what the turnover of goods subject to the Farm's levies was? But if we are uncertain

---

[81] David D. Bien, "The *secrétaires du roi*: Absolutism, Corps, and Privilege under the Ancien Régime," in Ernst Hinricks et al., eds., *Vom Ancien Régime zur Französischen Revolution* (Göttingen, 1978), 155.

[82] Henri Legohérel, *Les trésoriers généraux de la marine (1517-1788)* (Paris, [1965]), 318 and 319.

[83] Bien, "The *secrétaires du roi*," 160-61.

about this, we cannot fail to notice that income and property taxes—the *taille*, the *capitation*, and the *vingtième*—all yielded less than the Farm's comparatively minor taxes. The *gabelle* alone produced more than either the *capitation* or the *vingtième*. No wonder critics condemned "cette insatiable avidité du fermier."[84]

Intolerance toward the General Farm—the cry that the taxes should be collected by men willing to sacrifice compensation for the national good—helps explain the love-hate relationship the French experienced with their controllers general. Each controller general (except Necker) came to office pure, as a venal officer in the judiciary; thus everyone who came to office promising reforms could be celebrated as an heroic figure about to do battle with corruption. But the new controller general was immediately contaminated by taking office, for the mere entry into office shifted this individual from the realm of judicial purity into contact with the financial entrepreneur. A tireless theme of eighteenth-century French experience held that the *gens de finance* were scoundrels. Thus Machault had entered office in 1745 amidst high expectations about the reforms he would introduce, but had been corrupted not only by the deficit caused by war and the fiscal scrambling necessary to meet war costs, but also by the unavoidable association of every controller general with the greed of the *traitants*.[85] The same drama had been performed before, and would be performed again during the Seven Years War (by Silhouette and Bertin).

What is worthy of notice about the overhead in the collection of French taxes is not the high profits of the farmers general, or the immense scale of the so-called "faux frais du recouvrement" in general, but the low costs of collecting other taxes and all the taxes together. These costs apparently totalled less than 13 percent of revenues, and if the farmers general charged more, that is at least in part because they collected the taxes that were the most expensive to collect. The overhead might have been reduced by more stringent limits on General Farm profits. But the complete elimination of these profits—12 million a year—would have reduced collection costs only by a further 4 percent to about 9 percent. This is a signif-

[84] Bibliothèque de l'Arsenal, 4066B, 215.

[85] Marion, *Machault*, 377ff., discusses the attack, portraying it as evidence of the severity of Machault's program.

icant economy, but not one large enough to have paid off much of the debt or lowered taxes.

Furthermore, the eighteenth-century overhead represents a large gain in efficiency over the seventeenth century. Martin Wolfe estimates that collection costs around 1600 came to a quarter of total revenues, *not* including the profits of tax farmers and lenders, and that the most inefficient part of the system lay in its unnecessary venal officers, who performed no functions useful to the government except supplying credit.[86] Old regime France continued, on the surface, to manage its house and collect its taxes in much the same way. But the surface evidence is deceiving. Below it can be found large and important changes in the way officers functioned, and in the costs of the services they rendered.[87] In particular, the old regime monarchy made large strides in rendering its administrative performance more efficient by cutting the compensation of venal officers.

The problem created by the overhead lay less in the amounts involved than in its inequities. Even the privileged venal officeholders came to feel that the financial system was discriminatory. Perhaps the farmers general and other revenue officials collected still more than the sources consulted here admit. We must allow for that possibility. But the information the documents provide is revealing enough to see why the revenue system received so much criticism. We do not need to summon up the entirely hypothetical possibility of hidden profits.

To this point we have discerned a number of defects in the financial structure: the stability of the old tax base and a growing dependence on revenues collected by the General Farm, the rather small-scale extravagance of the court, the costs of privilege, and inequities in the collection system. But these defects do not add up either to a confirmation of Marion's explanation for France's financial problems or to a revised explanation placing less stress on the effects of privilege and more on other issues. This is so because the scale of the financial problem, represented by the debt, was much larger than the effect of each of these flaws, or of all of them together.

[86] Martin Wolfe, *The Fiscal System of Renaissance France* (New Haven, 1972), 248.
[87] Thus I disagree with Wolfe's view that the fiscal system established in the Ren-

CONCLUSION

The problem was obvious, so obvious that foreign observers understood it as well as did French officials. (No wonder. They had access
to the same documents.) As the Dutch ambassador to France since
1740, Mattheus Lestevenon, wrote to the pensionary of the province of Holland, Pieter Steyn, on February 13, 1755: the finances
"are not on a good foot, although France has many resources."[88]
Marion provides one answer to the question of why a land so rich
was poor in financial resources. The taxes, he says, were beset by
privilege, which let some escape assessment and reduced others to
misery. There is much truth in this view, of course. A mere glance
at the *taille* and *capitation*, or the *vingtième*, reveals how much less
they returned to the central government than warranted by taxable
resources in France. But this glance does not establish the costs of
privilege, which no one has claimed amounted to anything approaching the entire sum that the French did not pay in the *vingtième*, the *taille*, the *capitation*, and other levies. What is appealing
about Marion's interpretation is its call to principle and equity—the
taxes should be justly (if not progressively) distributed. But it is an
unrealistic view. A financial system in disarray cannot be reformed
by a call to principle—especially to principles alien to a society
which, at the middle of the eighteenth century, accepted the concept of privilege and had already made large strides toward bringing its effects in lost tax revenues under control. What, in practical
terms, could French authorities have done to draw on the rich resources of their land?

The first thing to notice is that France's financial plight was not
grave, or even serious, in the early 1750s. The last war had cost an
average of 90 to 100 million a year,[89] enough to prompt Machault
and many other observers to propose plans for reform. But France
emerged from the War of Austrian Succession in a position in which
expenditures exceeded revenues by small amounts, in which nearly

aissance changed very little thereafter, and with similar views expressed by Edward
Ames and Richard T. Rapp, "The Birth and Death of Taxes," *Journal of Economic History*, 27, no. 1 (Mar. 1977), 161-78.

[88] Algemeen Rijksarchief, Archief Pieter Steyn, 17.

[89] Algemeen Rijksarchief, Archief Fagel, 1571, excluding increases in ordinary
revenues, and including extraordinary spending during 1749 on grounds that war-
related spending continued into that year.

everyone saw the financial problem as a short-run difficulty to be surmounted by a few economies, increased taxes, and an ambitious plan of long-run debt amortization, in which the king was able to levy a peacetime *vingtième* in order to pay off the debt. The debt, counting only the part of it that was not self-extinguishing, totalled less than four times the amount of ordinary revenues plus the *vingtième* (260 million), and about twice the amount of all revenues collected under the king's authority (425 million in 1752). In the short-run, tax revenues were growing at a pace equal to output, but all the revenues collected under the king's authority claimed less than 14 to 16 percent of national output, which can be projected for mid-century at more than 2,600 to 3,000 million.[90]

Collecting the taxes in France cost surprisingly little. The old line taxes and the new levy on income, the *dixième/vingtième*, were gathered at modest expense. Only the General Farm cost the taxpayers a markedly higher rate. But it was only the General Farm that produced an increasing yield in revenues as incomes grew. The other

[90] The 1750 national product or output estimate is derived in the following way:

a) Two paths of per capita output in constant 1781-1790 prices are projected, the Bairoch path, and the O'Brien/Keyder path (as discussed in Chapter 1). Both depart from a 1781-1790 output estimate of 5.1 billion (including only agricultural and manufacturing output) but assume different rates of growth to that level and therefore different income levels for 1701-1710. The Bairoch estimate of the growth rate (0.3 percent) is nearly equal to French population growth so that it leads to very little change in the estimated per capita product for 1701-1710 in 1781-1790 prices. The O'Brien/Keyder estimate of the growth rate (1.0 percent) equals about 0.7 percent in per capita terms, and leads to a significantly lower figure for 1701-1710 output.

b) Following the discussion in Chapter 1, all per capita growth is assumed to have occurred before 1770. Aggregate output growth continued after 1770, but at a rate no greater than population growth.

c) The per capita estimates are:

	1701-1710	1770
Bairoch	182 l.t.	184 l.t.
O'Brien/Keyder	107	184

d) By straight-line interpolation, these estimates provide a range of per capita output as of 1750 of 160 to 183 l.t. in 1781-1790 prices.

e) Labrousse's index numbers (Ernest Labrousse, "Les 'bon prix' agricoles du XVIIIᵉ siècle," in Fernand Braudel and Ernest Labrousse, eds., *Histoire économique et sociale de la France* (Paris, 1970), II, 387) furnish a means of conversion to current values, comparing a thirteen-year average centered on 1750 (an index number of 68.7) with 1781-1789 prices (an index number of 103.7).

f) The per capita output range in 1750 prices is 106 to 121 l.t. With a population of 24.5 million, this leads to the estimate of 2,600 to 3,000 million l.t. for agricultural and manufacturing output alone.

levies returned approximately the same amounts year after year, and therefore their contribution to spending and their portion of national income diminished over time. The king could levy an additional *vingtième*, as his predecessor had (in effect) levied an additional *taille* in the form of the *capitation*. But his subjects would not admit to owing more to the royal treasury for individual taxes as their assets and incomes grew; they understood the system and its opportunities for evasion. Thus the treasury came to rely more and more on the levies collected by the General Farm, and on the farmers' enthusiasm to collect more than their lease required them to turn over to the king. It was this enthusiasm, which was lacking in other parts of the system, that enabled General Farm revenues to keep pace with the growth of national income. The farmers general may be condemned for having seized undeserved profits during the term of each lease. But their enthusiasm, or greed, was the leading force promoting growth in the ordinary revenues.

Marion condemned privilege, and the tax avoidance that this system allowed. Many people avoided taxes in a manner regarded as strictly legal. But the problem of avoidance should be distinguished from the problem of evasion. The *vingtièmes*, which contained fewer opportunities for avoidance than the *taille* or *capitation*, were nevertheless avoided or evaded by some 85 percent of the estimated national output of the 1750s.[91] The scale of evasion was massive, certainly larger in the aggregate than the scale of avoidance. This was the problem. Had the monarchy been able to eliminate evasion, then its revenues would have risen with incomes, and they would have been generous. But the monarchy could not deter evasion, for the French would not provide their government with the information necessary to detect income levels. One of the basic liberties claimed by the French was the right to preserve secrecy about family finances. This is the same liberty that blocked efforts by the royal government to take a census or to assess property values. In order to account for evasion on this scale, it is necessary to recognize that the entire populace practiced it.

The government lacked the means and the will to extract infor-

[91] That is, a single *vingtième* returned about 20 million when 5 percent of estimated national output (circa 2.8 billion, see the preceding note) amounted to some 140 million. In fact the shortfall will have been even greater, since French personal income, the theoretically taxable sum, will have exceeded agricultural and manufacturing product.

mation about incomes. From its point of view, the most efficacious policy was to levy a variety of taxes, which the government did, and to increase the weight of levies embedded in items of consumption. This too the government did through the General Farm. The very elements of the financial structure most often condemned by observers and historians are the elements that kept it going.

In practical terms, the finances could not be strengthened much by the elimination of privilege, because privilege was a cultural norm, and because it provided a motive for social and economic ambition. Nor could the overhead be reduced much, except at the cost of dampening revenue growth by removing from the General Farm the only incentive that promoted a significant growth in the ordinary revenues. It is more difficult to decide whether the extravagance of the court offered large opportunities for economy. Louis XIV had established that French kings had a role to play, and one part of the role was lavish display and spending. To what degree did the eighteenth-century monarchy require these financial symbols to maintain itself?

France emerged from the War of Austrian Succession with a larger debt and with larger tax revenues. Machault preserved the *dixième* in the form of a *vingtième*, against resistance from his former colleagues in the parlements. The objective, as Machault saw matters, was to pay off the debt. But Machault expected revenues from the peacetime *vingtième* to permit that. The financial authorities were confident that comparatively minor reforms would simultaneously stimulate French economic growth and resolve the old problem of financial weakness in a great and rich land. Machault did not see the problem clearly. At the heart of matters lies the unwillingness of the French to pay higher taxes except under extraordinary, and short-lived, circumstances, an unwillingness that assured new tension with each addition to the taxes. French kings could declare war at will, and could even expect their subjects to bear the added burden in taxes with less grumbling than greeted lower taxes in peacetime. But they could not expect their subjects to bear the burden of the war into peace. They could not overcome their subjects' aversion to paying taxes, and they could not overcome their subjects' feeling that basic liberties were at stake.

CHAPTER 3

THE SEVEN YEARS WAR

. . . lorsque la Nation parôit dans une espèce d'humiliation.[1]

*E*UROPEAN warfare was brought under control during the reign of Louis XIV.[2] The monarch who by his own admission loved war too much, who fought so many wars that his death in 1715 met rejoicing more or less equivalent to that which greeted the "miracle" of his birth in 1638, this monarch tamed war. The achievement may be assigned to Louis XIV and his ministers rather than to the times in general because of the single-mindedness with which Louis engaged in wars. A man given to occasional spiritual anxiety, Louis nevertheless did not let religion interfere with his decision to go to war or to make peace. The element that had impassioned war in the century before he came to the throne in 1661 was thus subdued. His ministers, Le Tellier and Louvois, introduced the bureaucratization of war and the conflict fought by seige-craft, supply, and position more than in pitched battles. The style of war created by Louis XIV, which lasted until 1792, knew wars fought for the comparatively simple and gentle objectives of gaining economic advantage, ag-

---

[1] *Journal encyclopédique*, Apr. 1, 1762, 98, from a poem by Colardeau.
[2] Michael Howard, *War in European History* (London, 1976), 54-74; John Childs, *Armies and Warfare in Europe, 1648-1789* (New York, 1982); and Theodore K. Rabb, *The Struggle for Stability in Early Modern Europe* (New York, 1975), 119-23. Another view is developed by Frederic C. Lane, *Profits from Power: Readings in Protection Rent and Violence-Controlling Enterprises* (Albany, N.Y., 1979), 13-15 and 36, who argues that the shift was from wars of plunder to wars designed to pursue economic advantages. These are discussed in terms of protection rents, best explained as costs added by military or naval enterprise to the business costs of rivals. William H. McNeill, *The Pursuit of Power: Technology, Armed Force, and Society since A.D. 1000* (Chicago, 1982), argues (e.g., 144) that European rulers bureaucratized military violence and found profit in global military expansion. It is difficult to decide what to make of Jack S. Levy's measurement of severity (in *War in the Modern Great Power System, 1495-1975* [Lexington, Ky., 1983], 121-49), in which battle deaths are a proxy. Battles deaths show no prominent trend until the very end of Levy's period, but Levy does not relate battle death figures to the size of the population or army at risk.

72

grandizing territory and power, or protecting prestige. But it also saw the introduction of standing armies and navies, so that war became a peacetime as well as a wartime business.

The king who loved war too much can be credited also with helping transform the geographical purview of conflict. Only a presentist affectation leads to a belief that world wars were fought first in the twentieth century. By threatening to fashion a European hegemony, Louis drew into his later wars an expanding array of powers, which had interests to pursue in Europe and elsewhere in the world. The Treaty of Utrecht in 1713 settled dynastic, territorial, and economic issues in Europe as well as North and South America. Eighteenth-century warfare would be distinguished both by a lower level of passion and a broader range of the theater of conflict.

Louis XV, born in 1710, was called in 1715 to his great-grandfather's deathbed to hear some advice ("I have loved war too much"), repeating one of those fascinating scenes of the era of ceremonial death in which Louis XIV likewise had participated at the age of five. We may wonder how much of what his great-grandfather said Louis XV understood, or remembered. In any case, the French appetite for war was exhausted in 1715. The regency, under the duc d'Orléans (1715-1723), passed with only a diplomatic conflict, with France, Britain, Austria, and the Dutch Republic allied against Spain in 1718-1720. Louis XV's personal reign began therefore in peace, which was not interrupted until the War of Polish Succession in 1733 and not in a serious way until the War of Austrian Succession in 1740.

The age of the old regime war lasted a century and a half. No one of its conflicts can be deemed representative, at least not without a more thoroughly developed theory of war than we yet possess. The next five chapters will examine one of these wars—the Seven Years War, a major rather than a minor example of old regime conflict—to discover whether this war involved large costs for the peacetime French economy, large displacements of resources. Did it sap the capacity for growth in the old regime economy? How did the government finance it? In the present chapter my goal is to summarize the story of French participation in the Seven Years War and to look for its effects in some of the most obvious places: the mobilization and export of money and men.

CONFLICT AND ITS MILITARY CONSEQUENCES

Hostilities opened in North America in June 1755 in a struggle that the Americans called the French and Indian War, identifying the enemy.[3] This portion of the war involved battles in two theaters, one above the fortieth parallel and the other largely below the twentieth. In the first, Anglo-American troops lost to the French at Fort Duquesne in July 1755, traded victories (and seized Fort Duquesne) in 1758, and took Quebec in September 1759, bringing a close to the struggle and to French rule in Canada. In the second theater, British forces attacked French and in 1762 Spanish possessions in the West Indies, enjoying a series of victories clustered in the later years of the war. Also in 1755 Britain began raiding French commerce.

European hostilities between Britain and France began in June 1756 when war was formally declared. In August Frederick II of Prussia, attempting a preemptive strike against Austria, which in May had concluded a defensive alliance with France in a maneuver known as the diplomatic revolution,[4] invaded Saxony and quickly defeated both the Saxons and the Austrians. Five months later, in January 1757, Austria and Russia agreed on a plan to partition Prussia, and Austria formally declared war on Prussia. By the middle of 1757 Britain was at war with France and Austria; and Prussia, with France, Austria, and Russia. Spain joined France in January 1762, but Britain and Russia remained at peace.[5] Lesser powers were also engaged. This struggle is sometimes called the Third Silesian War, which reveals the objectives of the central European belligerents. Austria wished to regain the prosperous region of Silesia,

[3] Useful sources on the war and its origins include: André Corvisier, *L'armée française de la fin du XVIIᵉ siècle au ministère de Choiseul* (2 vols ; Paris, 1964); Lee Kennett, *The French Armies in the Seven Years' War* (Durham, N.C., 1967); *Histoire de la dernière guerre, commencée l'an 1756* . . . (Cologne, 1770) (a pacifist tract); and Patrice Louis-René Higonnet, "The Origins of the Seven Years' War," *Journal of Modern History*, 40, no. 1 (Mar. 1968), 57-90. Sapin-Lignières, *Les troupes legérès de l'ancien régime. Les corsaires de roy de l'armée de terre* (n.p., 1979), esp. 57, is amusing for an argument that shortcomings in civilian morality during 1748-1756 sapped the army's strength.

[4] In other words, the war in North America began with France anticipating hostilities against Austria. See Mattheus Lestevenon van Berkenrode to Pieter Steyn, Jul. 23, 1755, in Algemeen Rijksarchief, The Hague, Archief Pieter Steyn, 17, where French plans for an attack on the Austrian Netherlands are discussed.

[5] H. M. Scott, "Great Britain, Poland and the Russian Alliance, 1763-1767," *Historical Journal*, 19, no. 1 (Mar. 1976), 60.

lost to Prussia in the War of Austrian Succession, which included the First and Second Silesian Wars, and to counter the rise of Prussian influence in Germany. Prussia wished to retain Silesia, to pursue its development as a great power, and to protect an extraordinarily weak geopolitical position. With a population of some 3.6 million, Prussia faced enemies in the Seven Years War with a combined population of some 70 million. Frederick's only major ally, Britain, could contribute only subsidies and troops from Hanover.

Frederick's preemptive strike in August 1756 gave Prussia the initial advantage, but it failed to win the war. Until the battle of Rossbach, November 5, 1757, the war seemed to be shifting to the favor of Austria, France, and Russia, which won victories, respectively, at Kolin in June, Hastenbeck in July, and Gross Jägersdorf also in July. But Frederick caught a combined Austro-French army by surprise at Rossbach and overwhelmed them. Thereafter his forces beat the Austrians at Leuthen (December), the French at Krefeld (June 1758), and the Russians at Zorndorf (August). Once again the fortunes of war shifted, and in 1759 and 1760 the Prussians were defeated on several occasions, and Berlin was burned by the Russians. At the moment of Frederick's greatest distress, after he had lost battles and the British subsidies, Elizabeth of Russia died (January 1762). She was succeeded by Peter III, who admired Frederick and quickly, in May, concluded a treaty with Prussia restoring all conquered territory and reducing the strategic problem that Frederick faced. In the last months of the war Frederick pushed the Austrians back, and France agreed to withdraw from Germany as a concession to an early peace.

For France this war was fought overseas and on foreign soil. In 1758 Britain seized French-controlled areas on the west coast of Africa near the mouth of the Senegal River, and in 1758-1760 French and British forces traded conquests in southern India and Bengal. For Europe the principal theater of conflict was Germany, with some activity also in eastern Portugal. In Germany the battles occurred chiefly between the Rhine and the Weser—the Franco-Prussian theater—and between the Elbe and the Oder with a pocket around Königsberg—the Austro-Prussian and Russo-Prussian theaters. No battles occurred within France, although British naval forces attacked at Quiberon Bay on the southern coast of Brittany, blockaded parts of the French fleet in Brest and Toulon, and attacked or assisted troop landings here and there on the French coast. In Toulouse, far enough inland to be free from fear of British invasion, the war and the absence of troops ordinarily quartered there (they were fighting in Germany) is said to have led to fears of Protestant subversion and thereby to have contributed to the conviction of Jean Calas, a Protestant, for the murder of his son, who was believed to have converted to Catholicism against his father's wishes.[6] But this was a representative old regime war in that, for Britain and Russia as well as France, the battles were fought elsewhere.

This war brought a major defeat to France and its allies. In the treaties of Paris and Hubertusburg in January 1763, France gave up Canada, Cape Breton Island, and Grenada, recognized the Mississippi River as the eastern boundary of its possessions in North America, then ceded those possessions to Spain. France also ceded Senegal, and lost enough influence and prospects in its colonies in general to lead to the dissolution in 1769 of the first Compagnie des Indes. Spain yielded Florida to Britain. Austria recognized once again the loss of Silesia. Both France and Spain also regained some territory lost to Britain during the war—France chiefly the islands of Guadeloupe and Martinique and Spain Havana. But much more was lost in the war than was regained in the treaty negotiations. These diplomatic successes for the French do, however, call attention to the scale of the French embarrassment in 1761 and 1762. At that moment the monarchy had lost more territory and prestige even than provided for in the Treaty of Paris. André Corvisier also finds profound military and political consequences of this defeat: a withdrawal of the army into itself and, simultaneously, a growth of support for military reform.[7]

MOBILIZATION FOR WAR

The Army

Eighteenth-century France maintained a standing army with French and foreign contingents, a militia, and a coast guard. In the

[6] David D. Bien, *The Calas Affair: Persecution, Toleration, and Heresy in Eighteenth-Century Toulouse* (Princeton, 1960), 71-75.
[7] Corvisier, *L'armée française*, I, 87, 90, and 129ff.

early 1750s the army numbered some 130,000 men, including only French forces in the regular army.[8] During the war all forces expanded:

regular army
French	200,000
non-French	70,000
militia	100,000

coast guard
effectives	42,000
watch companies and others	200,000
TOTAL	612,000

What is not entirely certain is how to evaluate the level and degree of peacetime service in the militia and coast guard. In peace both were staffed on paper more than in fact, and in a fashion that left most men free for civilian occupations. Here these troops are assumed to have been preeminently civilian in peacetime and military in wartime; in 1756 the coast guard began to be paid for active duty days during war and was often on alert or mobilized because of the threat of British landings and coastal raids.[9]

In the years before the Seven Years War the part of the army staffed by French soldiers—130,000—amounted to slightly more than one-half of 1 percent of the 1755 French population—25.0 million. In mobilizing for war, that portion was quadrupled—to some 540,000 French soldiers—until it totalled more than 2 percent of the population. Non-French forces rose from some 40,000 to 70,000, recruited mainly from Switzerland.[10] Each year also the va-

[8] *Ibid.*, I, 55, 57, 65, and 155; and André Corvisier, *Armies and Societies in Europe, 1494-1789*, trans. by Abigail T. Siddall (Bloomington, Ind., 1979), 113. These are approximate figures. Corvisier discusses problems with them in *L'armée française*, I, 54-55 and 65. Kennett, *French Armies*, 77, gives a total of 400,000, excluding the coast guard, and suggesting that this total may be too high. Several manuscript sources in foreign archives provide information on authorized (rather than actual) strength. E.g., the *état de militaire* for 1749 in Haus-, Hof- und Staatsarchiv, Vienna, Böhm-Supplement, Frankreich, Böhm 991-B717; and *id.*, Böhm 961-W923, for a memoir on the French navy in 1751. In the latter Ludwig von Zinzendorf remarked on the ease with which he could look into French naval warehouses and otherwise gather information.

[9] Charles Durand, *Les milices gardes-côtes de Bretagne de 1716 à 1792* (Rennes, 1927), 50, 53ff., 66-67, 70ff., 75ff., and 130-33.

[10] Corvisier, *L'armée française*, I, 155 and 259-74.

cancies created by deaths, wounds, desertions, capture by the enemy, and the completion of enlistment terms had to be filled. Thus war brought both a one-time increase in the army's demand for men and a larger annual quota of recruits.

The royal army drew its troops from the age group 16-40, recruiting first among unmarried males. Between 25 and 50 percent of the age group was ineligible for recruitment for physical reasons—they were infirm or too short. According to a reformist writer of the 1780s, Jean-Christophe des Pommelles, only some 600,000 men were then eligible among an estimated 1,450,000 unmarried males of appropriate age. Each year 339,000 men were identified as *miliciables*; of them, some 12,500 evaded the lottery-draft, and some 14,500 were drawn into the militia.[11] Exemptions were permitted also on grounds of economic utility, with individuals employed in trade, manufacturing, and public functions favored by the intendants who rendered such decisions. No exemptions were allowed for occupations in mining, and only a few arbitrarily determined exemptions were granted agriculturalists.[12] Most recruits thus came from the countryside, and most of those hailed from northeastern France.

Together with the navy, which was staffed chiefly by shifting men from the merchant marine and in which some 100,000 men served during this war,[13] men under arms at any one time during the Seven Years War totalled more than 2.5 percent of the population.[14] Another way to look at the manpower effects of war is to calculate the percentage of the prewar population serving during war. In these terms, French forces totalled the 650,000 to 700,000 men in the army and navy plus each year's replacements of at least 50,000 for the six years of actual hostilities, another 300,000.[15] Nearly a million Frenchmen—about 4 percent of the prewar population—served in

[11] *Ibid.*, I, 220-21 and 229; and [Jean-Christophe Sandrier] des Pommelles, *Tableau de la population de toutes les provinces de France* . . . (Paris, 1789).

[12] Corvisier, *L'armée française*, I, 206-216.

[13] T.J.A. Le Goff, "Offre et productivité de la main-d'oeuvre dans les armements français au XVIIIème siècle," *Histoire, économie et société*, 2, no. 3 (1983), 457-73; and information generously supplied by James Pritchard, who is writing a book on the French navy in the Seven Years War. Also T.J.A. Le Goff, "L'Impact des prises effectuées par les Anglais sur la capacité en hommes de la marine française au XVIIIe siècle," forthcoming in *Marines de guerre européennes de 1650 à 1815*.

[14] The prewar population was 25 million.

[15] Kennett, *French Armies*, 77.

the Seven Years War. This portion may be compared with military service in a population fighting twentieth-century wars on foreign soil. When compared with the percentage of the prewar United States population serving in World War II (11.2 percent), the figures for eighteenth-century France underscore the less than total scale of old regime warfare. But the portion of the French population serving in the Seven Years War does not differ much from the part of the American population serving in World War I (4.6 percent), the Korean War (3.8 percent), and the Vietnam War (4.5 percent). As Lee Kennett has remarked, "the transition to total war had begun."[16] Furthermore, the portion of the French populace too infirm to fight may have been significantly greater than in some twentieth-century societies so that providing a smaller percentage of able-bodied men may have been difficult for old regime societies. The old regime population was youthful, but very nearly the same proportion of the late-eighteenth-century male populace—about 60 percent—fell outside recruitment ages as is true of the late-twentieth-century male populace.[17] And the old regime economy presumably possessed less leeway to shift resources from one use to another. However much weight may be attached to these qualifying factors, it is apparent that war brought large changes in the size of the civilian labor force, and in the demand for grain and other necessities from people who no longer played much part in production. It is also apparent, from the evidence about exemptions, that the reallocation of men to the army fell heavily on agriculture. This is so because the proportion of peasants in the army increased in wartime,[18] because there were few exemptions for agriculturalists,

[16] *Ibid.*, xiii. The percentages of people in military service in the United States are drawn from Arthur A. Stein, *The Nation at War* (Baltimore, 1978), 35.

[17] This assertion is based on comparing the age profile of the male population of the province of Burgundy from the census of 1786, which is a rare detailed old regime age profile, with the profile of the male population of France at the beginning of 1982. In 1785, 48.4 percent of the male population under 80 was aged 0-15 or 50 and over (the age group 40-50 is part of the group 30-50 in Reinhard's report of this enumeration), whereas in 1982 48.1 percent of the male population under 80 was aged 0-15 or 50 and over. Marcel R. Reinhard, et al., *Histoire générale de la population mondiale* (3rd ed.; Paris, 1968), 249; and *Annuaire statistique de la France* (Paris, 1983), 27. Under a straight-line interpolation of the 1785 Burgundy population aged 30-50, 61 percent fall outside the ages 15-40, compared to 60 percent of the 1982 population.

[18] Samuel F. Scott, *The Response of the Royal Army to the French Revolution* (Oxford, 1978), 16.

and because agriculture included a large proportion of unmarried men—the so-called army of landless laborers who sought seasonal employment.

The Navy

Although the warring state of the old regime allotted two-thirds of its ordinary revenues to military spending—allocations for the army and navy, plus service on debts accumulated principally in war—and although French revenues exceeded those of any other mid-eighteenth-century European state, France could not afford to fund both an army large enough to rival the armies of Austria, Prussia, and Russia, and a navy as large as Britain's. In the reign of Louis XV France usually elected to favor the army, although Maurepas, secretary of state for the navy, and Fleury attempted in the 1730s and early 1740s to expand the navy. French strategic thinking held, sensibly enough, that the navy need not be as large as the British fleet in order to contest British forces at sea. But the French never managed to attain a level of strength sufficient to match Britain in areas of confrontation selected by the French. Thus the French empire in North America, the West Indies, Africa, and Asia, and French trade routes, connecting these places with the metropole and tying French ports to Baltic, Atlantic, and Mediterranean trading partners, stood open to British attack.

In 1754 France had a fleet of eighty-one vessels with twenty-four or more cannon—mostly ships of the line with some frigates. Antoine Louis Rouillé, secrétaire d'état de la marine from 1749, and Machault, transferred to that post from the controller generalship in 1754, directed a building program intended to expand the fleet to sixty-three ships of the line. But this energetic program faded in 1757 when, entangled in the Damiens affair with the marquise de Pompadour, the king's mistress and friend, Machault's public life ended. (Machault, keeper of the seals, rushed to the prison where Damiens was held and ordered torture with heated pincers, seeking to identify fellow conspirators. Later he was dismissed for designing the policy behind a confrontation with the parlement of Paris over the refusal of the sacraments controversy.)[19] In the interim more

[19] Dale K. Van Kley, *The Damiens Affair and the Unraveling of the "Ancien Régime,"* *1750-1770* (Princeton, 1984), 9, 152, and *passim*.

had been planned than achieved. In 1756 France could put to sea forty-five ships of the line and thirty frigates against Britain's sixty ships of the line (of eighty-nine in paper strength) and fifty frigates (of seventy).[20]

This was not enough. Indeed, it was so far below that hypothetical level of equivalent strength that France lost a large part of its fleet and its historical control over the Mediterranean in war. After a victory at Minorca in 1756, the French fleet was sometimes blockaded in port or its exit from the Mediterranean blocked at Gibraltar. It was also poorly led. Pursuing Choiseul's plan to invade England in 1759, the Mediterranean fleet was destroyed off Portugal in August, and the Brest fleet off Quiberon Bay in November. By the time Choiseul was named secretary of state for the navy in late 1761, the naval war had ended. Choiseul inaugurated another program of reconstruction and expansion, one that lasted up to 1770. In the opinion of Henri Legohérel, France had elected the wrong policy, pursuing military objectives in central Europe in preference to finer prizes to be obtained from war at sea with Britain.[21]

To assess the effect of the Seven Years War on the French navy is difficult. As naval historians remark, the fleet was nearly destroyed in 1759. But, new vessels and old, it was already an aging fleet in 1754, a time when vessels were made of wood and possessed a useful life ranging from eight to fifteen years, depending largely on the temperature of waters in which they served.[22] Some of the 1754 fleet did not survive because of their age rather than because of British action or, more often, accidents after engagements. Under Choiseul the French elected to build a larger navy: by 1770 the fleet contained sixty ships of the line and forty-five frigates, and was better led.[23] This massive program did not so much restore earlier power as create a fleet large enough to rival Britain's, which it was able to do in the War of the American Revolution.

[20] G. Lacour-Gayet, La marine militaire de la France sous Louis XV (2nd ed., Paris, 1910), 226, 235, and 261.

[21] Henri Legohérel, Les trésoriers généraux de la marine (1517-1788) (Paris, [1965]), 216-24.

[22] Patrick Villiers, Le commerce colonial atlantique et la guerre d'indépendance des Etats Unis d'Amérique, 1778-1783 (New York, 1977), 134 and 136; and T.J.A. Le Goff and Jean Meyer, "Les constructions navales en France pendant la seconde moitié du XVIIIᵉ siècle," Annales E.S.C., 26, no. 1 (Jan.-Feb. 1971), 185.

[23] Legohérel, Les trésoriers généraux, 221. Also Algemeen Rijksarchief, Archief Pieter Steyn, 343.

Losses in the navy did not curtail French trade. To maintain peacetime trade routes and quantities in war was beyond the power even of the French navy of 1778-1783, and certainly beyond anyone's expectation of what the navy would do during the Seven Years War. French merchants, like French naval tacticians, understood that the declaration of war would bring a brief interlude in which British naval strength was built up, and during which the leading risk came from privateers rather than men-of-war. After those months the British would control the seas. What France lost therefore was the navy itself—the remaining useful life of the fixed capital constituting the navy of 1755. Forbin believed in 1763 that 200 million livres would reestablish the navy.[24] The human capital—the sailors—largely survived.

What, in military and naval terms, did France lose between 1755 and 1763? For the army, casualties notwithstanding, the most significant consequences were psychological. Succeeding merely in trading victories with the outnumbered Prussians, French military men emerged from the war with a sense of the need for regeneration, a sense displayed in numerous publications finding fault and suggesting reforms.[25] Reform, which aimed to professionalize the officer corps, required decades to achieve, and remained incomplete in 1789, when it was interrupted. For the navy, this war cost France the bulk of its fleet, and thus required an expensive postwar rebuilding program. Mixed success on land and the failure of French arms at sea contributed to a crisis of confidence. Beginning in 1760, and with special intensity and openness in 1763, Frenchmen of many occupations and social orders investigated fundamental defects in the French polity. Their inquiries focused not only on the army or navy but also on finance. The failures of the war were attributed not to inadequacies in French military insight, but to the blunders of a leadership unable to furnish adequate funds and to manage them properly. Legohérel's judgment, that the French made the wrong choice in preferring to fund an army rather than a navy, seemed less

[24] [Gaspard François Anne de] F[orbin], *Système d'imposition et de liquidation de dettes d'état, établi par la raison* (n.p., 1763), 113.
[25] Kennett, *French Armies*, 139.

persuasive to observers of the day than the belief that the necessary amounts of money could be provided if only the finances were administered properly.

THE ECONOMICS OF WAR

To strategic thinkers in the army and navy, war is a question of resources, and thus, in the end, of financial wherewithal. To the civilians who direct financial and economic policy, however, war has another side. In the old regime as in later ages, civilian leaders attended not only to taxing and borrowing but also to certain economic issues that influence the capacity of a populace to pay taxes and lend. To mid-eighteenth-century observers the issues requiring closest attention were three: the net flow of specie and bullion, the cost of credit (usually expressed confusingly in terms of the availability of money), and the price of basic goods.

Money Flows

The net movement of precious metals concerned eighteenth-century statesmen in war and peace. It is a mistake to believe, as Mirabeau and Quesnay argued in 1763,[26] that informed commentators still measured the wealth of a nation by the volume of its precious metals. But mercantilists, physiocrats, and others alike recognized the inability of a country like France to produce precious metals on its own in sufficient quantity to provide a money stock, and the role of money as an engine of economic activity. Mid-eighteenth-century theorists and policy makers wished to augment the volume of specie in France, and they understood and were apprehensive about the tendency of war to lead to an outflow of specie and bullion.

Sources on old regime specie and bullion flows reveal trends clearly but are usually silent about magnitude.[27] In peace, France

[26] [Victor de Riquetti de Mirabeau], *Philosophie rurale, ou économie générale & politique de l'agriculture* . . . (Amsterdam, 1763), 395. Quesnay is said to have overseen Mirabeau's work on this book, the first general statement of physiocratic ideas.

[27] James C. Riley and John J. McCusker, "Money Supply, Economic Growth, and the Quantity Theory of Money: France, 1650-1788," *Explorations in Economic History*, 20 (1983), 274-93. Of eighteenth-century literature see especially [Buchet du Pavillon], *Essai sur les causes de la diversité des taux de l'intérêt de l'argent chez les peuples* (Lon-

enjoyed a large current account surplus, the result of exporting more than it imported in goods and services[28] and of net tourist spending in France. This current account surplus was apparently augmented by a capital account flow into France. Foreign investors and lenders spent more money in France than French investors and lenders spent abroad. Because the evidence—French mint output figures and exchange rates—indicates that the French specie stock expanded during the century, it can be inferred (everything else being equal) that the corresponding current account debit created by interest payments on these loans and investments did not match the current and capital account surplus. There would have been in the long run a transfer of bullion and specie to France to balance commercial and financial flows. The French coin stock grew from an estimated 500 million l.t. in 1683 to between 1,600 and 2,600 million a century later. (In the interim, up to 1726, the silver and gold equivalences of the livre also declined, but at a slower pace than the money stock grew. Holding the silver equivalence constant at post 1726 values, France's coin stock is estimated to have grown from some 936 million in 1683 to between 1,600 and 2,600 million in the 1780s.[29])

In war, as Michel Morineau has suggested,[30] the net flow was likely to shift toward an export of bullion and specie from France. There are two leading reasons. France had to export specie (or the equivalent) in order to pay its troops fighting abroad—chiefly in Germany—and to provide subsidies to its allies. The net flow turned against France also because war curtailed French trade, diminishing

---

don, 1757), 9-11, for a prose statement of the equation $P = f(M,V,T)$, where P is the price level, M the money stock, V the velocity of circulation, and T the volume of transactions.

[28] Estimates are offered by the *Journal de commerce et d'agriculture*, Dec. 1761, 33, and Jan. 1759, 118; [Ambroise Marie] Arnould, *De la balance du commerce et des relations commerciales extérieures de la France* ... (2 vols.; Paris, 1791), II, 168; and, for 1753, Riksarkivet, Stockholm, Skoklostersamling E 9027, 147-53, dealing with specie flows in trade.

[29] Riley and McCusker, "Money Supply," 277.

[30] Michel Morineau, "Pour une reconsidération des mouvements de longue durée et, notamment, des mouvements dits de Kondratieff," unpublished essay, 4; and id., "Quelques recherches relatives à la balance du commerce extérieur français au XVIIIᵉ siècle: Ou cette fois un égale deux," in Pierre Léon, ed., *Aires et structures du commerce français au XVIIIᵉ siècle* (Paris, 1975), 20. Also Abel Poitrineau, *La vie rurale en Basse-Auvergne au XVIIIᵉ siècle (1726-1789)* (2 vols.; Paris, 1965), I, 499-500.

the current account surplus. Thus France, whose trade experienced boom and bust fluctuations with peace and war, knew a far more unstable specie flow pattern than did Britain, whose trade was little influenced by war.[31] During the Seven Years War foreign lenders expanded their investments in French securities, enlarging the capital account inflow. Possibly this expansion was not enough to counter exports of specie and bullion from France. In the opinion of observers at the time the French money stock shrank significantly during the war.[32] This is an important issue in judging the economic effects of the Seven Years War. Did France's money stock actually shrink? Were apprehensions of economic paralysis owing to an inadequate money stock warranted?

Answers to these questions will not come easily and must, because of the nature of the evidence, be tentative. Only a rough approximation of money flows can be given. France exported specie to pay its regular army troops abroad. The records of these transactions are not available, but for this, the largest item in the wartime capital account, a rough idea can be obtained from estimates of the cost of maintaining French troops during the War of Austrian Succession. Corvisier reveals that in the 1740s these annual costs prevailed: 122,11 l.t. per native and 160 to 178,11 per alien soldier.[33] At this level the 200,000 French troops operating mostly abroad between 1757 and 1762 cost up to 24.5 million a year, and the 70,000 alien troops as much as 12.5 million—together 37 million. Other estimates range as high as 500 l.t. per man, which is derived by dividing total military and naval expenditures by manpower and is excessive for purposes of this discussion.[34] French officials projected military and naval spending at a rate of 212 million for 1759—or 300 to 325

---

[31] H.S.K. Kent, *War and Trade in Northern Seas: Anglo-Scandinavian Economic Relations in the Mid-Eighteenth Century* (Cambridge, 1973), 79 and *passim*, especially the appendices. However, Britain suffered losses in invisibles. Id., 137-38. Also Larry Neal, "Interpreting Power and Profit in Economic History: A Case Study of the Seven Years War," *Journal of Economic History*, 27, no. 1 (Mar. 1977), 20-35, esp. 35, on the impact of Dutch investment in Britain.

[32] E.g., *Mes rêveries sur les Doutes modestes, à l'occasion des Richesses de l'état, par M. B***...*, in *Richesse de l'état, à laquelle on a ajouté* ... (Amsterdam, 1764), 106; [François Marie Arouet de] Voltaire, *The Age of Louis XV*, trans. (2 vols.; London, 1770), II, 290; and Bedford to Egremont, Sept. 15, 1762, Huntington Library, Huntington, California, Stowe Collection: Grenville Correspondence, STG Box 16.

[33] Corvisier, *L'armée française*, I, 260.

[34] Kennett, *French Armies*, 97.

l.t. for each of the approximately 650,000 to 700,000 men under arms.[35] The French bought some war supplies abroad—gunpowder in the Dutch Republic, and some food and forage in Germany, and soldiers were paid where they were quartered.[36] But only part of aggregate military and naval spending went abroad. The annual outflow probably exceeded 37 million, but did not amount to as much as the added extraordinary spending of wartime—some 100 million over ordinary peacetime allocations.[37]

In war France also paid subsidies to its allies (which in the previous conflict had peaked at 55 million a year and which in 1756 amounted to about 55 million)[38] and continued customary peacetime capital account transfers: payments to the court of Rome, which are estimated in one source at 3.6 million l.t. in 1765,[39] and diplomatic costs, included in the subsidy estimate. Against these movements the largest credit item was foreign investment in French government loans, which is known to have been substantial even if its size remains unclear. This flow was, however, counterbalanced to some degree by service payments on prior loans so that the net lending flow was less than the amount of fresh credit from abroad.

These rough figures leave in doubt the amount of the outflow. Nevertheless, payments abroad—between 37 and 100 million for troops and supplies, perhaps 55 million for subsidies, 3.6 million for regular flows to Rome, and other items—certainly exceeded net foreign lending to France, presumably by several tens of millions, and in most years probably exceeded the capital account inflow and the current account surplus as ordinarily measured. During this war a large annual drain of specie and bullion was therefore necessary to bring current and capital account flows into balance.

[35] [Mathon de la Cour], *Collection de comptes-rendus* . . . (Lausanne, 1788), 47, supplies the spending figure, which is combined with the manpower estimate given above.

[36] Kennett, *French Armies*, 99-119, discusses supply.

[37] Compare the 1759 projection in [Mathon de la Cour], *Comptes-rendus*, 47, with figures on ordinary military and naval spending for preceding and succeeding years in University Library, London, Palæography Room, 127 (2); and Bibliothèque Mazarine, Paris, 2825.

[38] Algemeen Rijksarchief, Legatiearchief, Eerste Afdeling, Frankrijk, 776, reporting French subsidies during 1730-1750 in combination with French diplomatic costs abroad; and René-Louis de Voyer d'Argenson, *Journal et mémoires*, ed. by E.J.B. Rathery (9 vols.; Paris, 1859-1867), IX, 345.

[39] University Library, London, 127 (2).

At the middle of the century France's coin stock is estimated to have totalled some 1,500 million livres. A net outflow of 50 million, which seems plausible, therefore constituted a loss of more than 3 percent of the coin stock. Over six years, the flow could total 20 percent or more of the stock. But the fiscal authorities watched this problem and countered the tendency of war to deplete France's coin stock by calling on the king's subjects to bring unminted metal, chiefly plate and jewelry, to the mints. In 1759, according to Hume's translator, some 50 million was converted from non-monetary form to gold and silver coins. Mint activity continued during the war, thereby counterbalancing some of the outflow of coins and bullion. More research is clearly needed to provide firm estimates of key quantities, but it is apparent that eighteenth-century alarmists noticed the outflow without paying heed to the countervailing inflow.[40] For the moment, however, it seems most plausible to infer that war in general, and the Seven Years War in particular, occasioned both a net outflow of bullion and coins and a decline in the French coin stock. In the chapter that follows, after examining trade flows, we shall return to this issue.

Was there, however, an equivalent drop in the French money supply? Answering this question is complicated by the vagueness with which eighteenth-century observers discussed monetary issues and interest rates. Merchants, bankers, and theorists alike often complained about a shortage of money, but rarely in a specific way about high interest rates. Since interest rates are known to have fluctuated and some laments about tight money occurred in periods of a rapidly expanding specie stock, it is evident that this complaint spoke also to the cost of credit. The anonymous translator of David Hume's commercial essays confirms this, pointing out that interest rates are a function of the demand for and supply of credit, and that commentators have this in mind when they speak of money being scarce or plentiful.[41] In the Seven Years War French authorities augmented their issues of paper: the *billets des fermes* of the General Farm, the *rescriptions* of the tax receivers, the *lettres réquisitoriales* given suppliers of food and forage in Germany, the *billets de caisse*

[40] One extreme version, which appears at the end of one of the Seven Years War *états* (British Library, Additional Manuscripts, 40759), estimated France's specie losses during the war at 500 million.

[41] David Hume, *Essais sur le commerce* . . . (trans.; Paris, 1767), 117-18.

used to pay other army suppliers, and a wide variety of negotiable paper.[42] By 1764 the short-term debt, comprised of negotiable paper outstanding from the war, totalled at least 314 million.[43] All this paper may be counted as money, but it should not be counted to the same degree as specie; paper circulated in narrower limits and often in high denominations. Likewise the securities issued by France before and during the war, especially lottery tickets but also the various paper of long-term loans, possessed some negotiability. One source—a memoir by one Calsabigi—indicates that in 1761 France had 3 billion l.t. in paper in circulation.[44] Such a figure would include paper of severely limited negotiability, however, such as life annuities and tontines, and some patents of offices returning *gages*.

We stand at a great distance from the object to be measured, and use information that leaves several degrees of error and, in the end, only the roughest of notions. France's specie stock, about 1,500 million l.t. before the war, suffered some drain during the years of diminished trade activity and fighting abroad, 1757 through 1762.[45] But this drain was countered by paper issues on a scale apparently large enough to have augmented the overall money stock. After the war observers believed that the specie stock was changed little from its prewar level, despite interim losses. Specie temporarily drained abroad was compensated for by newly minted plate and, quite fortuitously, by a growing volume of negotiable paper in circulation in France; it was quickly made up by postwar trade surpluses and bullion inflow. French authorities did not issue paper with the intention of replacing lost specie. But they did issue specie substitutes in large enough volume to indicate that the economic effects to be feared

---

[42] Haus-, Hof- und Staatsarchiv, Böhm 960-W922 lists the *effets* in circulation in France in 1767. Paul Harsin, *Crédit public et banque d'état en France du XVIᵉ au XVIIIᵉ siècle* (Paris, 1933), 64-81, showed a half-century ago that the French debated paper currency issues before and after Law, and were less affected by the Law system issues than is still commonly supposed. Paul Butel, "Contribution à l'étude de la circulation de l'argent en Aquitaine au XVIIIᵉ siècle: Le commerce des rescriptions sur les recettes des finances," *Revue d'histoire économique et sociale*, 52, no. 1 (1974), 83-109, discusses trade in the *rescriptions* and internal money flows.

[43] See Table 6.6, combining the debts of government departments and the anticipations of future revenues.

[44] Haus-, Hof- und Staatsarchiv, Staatskanzlei, 5, 252. Calsabigi argued that French success in issuing paper suggested an opportunity for Austria.

[45] Riley and McCusker, "Money Supply," 277. See Chapter 5 on trade flows.

may have been inflation from a suddenly growing money stock rather than deflation from a sudden contraction of the stock. Let us set this question aside for a brief time.

Interest Rates

French borrowing expanded sharply in 1756, as the royal treasury turned to the capital markets of France, and obliged other institutions, chiefly the General Farm, the provinces, and the municipalities, also to borrow on its behalf. Such pressures on demand will be expected to push interest rates upward. But the measurement of rates is made difficult by the persistence of a ceiling on interest rates in private contracts, set by central government and regional order,[46] by the tendency of officials to use the ceiling (5 percent) as a standard rate in discussing interest, and by the scarcity of securities quotations. In that age only the London market possessed a regularly published list of securities prices. Even Amsterdam, the largest capital market in Europe, lacked such lists except for certain domestic government securities and the English funds. French securities prices were published occasionally in periodicals devoted to commercial news and discussions of commercial and economic issues as an irregular service to readers rather than under official auspices. (An official price current appeared only in the 1790s.) None of the lists I have encountered provides prices for the early war years. Thus the point of departure is the prewar yield on government securities, in 1749 some 4.7 percent and probably at lower levels between then and 1755.[47]

The first prices found during the war begin in January 1760 when the *Journal de commerce et d'agriculture*, published in Brussels, quoted a selection of prices from Amsterdam, Brussels, and Paris.[48]

---

[46] See n. 57 in Chapter 1. The ceiling rate in private transactions has the effect of obscuring both up and down movements under the 5 percent ceiling.

[47] See Chapter 6. The war years were a period of active discussion in France of the theory and practice of interest. [Buchet du Pavillon], *Essai*; [Simon] Clicquot [de] Blervache, *Dissertations sur les effets qui produit le taux de l'intérest de l'argent* . . . (Amiens, 1755); and [Henry de Goyon de la Plombanie], *Vues politiques sur le commerce* . . . (Amsterdam, 1759).

[48] Jan. 1760, 214, and *passim* in later numbers. This magazine formerly carried the title *Journal de commerce*.

Like all such lists, this one provides quotations in current prices or in the discount or premium from nominal value. Thus it is necessary to know the nominal value and yield in order to calculate the effective yield: the nominal yield divided by the market price. At a time when Dutch government securities paying 2.5 percent traded close to or at par, and with little change from month to month, French securities fluctuated in value and traded well below par. Cryptic descriptions make it difficult to identify all varieties of paper for which at least one quotation is given. Compagnie des Indes loan *billets*, bearing a nominal value of 500 l.t. and a yield of 5 percent,[49] traded at the following rates:

February 1760	395	(6.3 percent)
March 1761	398	(6.3)
May 1761	380-381	(6.6)
July 1761	405	(6.2)

This sparse information about a proxy borrower for the royal treasury—the Compagnie des Indes—agrees with indications from other sources. Silhouette, the controller general, complained toward the end of 1759 that subscriptions on royal loans had slowed, which is to say that lenders had stopped advancing money at the yields offered. Thereafter the dearth moderated as the treasury augmented yields.[50] With the end of war effective yields fell toward the 5 percent level so dear to official thought. By April 1763, when the *Gazette du commerce* of Paris began publication, French securities were paying 5.1 to 5.3 percent.[51] (Since, based on grain prices, the wartime price trend was ultimately stable, and since we lack the composite index necessary to compute real interest rates on a short-run basis, it is reasonable to see these nominal rates as close to real rates.)

French financial authorities were well advised to concern themselves about interest rates. Increases at these levels, which probably

---

[49] Haus-, Hof- und Staatsarchiv, Böhm 960-W922.

[50] Jacob Nicolas Moreau, *Mes souvenirs*, ed. by Camille Hermelin (2 vols.; Paris, 1898-1901), I, 78; and n. 48 above.

[51] April 1, 1763, listing prices for March 24: e.g., *rentes* on the Paris hôtel de ville with a nominal yield of 2.5 percent at 48, those secured on revenues from a tax on hides with a nominal yield of 3 percent at 56.5, and the 5 percent *rescriptions* at a 6 percent discount. This information comes from the Paris edition. Briefly the *Gazette* also issued a provincial edition, which provides additional data.

overstate the prewar effective yield and understate the wartime high,[52] and thus underestimate the increased cost of war borrowing, amount nonetheless to a rise of 40 percent in the cost to the government of financing loans. Thus at the same time that aggregate service payments rose with additional borrowing, the cost of buying credit advanced. An increase at this level does not exceed the increase faced by Britain. But France borrowed large sums at far more generous yields than these, as will appear below. For the moment, therefore, our focus is not on these effective returns as statements about the cost of borrowing so much as it is on what changes in securities prices and effective yields suggest about pressures in the money markets. These developments promote a suspicion that the government's need to borrow squeezed out some private investment. At the very least, we can hypothesize that investors considering fixed capital assets—shipping, warehouses, mining equipment, land, and the like—may have begun to reconsider during the war in the face of generous and rising yields from government securities.

Prices

In the eighteenth century the leading price issue is no longer the classic *crise de subsistance*—the coincidence of dearth, higher prices, and higher mortality—which disappeared toward the end of the reign of Louis XIV.[53] It is rather the question of the distribution of wealth. The reigning hypothesis, initially formulated by Ernest Labrousse, and recently restated by Emmanuel Le Roy Ladurie, Colin Jones, and others, is that the end of the subsistence crises contributed to the rise of mere poverty.[54] According to this interpretation, augmentations in the per capita quantity of income and wealth were distributed unevenly. Real income among the lower economic classes diminished during an era of general economic growth,

[52] Certainly they understate it on the life annuities and tontines, which before and during the war paid much higher yields. Here I am concerned to compare paper of similar type. See Chapter 6 on the life annuity problem.

[53] Jean Meuvret, "Les crises de subsistances et la démographie de la France d'ancien régime," *Population*, 1, no. 4 (Oct.-Dec. 1946), 643-50.

[54] Emmanuel Le Roy Ladurie, *Les paysans de Languedoc* (2 vols.; Paris, 1966), I, 484ff., in terms of a large long-run shift of wealth and income from countryside to town in seventeenth- and eighteenth-century France; and Colin Jones, *Charity and "Bienfaisance": The Treatment of the Poor in the Montpellier Region, 1740-1815* (Cambridge, 1982), 29.

which persisted from the 1720s or earlier until at least the eve of the Seven Years War. The rich got richer, and the poor poorer. Two forces were at work. The overall increase in real income was seized by the rich, or perhaps by the rich and the public sector in combination. At the same time, the real income of the poor shrivelled, which is to say that the rich got richer at a faster rate than income grew.

This interpretation, which can be styled the "immiseration hypothesis," conflicts with an idea articulated by a political scientist, Arthur A. Stein. Thinking most especially about twentieth-century wars involving the United States, Stein suggests that war mobilization dampens inequalities in society because manpower mobilization diminishes unemployment and thereby reduces income inequalities. War may also augment the money supply and promote inflation, as the authorities borrow. And Stein believes that inflation hurts the rich more than the poor because it aids debtors and penalizes creditors. Finally, wartime taxation is likely to be more direct and progressive than peacetime taxation, which is another blow to the rich.[55] This can be styled the "democratization hypothesis."

Neither interpretation can be fully tested. The immiseration hypothesis needs to be articulated in more detail. Where should the gains to the rich and the losses to the poor be expected to show up? It is also a hypothesis about the long-run trend of the division of income, while the issues raised here deal with short-run movements influenced by war. Both hypotheses would benefit from data about wages, which is notoriously difficult to produce in a form that allows comparisons over time. Nevertheless, it will be useful to examine price data during the Seven Years War and in the years surrounding it in search of evidence that will imply something about these hypotheses and answer two other interesting questions. First, France was both an importer and an exporter of grain at the middle of the eighteenth century. Did war, which disrupted peacetime trade flows and routes, reduce the level of integration that French grain markets had achieved by the middle of the eighteenth century? A lower level of integration—that is, a decline in the efficiency of French grain markets—might be expected to disrupt any peacetime trend

[55] Stein, *Nation at War*, 22-23. Stein's counterhypothesis of war financed by economizing social services does not apply to eighteenth-century France, where the private sector shouldered most social services.

in income distribution. If, as the immiseration hypothesis suggests, the income trend was toward greater unevenness, then a lower level of integration across domestic markets and between domestic and foreign markets would be expected to reduce the capacity of land-owners and merchants—the rich—to profit from grain production and trade at the expense of peasants, haulers, and others—the poor—engaged in the same activities.[56] Second, did either the initiation or the conclusion of conflict show up in prices? Both displaced large numbers of people who were taken from the civilian labor force at the beginning of conflict and returned to it at the end. Both altered the scale at which grain was consumed by people who had little or nothing to do with its production—the wartime army, and to a lesser extent the militia and coast guard. At the initiation of war, before the army was sent abroad, the large increase in military man-power had to be fed chiefly from French grain resources. An increase in prices, stimulated by war or other forces, would have simplified any shift toward unevenness in income distribution by giving grain producers and traders—the rich—larger short-run profits. These questions can be addressed with evidence from grain price series. To those data already examined by scholars can be added a series recently acquired by the Kress Library of Business and Economics.

Before consulting the evidence, it will be useful to acknowledge some of its characteristics, and the contentious nature of the idea of market integration. French agriculturalists produced a variety of basic grains, of which wheat and rye were, in quantity and price, far and away the most important.[57] Their quality, and weights and measures, varied from region to region. What is at issue here is change in the closeness with which prices moved together among markets. Conversions to the same quality and quantity are unnecessary. All that is required is to examine the movement of variances

[56] That is, significantly less integration would be expected to shift the focus of trade from large-scale regional producers and traders to small-scale local producers and traders.

[57] Using information from J.-C. Toutain, O'Brien estimates these two at 77 percent of the four-grain basket he developed. From J[acques] Dupâquier, M[arcel] Lachiver, and J[ean] Meuvret, *Mercuriales du pays de France et du vexin français (1640-1792)* (Paris, 1968), 230-31, it appears that wheat and rye, sold separately or in combination, accounted for nearly 83 percent of grain sold in Pontoise during 1752-1761.

between prices on different markets. That a particular level of integration had been achieved by French markets before the eighteenth century prompts suspicion among some historians, despite the work of Louise Tilly, Jacques Dupâquier, and others on market integration.[58] The suspicion seems to arise from a recognition that grain, a bulky good, did not travel readily across France, and that areas of dearth sometimes appeared only a few leagues away from areas of plenty. It is true that the overland transport of grain remained expensive, and thus feasible only under conditions in which the price differential between two markets compensated the shipper. And it is true also that France was divided into regional market areas, some of which had important linkages with territories outside France. But the actual movement of goods is not the only ingredient in market integration. Here we are dealing with markets imperfectly integrated, markets where, in some cases at least, information flows will have had more effect than actual movements of grain, and where in any case there is no need to assume that the Paris market dominated other French markets, as Tilly does, or that the evolution toward small variances across markets implies very much about political or cultural integration, as skeptics seem to fear. Prices from other centers will be compared to those in Paris, but my notion is that the level of variance was fixed not only by the scale of the Paris market but also by a variety of factors, some of which issued from outside France.

The area under investigation stretches from the Levant and Spain, which supplied Marseilles, to the Baltic coast, which supplied Amsterdam. An underlying portion of any coefficient of correlation may be the product of similarities in climate and thus in harvest fluctuations. But high levels of association in markets not close together, as these were not, signals similarities among those markets in setting prices, though it does not reveal the reasons for these similarities. Another portion of the association can be accounted for by mutual

[58] Louise A. Tilly, "The Food Riot as a Form of Political Conflict in France," *Journal of Interdisciplinary History*, 2, no. 1 (Summer 1971), 23-57, esp. 45 and 45n47; Dupâquier, Lachiver, and Meuvret, *Mercuriales*, 9-10; and Pierre Léon, *Aires et structures du commerce français au XVIII siècle* (Paris, 1975), xxi-xxii. Léon shows that the hinterland of ports functioned both as a source of goods for export and a center of demand for imports.

participation of all these markets in a long-run inflationary price trend. What is at issue here is not the trend of prices but differences in the degree of integration.

Our tools of analysis are not ideally suited to probing these issues. Warring states did not either fight or keep the peace in long runs of years. It is necessary to examine the relationship between markets for years that include peace and war. French historians have provided a number of price series, although not all series give annual data for the years of concern here, 1730-1770.[59] And some series merely repeat what is known from others because they are drawn from markets in very close proximity.[60] Of particular interest here are prices in the mobilization region of France, which is, according to Kennett's discussion of the territory within France from which food and forage were drawn, the area east of Paris. Two price series draw our attention. One, dealing with the Charleville market near the Austrian Netherlands frontier, has recently been analyzed by Morineau. The other is a new series giving usually twice-weekly readings for the wholesale market in the town of Tonnerre, on the Armançon River southeast of Paris.[61] Together with Paris and Pontoise, these markets demarcate a horn of plenty, the district producing fodder and grain for the war effort. They should be more sensitive to any war-related price effects than the other French markets examined—Marseilles, which imported from the eastern Mediterranean and Toulouse, center of the grain-rich Garonne Valley. But they may be less sensitive to the war than Amsterdam prices, which are also included in Table 3.1 both as a way of checking associations between French and non-French markets and as a test, with the

[59] Here I elected to deal with wheat prices alone. Series for commodities other than grains are unavailable, and the choice is limited in some cases to wheat alone and in others to a combination of wheat, rye, barley, and oats. As suggested above, wheat and rye, especially wheat, dominated the grain markets. The common people ate bread made of a combination of wheat and rye, but grew wheat to sell for its more generous return, a consequence of the urban preference for wheat bread. Many authorities have noticed that wheat and rye prices moved in close association, so that wheat also speaks as a proxy for rye.

[60] E.g., René Baehrel, *La Basse-Provence rurale (fin XVIe siècle-1789)* (2 vols.; Paris, 1961), I, 535ff.; and Dupâquier, Lachiver, and Meuvret, *Mercuriales*.

[61] The identification of this series with Tonnerre rests on the association of the compiler, Nicolas François, with that town, an association announced in the manuscript early in the 1762 series.

TABLE 3.1

Associations between Paris and Other Grain Markets

(r values)

	Pontoise	Charleville	Tonnerre	Toulouse	Marseilles	Amsterdam
1730-1749	.875	.926	—	.222	.025	.735
1740-1759	.880	.942	—	.217	−.023	.732
1753-1771	—	—	.889	—	—	—
1750-1769	.937	.850	—	.565	—	.700
1760-1779	.964	.919	—	.661	—	.770

SOURCES: Micheline Baulant, "Le prix des grains à Paris de 1431 à 1789," *Annales E.S.C.*, 23, no. 3 (May-Jun. 1968), 540; N. W. Posthumus, *Inquiry into the History of Prices in Holland* (2 vols.; Leiden, 1946-1964), I, 2-3; Michel Morineau, "A la halle de Charleville: Fourniture et prix des grains ou les mécanismes du marché (1647-1821)," *Actes du 95ᵉ Congrès national des sociétés savantes*, Section d'histoire moderne et contemporaine (Reims, 1970), II, 194-98; René Baehrel, *Une croissance. La Basse-provence rurale (fin XVIᵉ siècle-1789)* (2 vols.; Paris, 1961), I, 545; Georges and Geneviève Frêche, *Les prix des grains, des vins et des légumes à Toulouse (1486-1868)* (Paris, 1967), 89-90; J[acques] Dupâquier, M[arcel] Lachiver, and J[ean] Meuvret, *Mercuriales du pays de France et du vexin français (1640-1792)* (Paris, 1968), 71-93; and the manuscript entitled "Taux des gros fruits commencé le 20 Juin 1753 et finis le 18 Xbre [December] 1762," Kress Library of Business and Economics, Boston. The manuscript actually continues until June 22, 1771 No information is available for Tonnerre before 1753 or after 1771, and only fragmentary information is available for Marseilles import prices after 1759.

Marseilles series, of the effects of war on French participation in the international grain trade.

These coefficients of correlation describe the degree of association between two variables, prices in Paris and each other market listed. The possible range of degrees of association is − 1.0 to 1.0, with a coefficient close to 0.0 indicating no association and a coefficient close to 1.0 indicating a close association. Of course these coefficients do not speak to the causes behind the close or distant association; that is left to the insight of the historian. Here one must expect to consider climate, which influenced output levels in a similar manner across northeastern France, the physical movement of grain to Paris along the river and canal network of the north, and the even larger flow of information among trading centers. Several trends are apparent. The Paris and Pontoise markets were moving toward even closer association, having already achieved a high degree of integration. Likewise Toulouse, which Tilly found to have oscillated with Paris during the seventeenth century, continued to oscillate in the eighteenth. Like Marseilles, Toulouse was situated in a region distant from northern European trade and information flows. Two periods of association for Paris and Marseilles, 1730-

1749 and 1740-1759, bear out this detachment of the north from the south in grain pricing. Marseilles import prices do not show any significant association with Paris prices, although prices on the Paris market moved in close association with those in Amsterdam.

No clear trend is evident in the Paris/Amsterdam comparison. The high degree of integration achieved by 1730 does not seem to have changed much thereafter. But both Amsterdam and Charleville prices show a small movement away from integration during 1750-1769, when any effects of the Seven Years War would be expected to show up most strongly. Earlier wars, the War of Polish Succession and the War of Austrian Succession, which are reflected in the coefficients for 1730-1749 and 1740-1759, establish a normative pattern of levels of market integration during mixed periods of peace and war. And both comparisons show a restoration of higher levels of integration in the mostly postwar years of 1760-1779. Apparently the Seven Years War influenced both internal and international markets in northern France. But the disruption affected distant rather than proximate markets: it did not show up in Pontoise, adjacent to Paris.

If the war had an effect in the northeast, where recruitment was concentrated, the scale of the effect was not large. Neither Amsterdam nor Charleville prices lost their close association with the Paris market. Thus the war, which did interfere with peacetime trade flows in other goods by curtailing French shipping toward Amsterdam and presumably also by drawing grain and fodder produced in northeastern France off to French armies, did not significantly reduce the level of integration between French markets and Paris, or between Amsterdam and Paris. It is in particular this latter association which indicates that French markets continued to operate within previous levels of efficiency. The war did not add much to the costs of doing business in grain and thus did not erode the profits of producers or merchants. The reason for this may well be the extraordinary run of satisfactory or better harvests that France enjoyed between the dearths of 1740-1741 and 1766-1775. That is, Nature may have made up for effects that would otherwise have been felt. In any case, the investigation of market integration does not suggest that the Seven Years War influenced either the distribution of wealth within France or other aspects of the relationship between producers and consumers.

We know, however, that France mobilized a large part of its population to fight in Germany, and that recruits were drawn more often from the large reservoir of agricultural labor than from the small reservoir of unskilled urban labor. Shifting from the issue of markets to that of price levels, did the war have an impact? In earlier sections the long-run trend of prices has been examined. Here attention shifts to the short-run trend, which can be studied in a brief but important twice-weekly series for Tonnerre as well as in other markets for which annual data are at hand. Chart 3.1 provides an annual wheat price series for the period 1745-1775, and Chart 3.2 monthly quotations for periods of mobilization and demobilization, 1756-1757 and 1762-1765.

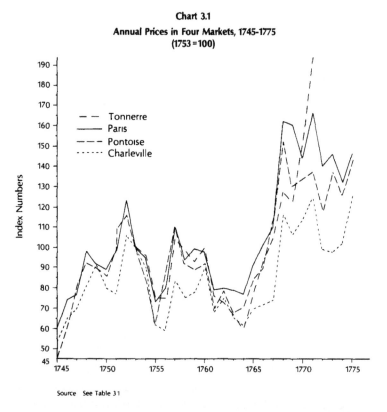

Chart 3.1

Annual Prices in Four Markets, 1745-1775

(1753 = 100)

Source See Table 31

In circumstances such as these, where meteorological and other factors are mixed with war effects, it is difficult to isolate one set of forces from another. The Seven Years War might be expected to

Chart 3.2

Monthly Prices in Tonnerre during Mobilization and Demobilization

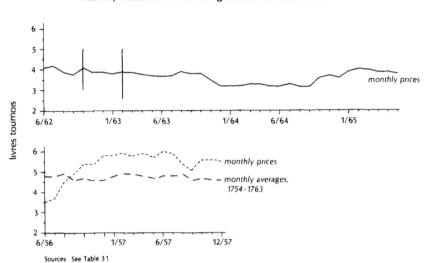

Sources See Table 31

have produced a bowl-shaped effect, with prices rising to the lip of the bowl during mobilization, when troops were drawn chiefly from agriculture into the army, falling during the years of warfare, when the troops fighting abroad were supplied from German sources, and rising again with demobilization between the time troops were repatriated and their reabsorption into the civilian labor force. In four price lines that tell a similar story of fluctuations, mobilization and demobilization effects cannot be ruled out. During 1756 and 1757, especially in 1757, when France was gathering an army to fight abroad, wheat prices rose in markets forming the corners of the horn or triangle, Charleville, Paris/Pontoise, and Tonnerre. And in 1762 prices rose slightly before falling in 1763-1764, as they had also in 1748-1750, after the War of Austrian Succession.

Did these movements occur because of mobilization and demobilization? For France this war began hesitantly, the process impeded by the desire of imcompetent French and British diplomats to preserve peace and by the rearrangement of European alliances. Frederick II invaded Saxony in August 1756, but French forces did not push into Germany until 1757. Initially French mobilization aimed to put only a small army into the field. Thus the mobilization period covers the months of rising prices—from mid-year

1756 to mid-year 1757—when wheat prices on the Tonnerre market rose sharply and did not peak until June, well after the customary peak in March, which occurred before the winter wheat harvest came in. Moreover, Tonnerre prices remained high until 1759 (in comparison to the monthly average during 1754-1763, also given in Chart 3.2). Demobilization occurred in a shorter space, from about October 1762 to February 1763. It coincided with a mild counter-cyclical decline in wheat prices during a portion of the year when prices ordinarily advanced from the fall harvest low.

To return now to a question raised earlier in this chapter, do the short-run price data show a pattern of war inflation or deflation? France's money stock, defined broadly to include specie substitutes, expanded in every year of the war. Revenues began to run short especially in 1759 and thereafter, prompting the authorities to place more reliance on short-term paper. The type of paper most closely approximating money—the various interest-bearing and non-interest-bearing receipts that circulated like bills of exchange—increased most rapidly during the deflationary phase of the price cycle after 1757. Wheat prices continued to fall until 1764 (Chart 3.1). Thus the price effects of wartime money flows seem to have been deflationary despite the apparent maintenance of the prewar money stock through specie substitute issues that counterbalanced specie exports, and despite also the apparently rapid postwar restoration of the French specie stock to prewar levels. It will be wise to recall that these are tentative conclusions, and that, in the absence of information about harvest quantities, no one can say whether an inflationary effect is buried under the deflationary impact of generous harvests. Nevertheless, these data sustain Earl J. Hamilton's argument that early modern wars "generated little, if any, price inflation."[62] But the reason Hamilton gives, that only a small part of resources was devoted to war, is open to dispute in this instance. France shifted a substantial part of its manpower resources to the war effort. In this case countervailing monetary flows, and the leading role still played by specie over paper, seem to have undermined inflationary pressures.

Who gained and who lost in these price trends? The war occurred during a brief period of falling wheat prices embedded within a

[62] Earl J. Hamilton, "The Role of War in Modern Inflation," *Journal of Modern History*, 37, no. 1 (Mar. 1977), 13-19.

longer era of inflation (Chart 3.1). Without evidence about income distribution, I find it difficult to accept the immiseration hypothesis for this part of the eighteenth century. Where are the concrete signs of growing unevenness in the distribution of income? This skepticism notwithstanding, the coincidence of war and declining prices suggests, in terms of this hypothesis, a reversal of trend. The war appears as a force for the democratization of income, as Stein argues about modern wars. Mobilization dampened inequalities in economic life, although not in society, by diminishing unemployment and underemployment among young adult males who lacked an economic or marital stake—landless agricultural laborers, migrant laborers, and unskilled workers.[63] Although mobilization forced up wheat prices in the region of France most sensitive to preparations for a conflict in Germany, and therefore temporarily increased living costs, the war as a whole seems to have dampened income inequalities. The implication is that the 200,000 or more men fighting abroad had previously, when living in France, consumed more than they produced, so that their departure from France in 1757 improved the ratio of outputs (grain) to inputs (land and labor). Thus we encounter the curious phenomenon of beneficent war. Whereas the earlier religious wars had most severely burdened the poorer classes,[64] this old regime war seems to have been a good thing for the common people of France. Some of the unemployed and underemployed obtained jobs in the army, and their departure did not disrupt the rural equilibrium of prices or wages.

CONCLUSION

The search has begun. In what areas of the economy and state finance did old regime war bring significant effects? In the Seven Years War France lost its colonies in North America and West Africa together with much of its prestige and the national confidence of its

[63] According to "Mémoires de la situation actuelle des Peuples du Roy.me de France, Année 1745" (Det Kongelige Bibliotek, Copenhagen, Manuscript Department, Ny kgl. S. 495[a], 28), "les biens de la guerre sont l'enlèvement des garçons inutiles qui ne causent que du désordre dans les villes et dans les Campagnes."

[64] Christopher R. Friedrichs, *Urban Society in an Age of War: Nordlingen, 1580-1720* (Princeton, 1979), 123-24; and, on France, Michel Morineau, "Les noeuds d'angoisse de l'Europe," in P. Léon and J. Jacquart, eds., *Histoire économique et sociale du monde* (Paris, 1978), II, 183-84.

people. After the war the French celebrated Frederick II in prose and verse rather than Louis XV,[65] of whom an equestrian statue was unveiled at an untimely moment a few months after the peace. As a consequence of the ineptness with which observers perceived the war to have been conducted, it became fashionable to make fun of French officials. The poet Colardeau, a tiresome windbag, captured the public feeling with a poem "Le Patriotisme," of which selections appeared in April 1762. Amidst praise for the king so heavy-handed and repetitious as to seem ironic, the poet remarked on the humiliation of "la Nation."[66]

France mobilized a large portion of its populace for the 1757-1762 war in Germany. The mobilization drew manpower from the countryside especially, where some 82 percent of the populace lived. It augmented the standing army and sharply expanded the scale of militia and coast guard forces. Markets like Charleville might be expected to have been affected by mobilization. And Paris, with which other grain markets in northeastern France and Amsterdam were closely linked, might also have reflected the combined effects of shrinkage in the agricultural labor force and a sudden increase in the military demand for foodstuffs. To the extent that they were rural dwellers, recruits metamorphosed from people who dealt with the market for only a part of their grain consumption and who produced and consumed the remainder, or who received grain as wages, into people who consumed all grain through the market. To all appearances France managed to mobilize about 2.5 percent of its population. Altogether about 4 percent of the prewar population served in arms during the Seven Years War, a portion not very different from American experience in three of its four twentieth-century wars.

Search as diligently as we may, however, it is difficult to detect large price or money flow effects from this war. Interest rates rose as government borrowing increased, and they may also have made private sector borrowing, and thus capital formation, more expensive. But prices, after jumping upward sharply in 1757, declined to a postwar floor. The flow of specie out of France to pay and supply troops serving abroad, to service loans owed foreigners, to pay sub-

[65] H[enri] Carré, *Le règne de Louis XV (1715-1774)*, vol. 8, pt. 2, of *Histoire de France*, ed. by Ernest Lavisse (Paris, 1909), 288.

[66] *Journal encyclopédique*, Apr. 1, 1762, pp. 98-102.

sidies to allies, and to cover ordinary capital flows seemed to observers at the time to have reversed the customary flow of specie and
bullion into France. Losses of specie seem to show up more forcefully in the short-run price trend, which was deflationary, than do
additions of specie substitutes from government borrowing. Any inflationary effects of large issues of these substitutes were counter-
manded by a temporary decline in the specie stock. But not long
after the conclusion of the war, informed estimates of the specie
stock suggest a higher level than before the war.

This comparatively primitive economy, in which harvests remained the most important events of the year, managed to mobilize
4 percent of its population to fight with only mild price and money
effects. How is it possible that so many men were taken into the
army without more effect? The answer must lie with the characteristics of the soldiers. They may not have been the dregs of society,
and Corvisier argues that regular army recruits (as opposed to militia recruits) were not. But they were men whose labor could be
reallocated with minimal effects. Such a reallocation is imaginable
only in an economy with a large underemployment of human capital resources. Within certain limits, the old regime economy could
shift vast resources to wars which seem, on the basis of suggestive
rather than conclusive evidence, to have been an egalitarian economic force in a society marked by inequality.

CHAPTER 4

THE SEVEN YEARS WAR AND THE
FRENCH ECONOMY

*"I had a much better opinion of the Country of France this
time than the last."* [1]

HISTORIANS have disagreed about the economic effects of
old regime wars in general and in particular. But through
their disagreements runs one point of universal consent: these wars
seriously damaged trade. Nowhere is this held to be more evident
than in the case of France in the Seven Years War. Even Charles
Carrière, who wishes to temper the interpretation of the effects of
war on trade, has to admit that trade was brutally disrupted by war.[2]
Curiosity is pricked especially by the problem of measuring losses in
the commercial sector.

WAR AND THE INTERNATIONAL ECONOMY

"Au XVIIIe siècle, une Europe sans rivages a développé ses
échanges avec les autres continents, fondant ainsi les conditions
d'un enrichissement sans précédent."[3] In France, which shared in
this groundswell toward prosperity, the most dynamic sector of the
old regime economy was the sector of trade. Yet its path of growth
was irregular. In the customary interpretation this irregularity is
said to have had less to do with changes in the pace of growth in the
domestic economy than with maritime wars, in which France in the
eighteenth century found itself in confrontation with the largest naval power of the age, Britain. During conflicts, the British navy regularly sought to block the commerce of its rival, France, and British
privateers took as many French ships as they could find and cap-

---

[1] See n. 58 below.

[2] Charles Carrière, *Négociants marseillais au XVIIIe siècle* (2 vols.; n.p., n.d.), I, 395.

[3] Paul Butel's view in "Les Amériques et l'Europe," in Pierre Léon, ed., *Histoire
économique et sociale du monde* (Paris, 1978), II, 51.

ture. In the Seven Years War Britain also occupied several French colonies (Canada, Guadeloupe, Domingue, and Martinique). The image of the effect of war, and especially the Seven Years War, on French trade is nearly uniform in the literature: seriously disruptive,[4] "brutale,"[5] brutally disruptive,[6] "vraiment désastreuse,"[7] "très préjudiciable,"[8] "unmitigated disaster";[9] "The Seven Years' War battered the economies of France's maritime centers."[10] Where differences of opinion are evident is in the scale of the catastrophe and in its timing.[11]

Yet, as is evident from Chart 4.1, which depicts French trade in current values, the trend of commercial activity was one of impressive growth in an age of war.[12] Between 1716 and 1720, when the first balances are available, aggregate trade activity (imports plus ex-

[4] Théophile Malvezin, *Histoire du commerce de Bordeaux, depuis les origines jusqu'à nos jours* (3 vols.; Bordeaux, 1892), III, 42.

[5] Carrière, *Négociants marseillais*, I, 395.

[6] François Crouzet, "Angleterre et France au XVIIIᵉ siècle: Essai d'analyse comparée de deux croissances économiques," *Annales E.S.C.*, 21, no. 2 (Mar.-Apr. 1966), 264.

[7] François Crouzet, "La conjoncture bordelaise," in François-Georges Pariset, *Bordeaux au XVIIIᵉ siècle* (Bordeaux, 1968), 299.

[8] Pierre Dardel, *Navires et marchandises dans les ports de Rouen et du Havre au XVIIIᵉ siècle* (Paris, 1963), 50.

[9] John G. Clark, *La Rochelle and the Atlantic Economy during the Eighteenth Century* (Baltimore, 1981), 17. Also Jacob M. Price, *France and the Chesapeake: A History of the French Tobacco Monopoly* . . . (2 vols.; Ann Arbor, 1973), I, 392; and Jean Tarrade, *Le commerce colonial de la France à la fin de l'ancien régime: L'évolution du régime de "l'Exclusif" de 1763 à 1789* (Paris, 1972), II, 774.

[10] Clark, *La Rochelle*, 157.

[11] Unlike most authorities, Carrière, Meyer, and Villiers emphasize rapid postwar recoveries and argue that the effects of war were not as severe as is often said. Carrière, *Négociants marseillais*, 395ff. and 521; Jean Meyer, *L'armement nantais dans la deuxième moitié du XVIIIᵉ siècle* (Paris, 1969), 82; and Patrick Villiers, *Le commerce colonial atlantique et la guerre d'indépendance des Etats Unis d'Amérique, 1778-1783* (New York, 1977), 457. Also Crouzet, "La conjoncture bordelaise," 300-301 and 302, notes the rapidity of postwar recovery but insists on a bleak image of war costs.

[12] This chart is based on data supplied by Ruggiero Romano, "Documenti e prime considerazioni intorno alla 'Balance du commerce' della Francia dal 1716 al 1780," *Studi in onore di Armando Sapori* (2 vols.; Milan, 1957), II, 1,267-1,298. Ruggiero corrects the data gathered by [Ambroise Marie] Arnould, *De la balance du commerce et des relations commerciales extérieures de la France* . . . (2 vols.; Paris, 1791). Although other authorities have offered some additional corrections, Romano's series has become the standard for representing orders of magnitude in French trade. On corrections, see especially Pierre Léon, "L'élan industriel et commercial," in Fernand Braudel and Ernest Labrousse, eds., *Histoire économique et sociale de la France* (Paris: 1970), II, 500n and 501, for a corrected curve with some additions to Romano's figures. However,

Chart 4.1

Aggregate French Trade in Current Values, 1726-1780
(millions of l.t.)

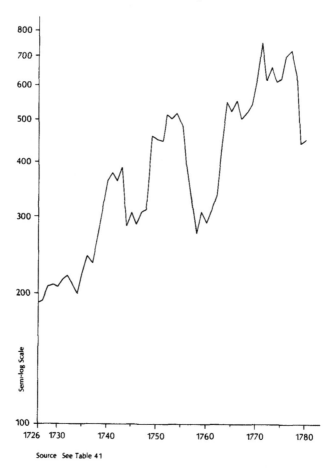

Source See Table 41

Léon and Carrière do not furnish the new numbers, which, in any case, do not alter the "order of magnitude" of Romano's figures but add more data on trade with French Guinea and Asia. On how the trade data were compiled in the eighteenth century, see Romano, "Documenti," 1,293-1,299; and Dardel, *Navires et marchandises*, 15-16. Among numerous judgments in favor of the reliability of these data for their order of magnitude, see Michel Morineau, "La balance du commerce franco-néerlandais et le reserrement économique des Provinces-Unis au XVIIIème siècle," *Economisch-historisch jaarboek*, 1965, 30 (1965), 181-87; and Crouzet, "Angleterre et France," 261n1. Léon, "L'élan industriel," 500n1, deems the errors in the *états* to have

ports) averaged slightly more than 125 million l.t. per annum; by 1775 this total had increased to 625 million.[13] After falling off during the War of American Independence, activity expanded again quickly; by 1789 the aggregate amounted to more than 1 billion l.t.[14] Both exports and imports flourished, and until about 1770 France's surplus trade balance also tended to expand. Crouzet has asserted that French trade grew more rapidly than British.[15] Moreover, France's trade contacts became more balanced during the century. At the beginning of the period for which data are available, about 88 percent of France's trade was with other European ports, 3 percent with the Levant, and 8 percent with other regions, chiefly French islands and colonies in the Americas.[16] By 1775 the European percentage had fallen and all other portions grown. In other respects too, France's commercial sector had both grown and become healthier. French shipbuilding, insurance underwriting, and other shipping services expanded with shipping itself. Despite the consequences for the smaller ports such as La Rochelle, one might

---

been more or less constant. Of course, the series omits smuggling. Price (*France and the Chesapeake*, I, 391) believes that the *états* were altered to understate French tobacco imports from Britain. It is also known that the prices furnished by merchants sometimes deviated from current prices (Dardel, *Navires et marchandises*, 19 and 547), and that the destination ports given by shippers were sometimes misleading (Pierre Jeannin, "Les marchés du nord dans le commerce français au XVIIIᵉ siècle," in Pierre Léon, ed., *Aires et structures du commerce français au XVIIIᵉ siècle* [Paris, 1975], 53-54). But Morineau, "La balance," 184, decides that "les prix, portés sur les Etats de la Balance du Commerce doivent être acceptés comme représentatifs." Tarrade criticizes Arnould's series for the colonies as being too harmonious from year to year, suggesting that Arnould corrected earlier figures. Tarrade prefers to use a table prepared by one of the eighteenth-century directors of the Bureau du Commerce, Bruyard, which he believes was Arnould's source. His values (*Le commerce colonial*, II, 739) agree with Romano's ("Documenti," 1,291).

[13] Romano, "Documenti," 1,274. It is known, however, that the balances for early years underreport activity. Michel Morineau, "Trois contributions au colloque de Göttingen: II. 1750, 1787: Un changement important des structures de l'exportation française dans le monde saisi d'après les états de la balance du commerce," in Ernst Hinrichs et al., eds., *Vom Ancien Régime zur Französischen Revolution* (Göttingen, 1978), 397.

[14] Léon, "L'élan industriel," 502; and Michel Morineau, "Quelques recherches relatives à la balance du commerce extérieur français au XVIIIᵉ siècle: Ou cette fois un égale deux," in Léon, ed., *Aires et structures du commerce*, 4, providing data for 1787-1789 to supplement Romano's tables.

[15] Crouzet, "Angleterre et France," 260-61.

[16] Romano, "Documenti," 1,275.

also see the faster growth of large ports as a healthy development for the economies of scale that this move involved for ports and firms specializing in maritime trade.[17]

The curve of French trade activity (Chart 4.1) immediately exposes the apparent sensitivity of imports and exports to maritime war. During 1744-1748, 1756-1763, and 1779-1780 (and undoubtedly afterward; the data for 1781-1786 are lacking), ship movements fell off sharply. Here the objective is to pose a counterfactual hypothesis: what if one of these wars, the Seven Years War, had not occurred? What losses in commercial activity may be convincingly assigned to this war, and what others may plausibly be assigned to it?

The first step in seeking answers is to shift the frame of reference to livres of constant value. In French historiography it has become customary to discuss trade activity in livres of current value. Thus the data supplied by the Balance du Commerce, which assessed trade flows and supplied prices for trade volume, are used to gauge changes in trade volume for years when data on quantities are lacking. Since that holds for most years, the discussion is typically in current values. But almost all scholars who have worked on this issue have been sensitive to the importance of the price movement and the danger of money illusion. Comparisons of early with late century trade volume, such as supplied by Crouzet, cite the need to adjust for price changes.[18] Lacking price series of the goods in trade, or a satisfactory substitute measure of prices in France, these adjustments remain rough. Using an index for French agriculture, Crouzet suggests that prices inflated by about 60 percent from 1716-1720 to 1784-1788. But of course the goods represented in Labrousse's national survey of agricultural prices do not much resemble French trade goods. The analysis of markets in the previous chapter has shown that Amsterdam was closely integrated with northern French grain markets, implying that markets in other goods less costly to transport than grain would have been even more closely integrated. Thus for purposes of long-run comparisons, it is preferable to turn to Posthumus' price index built on goods in trade in Amsterdam rather than to a French agricultural price index. Am-

[17] Meyer, *L'armement nantais*, 77, ranks French ports in 1792 by number of ships and tonnage.

[18] Crouzet, "Angleterre et France," 260-61.

sterdam traded in many of the same commodities as French ports, serving as a hub between southern and northern European trade as well as maintaining its own links with West Indian colonies in competition with the French.[19]

In Table 4.1 the series used to build Chart 4.1 are converted into constant prices. Chart 4.2 provides a graphic view of these values, one that preserves the image of war-depleted trade.[20] The years 1744-1748, 1755-1763, and 1778-1780 show severe trade losses and a drop to the low trade values of the late 1720s and early 1730s. The chart also raises some interesting questions. How are the costs of war to be measured? Should the counterfactual trend line be sketched from peak to peak, as is sometimes done or implied?

TABLE 4.1
French Trade in Constant Values
(millions of l.t.)

	imports	exports	balance
1726	81.5	108.0	26.4
1727	80.8	108.0	27.3
1728	84.1	122.8	38.7
1729	85.1	126.5	41.4
1730	93.1	118.5	25.4
1731	94.4	128.3	33.9
1732	102.0	128.9	26.9
1733	92.2	129.5	37.3
1734	87.5	121.9	34.4
1735	94.3	140.5	46.2
1736	111.9	147.2	35.4
1737	114.3	134.9	20.6
1738	123.7	151.0	27.3
1739	147.6	161.0	13.4
1740	151.8	196.4	44.5
1741	152.0	199.4	47.5
1742	138.7	187.1	48.4
1743	153.5	199.0	45.5
1744	110.2	151.9	41.7
1745	115.3	168.9	53.6
1746	106.2	163.1	56.9
1747	120.6	169.7	49.2

[19] The issue of substituting Posthumus' Amsterdam series is discussed further in Appendix 1. It is worth noting that the aggregate price increase derived from Posthumus' data for 1715-1719 to 1785-1789 is 62 percent, thus very close to Crouzet's figure. But the interim course of the agricultural index does not closely resemble the interim course of Posthumus' trade index.

[20] The unusual import curve for 1771 is the result of heavy French grain imports.

TABLE 4.1 (cont.)
French Trade in Constant Values
(millions of l.t.)

	imports	exports	balance
1748	127.7	167.3	39.6
1749	198.2	237.1	38.9
1750	193.5	234.5	41.0
1751	184.8	240.0	55.2
1752	216.8	275.1	58.4
1753	208.1	269.3	61.2
1754	211.5	272.0	60.5
1755	207.4	240.5	33.1
1756	141.4	215.7	74.2
1757	132.5	168.6	36.0
1758	98.0	143.8	45.8
1759	103.5	160.3	56.8
1760	96.7	147.1	50.3
1761	109.7	144.6	34.9
1762	112.2	157.0	44.9
1763	145.2	203.7	58.5
1764	180.2	248.9	68.7
1765	163.6	241.7	78.1
1766	156.8	261.6	104.8
1767	167.0	210.9	43.9
1768	177.9	213.0	35.1
1769	199.6	206.4	6.7
1770	243.5	223.5	− 19.9
1771	314.6	249.8	− 64.9
1772	225.7	240.3	14.6
1773	245.5	247.6	2.0
1774	216.4	233.5	17.1
1775	211.8	239.9	28.1
1776	264.6	235.5	− 29.0
1777	250.5	258.9	8.5
1778	243.4	190.2	− 53.2
1779	139.9	157.9	18.0
1780	142.0	154.9	12.9

SOURCES: Ruggiero Romano, "Documenti e prime considerazioni intorno alla 'Balance du commerce' della Francia dal 1716 al 1780," in *Studi in onore di Armando Sapori* (2 vols.; Milan, 1957), 1,274, deflated with interpolated annual index numbers (1721-1745 = 100) from N. W. Posthumus, *Inquiry into the History of Prices in Holland* (2 vols.; Leiden, 1946-1964), I, ci, col. H. Column 3 has been calculated separately, leading to what appear to be rounding errors. See also Appendix 1 to this volume.

Thomas M. Doerflinger estimates that the Seven Years War reduced French colonial trade by 81 percent, taking the difference between "wartime and peacetime levels as a percentage of peacetime levels."[21] Robert Louis Stein prefers a figure of 90 percent.[22] Or should this line be drawn along some other path?

Chart 4.2
French Trade in Constant Values

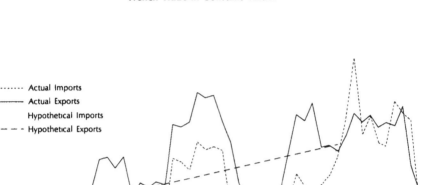

The chart shows that trade values and therefore volume peaked *before and after* wars. Do the prewar peaks of 1739-1743, 1752-1755, and 1776-1778, which are more sharply defined in the constant than the current value reconstruction of French trade,[23] reveal that merchants anticipated wars, laying in stocks of imports and persuading their commercial associates to take extra quantities of exports? Whether or not merchants anticipated wars, the trend line of trade must be sketched at a lower level than is ordinarily done. Drawing it from peak to peak exaggerates the counterfactual trend of trade because it depicts unusually heavy postwar trade to be a

[21] Thomas M. Doerflinger, "The Antilles Trade of the Old Regime: A Statistical Overview," *Journal of Interdisciplinary History*, 6, no. 3 (Winter 1976), 401.

[22] Robert Louis Stein, *The French Slave Trade in the Eighteenth Century: An Old Regime Business* (Madison, Wis., 1979), 109.

[23] Compare with the current livre value charts in Charles Carrière and Marcel Courdurie, "L'espace commercial marseillais aux XVIIᵉ et XVIIIᵉ siècles," in Léon, ed., *Aires et structures du commerce*, 106.

normal course of affairs. Here a second hypothesis will be developed: there was both a postwar period of compensatory trade, as all authorities acknowledge, and a prewar period of anticipatory trade. Unless both are taken into account, the putative volume of trade in the absence of war will be exaggerated.

Hypothesis 1: The High Road—Maximum Losses

In Table 4.2 the data presented above are used to estimate losses in French exports and imports under the assumption that the course of trade in the absence of the Seven Years War would have flowed from the prewar to the postwar peak. A straight-line interpolation of trade values between peak years, 1752 and 1764 for imports, 1752 and 1766 for exports, brings to light the putative progress of trade under this assumption. By subtracting actual trade values, the quantity of "losses" can be estimated (last column) in the manner apparently adopted by Doerflinger, Stein, and others. This calculation suggests aggregate "losses" of nearly 1.5 billion l.t., most of which occurred during 1755-1763. According to the "high road" hypothesis, the dramatic modifiers ordinarily employed to describe the effects of this conflict on trade are warranted. But is the high road hypothesis itself the most likely interpretation of the course of trade in the absence of the Seven Years War?

Hypothesis 2: The Low Road—Compensatory Trade

The idea of compensatory trade, which both anticipated war and sought to make up for war losses, is suggested by the pattern in Chart 4.2. In the years immediately before and after war French trade shifted to much higher constant values, then returned three or four years after the conflict to what appears to have been ordinary peacetime trade. That such a pattern may have existed is implied by Carrière's observations about the psychological element in the commercial mentality. Anxiety about wars, Carrière notices, was general even in eras of peace.[24] That such a feeling pervaded the merchant's view of the world is hardly surprising, given the frequency of war in the old regime, the degree to which war undoubtedly did influence the environment in which commercial and finan-

[24] Carrière, *Négociants marseillais*, I, 466-67.

TABLE 4.2

Hypothesis of Maximum Losses: Peak to Peak
(in millions of constant livres)

	actual values		interpolated values		"losses"		
	imports	exports	imports	exports	imports	exports	total losses
1752	217	275	217	275	0	0	0
1753	208	269	214	274	6	5	11
1754	212	272	211	273	(1)	1	0
1755	207	241	208	272	1	31	32
1756	141	216	205	271	64	55	119
1757	133	169	202	270	69	101	170
1758	98	144	199	269	101	125	226
1759	104	160	195	269	91	109	200
1760	97	147	192	268	95	121	216
1761	110	145	189	267	79	122	201
1762	112	157	186	266	74	109	183
1763	145	204	183	265	38	61	99
1764	180	249	180	264	0	15	15
1765	—	242	—	263	—	21	21
1766	—	262	—	262	—	0	0
TOTAL							1,493

1755-1763 total	1,446 million, or 161 million per annum
1756-1763 total	1,414 million, or 177 million per annum
1756-1762 total	1,315 million, or 188 million per annum

SOURCES: Table 4.1 and text.

cial profits were made or not, and the substantial resources devoted by merchants to the communication of commercial and especially political news.

What did the merchants watch in order to find signs of impending war? Frank C. Spooner, in a study of the Amsterdam insurance market, reveals that as war approached, orders for munitions went out from governments wanting to build stockpiles.[25] The trade in munitions, Swedish artillery and iron, Dutch saltpeter, and Baltic naval supplies was inevitably international so that these orders went to international merchants. Spooner suggests that on the Amsterdam insurance market the barometer of war was the price of gunpowder and saltpeter. Other signs existed in activity at domestic munitions plants. French arsenals began preparing for a new war with Britain in 1776, one and a half to two years before war was de-

[25] Frank C. Spooner, *Risks at Sea: Amsterdam Insurance and Maritime Europe, 1766-1780* (Cambridge, 1983), 98 and 100.

clared.[26] And there is also the otherwise curious slant of the commercial press toward political news. Why did the many commercial periodicals of eighteenth-century Europe supply so much political news? Because predicting the beginning of war was one of the most important issues to their merchant readers.

In Table 4.3 "losses" occasioned by the Seven Years War are estimated according to this second hypothesis. Here it is necessary to find trade values on both sides of the era of war and compensatory trade. The entire interwar years of 1749-1755 as well as briefer periods before the War of Austrian Succession and after the Seven Years War are years of compensatory trade. Thus the projection of trade in the absence of conflict is drawn from the average of imports and exports in 1736-1738 to the average in 1768-1770. The result is a wartime "loss" during 1756-1763 of some 665 million l.t. But these wartime losses are seen to have been more than compensated for in the long run by heavy prewar and postwar trade, especially during 1749-1755. In the longer period dealt with in Table 4.3 estimated gains thus exceed estimated losses by 472 million l.t.

The implication of the low road hypothesis is that eighteenth-century wars, including the Seven Years War, had minor effects on trade because of anticipation and compensation. Merchants maintained the growth path of French commerce in an era of recurrent international conflict because they could successfully foresee wars and because the demand for goods unavailable in the latter stages of wars did not go unsatisfied but was served, insofar as it could be deferred at all, by heavy postwar trade activity. This is a point that should not go unnoticed. The low road hypothesis suggests that consumers did not, in the long run, let war influence their use of trade goods but, as reserves were exhausted during war, allowed demand to build up. Certainly purchases of goods such as sugar and spices forgone late in war may not have been compensated entirely by heavier postwar consumption. But trade in these goods did expand sharply at the conclusion of war rather than begin again at ordinary peacetime levels. Thus war does not appear to have caused forgone demand so much as to have disturbed the pattern in which demand would be satisfied.

The low road hypothesis gives an image not of eighteenth-cen-

[26] George T. Matthews, *The Royal General Farms in Eighteenth-Century France* (New York, 1958), 252.

TABLE 4.3

Hypothesis of Losses under Compensatory Trade
(in millions of constant livres)

	actual values, imports plus exports	continuously compounded curve	"losses"
1736-1738	261	261	0
1739	309	269	(40)
1740	348	273	(75)
1741	351	277	(74)
1742	326	281	(45)
1743	353	286	(67)
1744	262	290	28
1745	284	294	10
1746	269	299	30
1747	290	303	13
1748	295	308	13
1749	435	312	(123)
1750	428	317	(111)
1751	425	322	(103)
1752	492	327	(165)
1753	477	332	(145)
1754	484	337	(147)
1755	448	342	(106)
1756	357	347	10
1757	301	352	51
1758	242	357	115
1759	264	363	99
1760	244	368	124
1761	254	374	120
1762	269	379	110
1763	349	385	36
1764	429	391	(38)
1765	405	397	(8)
1766	418	403	(15)
1767	378	409	31
1768-1770	421	421	0
TOTAL			(472)

1755-1763 total	559 million, or 62 million per annum
1756-1763 total	665 million, or 83 million per annum

SOURCES: Table 4.1 and text.

tury trade "brutally disrupted" by war but of trade affected only insofar as war exceeded, or fell short of, merchants' expectations about its effects. The scheme of overall growth in trade is preserved—indeed augmented, for the growth rate associated with this lower estimate of the volume of losses, 1.5 percent, is higher than the rate implied by the peak-to-peak hypothesis, and also closer to the estimate of long-run trade expansion (Chart 4.2: hypothetical imports and exports). But the path of growth is shifted downward to lower putative values.

Choosing Between the Hypotheses

Both hypotheses suggest that war was costly, but in different fashions. In the first, war is assumed to have been a shock unanticipated by merchants and to have quickly and sharply diminished trade in a fashion in which wartime losses were not compensated for by postwar trade. In the second, war is interpreted as an event to the anticipation of which probabilities might be assigned. Merchants are supposed always to have been sensitive to the possibility of war and peace and to have developed channels of information and indicators to help gauge these probabilities. When they judged war to impend, merchants are supposed to have built up stocks and after the war to have engaged in extraordinarily heavy compensatory trading to replenish depleted stocks and satisfy deferred consumer demand. Such a scheme of trade involved its own risks. In the years before the War of Austrian Succession French merchants apparently overcompensated, especially in exports (notice the unprecedented trade values in Chart 4.2 for 1740-1743). That such a thing might have happened is understandable in light of the unusually long period during which trade curtailment by this war could be anticipated, a period stretching from the unexpected loss of Captain Jenkins' ear in 1739 until 1744 when French trade volume was actually reduced by conflict. For French trade, this war lasted five years (1744 through 1748), long enough to deplete stocks and heighten demand for imports. The immediate postwar trade appears, under this hypothesis, as compensatory for the latter years of the last conflict.

When did compensation for the war just past shift toward anticipation of a renewal of conflict? The upward shift of imports and exports in 1752, and the generally higher level of trade during 1752-1754, as compared to 1749-1751, suggests a midway adjustment during these six years of peace. In 1755 the prospect of war became war itself at sea, as British naval vessels and privateers began to seize

French merchant ships. Presumably this was also a year of antici-patory trade, but one curtailed especially for French exports by British naval activity.

The hypothesis of compensatory trade, which produces a low road estimate of trade in the absence of war, fits the overall scheme of trade more satisfactorily than does the high road hypothesis. This is so especially because of the timing of peak trade—always im-mediately before and after conflict. If war was divorced from high trade volume, as the high road hypothesis implies, then such peaks should be randomly distributed among years of peace. They are not. Furthermore, high trade values after conflicts do not describe the normal course of peacetime trade, but clearly are compensation for wartime losses. This more or less intuitive approach, which at-tempts to recreate the logic of the merchant's view of war, can be supplemented by two tests of serial data.

One test, which investigates whether one large port experienced financial shocks in wartime and thus whether wars caught the com-mercial community unawares, is made possible by Carrière's exam-ination of bankruptcies in Marseilles during the eighteenth cen-tury.[27] If war, and especially the Seven Years War, had grave or devastating consequences for trade, then the bankruptcy records should show failures peaking during or toward the end of conflict. But the records actually show that failures peaked, among the mid-dle decades of the eighteenth century, in 1730 and 1774—years of peace. Between 1740 and 1770 the number of failures declined dur-ing the active phase of the War of Austrian Succession for French trade, peaked in 1755, before the new war reached the Mediterra-nean, and thereafter declined through the Seven Years War.[28]

What makes this pattern especially interesting is the heavy toll of

[27] Carrière, *Négociants marseillais*, I, 429-31, and II, 1056-57.

[28] R[uggiero] Romano, *Commerce et prix de blé à Marseille au XVIIIᵉ siècle* (Paris, 1956), 45: "la Méditerranée est d'ailleurs débarrassée de vaisseaux ennemis jusqu'à l'automne 1757." In 1763 Marseilles suffered little from the postwar financial adjust-ment that brought down several firms in Amsterdam and Hamburg. In the War of American Independence bankruptcies also declined, but on that occasion the post-war financial crisis evidently made itself felt in Marseilles, if rather lightly. In Dijon, center of the Burgundy wine trade and situated on the northeastern edge of the Mas-sif Central, bankruptcy peaks were distributed in periods of war and peace: 1724-1727, 1739-1743, 1750-1751, 1761-1762, and 1769-1773, and occurred more often in peace. P[ierre] de Saint Jacob, "Histoire économique et sociale dans les archives de la juridiction consulaire de Dijon (1715-1789)," *Bulletin de la Société d'histoire moderne*, 12th ser., 56, no. 4 (Oct. 6, 1957), 2-9.

the war in ships lost to enemy activity. The Marseilles records reveal 688 Marseilles and Provençal ships lost to the *guerre de course* during 1744-1749, 716 during 1755-1763, and 424 during 1778-1783.[29] Yet these extraordinary losses did not force a more than ordinary number of inhabitants into bankruptcy, despite the fact that insurance rates climbed from 2-4 percent before the war to as high as 50-60 percent during the war.[30] In time of war ships were generally insured,[31] whereas in peace merchants preferred sometimes to avoid this expense. On the basis of the Marseilles bankruptcy records, it seems that the Seven Years War produced no more losses than could be absorbed and that war was an event that merchants anticipated and protected themselves against.

Another way to test these hypotheses is to examine prices in French ports during conflict. If merchants anticipated conflicts and built up stocks, then prices of imports cut off by war would not show much increase in the early years of the conflict, but they would climb in the latter years, when these putative stocks were exhausted. Postwar prices would then be expected to fall sharply as compensatory trading replenished stocks and supplied pent up demand. For French exports the reverse should hold, as prices would be expected to decline as stocks accumulated during the war and rise as postwar demand abroad could be satisfied. Likewise prices of French exports in receiving ports should have been low during the early stages of conflict, because stocks had been built up, and should have risen during the conflict, after a lag during which stocks on hand were exhausted. Unfortunately, the price data against which these hypothetical possibilities can be tested are in short supply.

Romano's study of the Marseilles grain trade indicates that during the early years of the Seven Years War merchants held grain in depot in expectation of a price increase.[32] But even in 1762 grain stocks were so large that prices declined instead of rising. Marseilles grain prices fell during the war (except for 1760).[33] After the war the innovation of free trade in grain confused the picture, and damaged Marseilles interests by requiring the export of grain in French

[29] Carrière, *Négociants marseillais*, I, 481 and 483, excluding losses of ships belonging to aliens. The port also lost some vessels to shipwreck, fire, and the *course barbaresque*.
[30] *Ibid.*, I, 537.
[31] *Ibid.*, I, 484.
[32] Romano, *Commerce*, 45-47 and 57-59.
[33] *Ibid.*, 14 and 91.

vessels only. In any case, the war did not bring high grain prices in Marseilles, the port for Provence, which was not a major grain-producing region and which imported grain from the Levant, Italy, Spain, and elsewhere. Speculative efforts to take advantage of the British blockade failed and brought losses instead of profits. This is a weak test because of the small impact of Marseilles imports on grain prices. Nevertheless, it does provide an example of anticipatory action by merchants, even if of a plan that went awry.

Another test is made possible by some data rehabilitated by Jean Tarrade, concerning colonial wares imported into the three largest ports dealing in such goods on the Atlantic coast during 1749-1790.[34] Based on rates set for collection of *droits du domaine d'occident* and thus subject to conflicting pressures from tax authorities and merchants—as were the valuations of all imports and exports—these prices, in Tarrade's judgment, may be relied upon, because their reductions from actual market prices were relatively constant. Of the commodities surveyed, sugar provides a price picture most sensitive to the impact of war. As Chart 4.3 indicates, French sugar prices fell between 1749 and 1753, during compensatory importing for the war just past. They rose, especially in 1755, in anticipation of a renewal of conflict, then held steady during the first two full years of formal war, 1756-1757, and perhaps during 1758, for which data are lacking. In 1759 prices advanced sharply and remained high through 1763 before beginning a postwar decline lasting into 1766.[35] At least in the three ports of Bordeaux, La Rochelle, and Nantes, sugar prices lend further support to the low road interpretation of French trade in the absence of war. But the other goods for which prices are provided by Tarrade, goods generally traded in much smaller volume and value than sugar,[36] do not follow any price trend that can readily be related to the war.[37]

[34] Tarrade, *Le commerce colonial*, II, 760-72. Chart 4.3 reports an unweighted average of raw and semi-processed sugar. Morineau, "Quelques recherches," 44, reports that raw sugar imports accounted for 54.6 percent of the total in one sample, and white sugar for 45.4 percent.

[35] Presumably, reexports were curtailed in the early years of conflict but increased as neutral shipping substitutes were arranged. See Crouzet, "La conjuncture bordelaise," 300.

[36] Doerflinger, "The Antilles Trade," 404, reports the part of sugar in imports from the Antilles at four leading ports. In 1754 and 1764 sugar accounted for 62 and 67 percent of Rouen imports of six major Antilles products, and 49 and 71 percent of Bordeaux and Marseilles imports of all Antilles products.

[37] Cacao most closely followed the scheme outlined for sugar, but coffee, cotton,

Chart 4.3

Sugar Prices in Three Atlantic Ports, 1749-1768

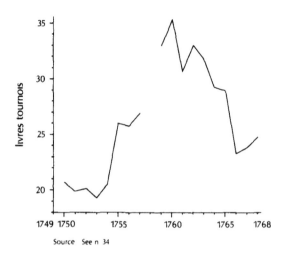

Source See n 34

These calculations are crude, but there is little doubt that the order of magnitude is correct. The high road hypothesis can be ruled out. Estimating trade losses from war by comparing wartime trade cut off by British control of the seas with postwar trade values will inevitably exaggerate the scale of losses. Thus the Seven Years War looks especially devastating if two periods of peak postwar trade are used to estimate war losses. Even the low road estimate of losses—665 million l.t.—is excessive unless postwar and prewar compensatory trade is folded in, in which case the overall war experience shows a continued pattern of growth. The commercial costs of the Seven Years War are to be found not in a simple measurement of trade activity apparently forgone because of British naval superiority but in the much smaller and more complex scale of activity disturbed by war-caused inefficiencies and in the more intricate problem of distinguishing commodities open to a deferred demand (such as textiles) from those not open. For compensatory trade to succeed, the merchant had to allot resources to storage, where imports were accumulated on the eve of conflict and exports during

and indigo all established their own schemes. Coffee peaked during the interwar years and recorded its lowest prices between 1750 and 1765 in 1761-1762. Cotton peaked in 1757 and then declined in price. Indigo peaked in 1755 and again in 1757 before falling.

conflict. Consumers may also have laid in stocks of goods. Merchants in the colonies, who stockpiled goods during war for export at its end,[38] had to pay for the costs of storage and for the shrinkage of foods stored over long periods. The merchant also had to maintain an elaborate information network to provide warnings of war.

Accepting the low road hypothesis also resolves a quandary. Expert opinion differs on the timing of the period of most rapid growth in French trade. Carrière, considering Marseilles, locates that period in the second half of the eighteenth century. Crouzet, considering French trade in general, situates it between 1736-1739 and 1749-1755. The quandary is that both place this period during eras of war while also maintaining that war brutally disrupted trade. By noticing that merchants both anticipated and compensated for maritime wars, we notice also how trade values could expand in an era of war.

Trade with Regions

Aggregate French trade activity, such as we have dealt with to this point, conceals irregularities in the order of magnitude of trade with individual partners. In the *états* of the Balance du Commerce entries were organized according to state and region. Examining some of the most important regional entries in the balances (Chart 4.4), a departure from the pattern of aggregate trade is immediately noticeable. Some trade links experienced considerably less effect from the war than others.

Two features in the chart are especially interesting. One is that exports were more sensitive to war than imports from areas not directly affected by naval conflict.[39] This observation can be qualified. Certain exports—Bordeaux wines are an example—were not seriously affected by war.[40] But of course the reexport of colonial goods was curtailed by the interruption of supplies. The second noteworthy feature lies in the organization of compensatory trade suggested in this chart. Two types of compensatory trade appear to have been engaged in. First, the existence of trade routes likely to be disrupted by war prompted merchants to expand shipments to and from Britain, the United Provinces, the Levant, the Baltic (Nord), Italy, and

[38] Crouzet, "La conjuncture bordelaise," 300.
[39] Presumably trade with Britain and the Levant especially was less open to substitution of neutral for French flag ships.
[40] Crouzet, "La conjuncture bordelaise," 288.

Chart 4.4
French Trade in Regions
(millions of l.t.)

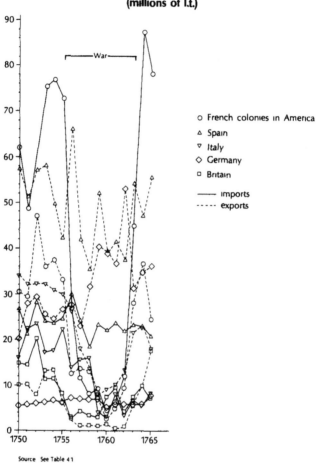

French colonies in America
Spain
Italy
Germany
Britain

——— imports
- - - - exports

Source See Table 4 1

the American colonies before and after the conflict.[41] Second, the
expansion of exports to Germany during the Seven Years War indicates that merchants could substitute markets. Substitution is
most notable in the case of Germany (even though the *états* exclude
trade to and from Alsace and Lorraine, which were at some distance
from the theater of conflict but adjacent to German territory)[42] but
also figured in trade with Spain. During the Seven Years War Span-

[41] Jean-Pierre Filippini, et al., *Dossiers sur le commerce français en Méditerranée orien-
tale au XVIIIe siècle* (Paris, 1976), provides more information on the Levant trade.
[42] Morineau, "La balance," 183.

ish trade declined less than trade with other major areas; and in some years, especially 1756, wartime trade with Spain, which centered on French textile exports, exceeded peacetime levels. Substitution involved only a fraction of the values in anticipatory and compensatory trade, which is to be explained by the unattractive costs of turning to neutral shippers to furnish the commercial services that the French preferred to supply. The trade balances tend to obscure the scale and the role of shipping services, which require discussion in their own right.

Trade Balances and Shipping Services

The Bureau de la Balance du Commerce initiated the evaluation of imports and exports to discover whether specie was entering or leaving the realm. Although we recognize that the *états* deal only with some current account items, we can see that they provide information essential to any estimate of the flow on capital account (such as in loans and financial services) and thus to the overall movement of bullion. One of the most remarkable features of French trade in the eighteenth century is the nearly continuous scheme of a surplus balance. Year in and year out, the French shipped more goods abroad than they imported. Only in five years between 1716 and 1780—1724, 1770-1771, 1776, and 1778—did imports exceed exports. Cumulatively, the surplus of exports was massive. Chart 4.1 and Table 4.1 show the growth of these surpluses into the 1760s, and especially during 1740-1766. From Table 4.1 a sense of the constant value scale of surpluses can be derived:

1726-1735	338 million l.t.
1736-1745	378
1746-1755	495
1756-1765	548

Even during war the balance was favorable to France. In the active years of the War of Austrian Succession, 1744-1748, the surplus totalled some 241 million l.t. During the Seven Years War (1756-1763) it reached 401 million, and increased slightly in annual average (from 48 to 50 million).

This pattern of enormous surpluses has intrigued and puzzled historians, for it seems to contradict David Hume's theory of a specie flow-price mechanism, according to which persistent surplus balances will force prices up and thereby reduce exports. But of course the trade balance data depict only the movement of goods, not that of commercial services or other items in the current account, just as Hume's theory neglects some of the forces operating on money and trade flows. Moreover, these data have nothing to say about capital account flows, which are matters of special importance during wars fought away from the metropole, as the Seven Years War was.

Evidence about the colonial trade supplied by Michel Morineau compounds the problem.[43] Noticing the large role played in the trade balance by the reexport of colonial goods and the vast deficit between the metropole and its colonies (Chart 4.4),[44] Morineau sought an explanation. He found it in a previously known but inadequately interpreted document of 1729 or 1730 in the Bibliothèque Mazarine. This document, detailing the experience of a vessel trading between Bordeaux and Léogane in Saint Domingue, shows how much the goods bought in France for shipment to the Antilles increased in value during the voyage. Goods bought in Bordeaux for some 37,000 l.t. brought more than 81,000 l.t. at their sale in Léogane—slightly more than twice their cost.[45] Of course the cargo and costs in Léogane were not the only expenses encountered. Other costs in Bordeaux, depreciation of the vessel, outfitting and equipment, wages, insurance, *désarmement*, and other expenses—together the so-called invisibles on current account—totalled some 31,000 l.t., leaving a credit of slightly more than 24,000 on the sum received at Bordeaux for the return cargo.[46]

The multiple of two between prices in France and the Antilles

[43] Morineau, "Quelques recherches."

[44] In the trade balance calculations, the French colonies in America were counted in the same way as other trading associates rather than as part of France. Thus the large deficit in trade with the colonies diminished the scale of the overall surplus, while the reexport of colonial goods added to the surplus.

[45] The French West Indies transacted in the livre tournois *monnaie du pays* worth, at par, two-thirds of the l.t. *monnaie de France*. John J. McCusker, *Money and Exchange in Europe and America, 1600-1775* (Chapel Hill, 1978), 280-90. I assume that Morineau's figures are in *monnaie de France*. Additional value was added, on a smaller scale, to the return cargo, so that the goods sold in Bordeaux brought almost exactly 2.5 times the original outlay in that same city for cargo.

[46] This "profit" figure includes costs at Léogane, which should be deducted. Morineau makes no attempt to calculate profits finally realized, a matter of some importance because goods were ordinarily sold in the colonies on credit, and some losses were suffered through defaults.

closely matches the difference in export and import values in the *états* for trade between the metropole and the Antilles. From the perspective of the colonies, therefore, the trade balance with France was in equilibrium because of the high value of the invisibles furnished by the metropole. Its disequilibrium in the French accounts included the costs of trade with the Antilles and more, which made this trade route so profitable for French and other merchants dealing with the West Indies.

What Morineau's treatment of this document captures is the important role of commercial services for an interpretation of the *états*. By virtue of the *exclusif*, which prohibited foreigners from trading with French colonies, French merchants controlled trade with the Antilles, and thus in peace had a nearly monopolistic hold on commercial services provided to that trade. On no other French trade routes, except perhaps Guinea and the Far East, was the provision of services so clearly in France's favor. In the case of the Antilles trade, insofar as it is revealed by this single enlightening document, France provided services valued by the shippers at 31,268 l.t. plus their profit, and Léogane provided services valued at 3,081,15 l.t.[47] In terms of all services furnished, France provided some 95 percent of the total, including profits to the shippers. Altogether services in France and Saint Domingue nearly matched the cost of the cargo. If profits are added to the value of these services, the total far exceeds the cost of cargo (nearly 150 percent).

The Balance du Commerce data for the Antilles subsume this provision of services, which appears as the largest part of the unfavorable balance of trade with the colonies when it should appear in the current account to France's credit. Thus the French current account surplus was even larger than the *états* suggest. With other trade associates in Europe, France provided some commercial services and some were furnished by the associate. Since French purchases of insurance and credit from elsewhere in Europe (for the European and colonial trade) exceeded the French supply of these services,[48] and since otherwise French services (e.g., equipment and

---

[47] That is, the cost at Bordeaux compared to the difference between the receipts from the sale of goods in Léogane and the cargo bought there. The services provided in France amounted to 84 percent of the cargo cost.

[48] Especially in services provided by the Dutch, on which see Jeannin, "Les marchés du nord," 71 and 71n50.

outfitting costs) more or less matched services provided by associates, a small part of the surplus balance enjoyed by French trade in the eighteenth century may be accounted for by French purchases of commercial services elsewhere in Europe.

Between peace and war the provision of services shifted against France, especially as neutral ships took over a larger part of total trade activity.[49] Nevertheless, as Table 4.1 demonstrates, the favorable trade balance in the visibles was maintained during war. In part, for the reasons exposed above, this is merely an artifact of the way the balances were calculated. Since French commercial services to the Antilles figured in the balances as part of France's imports, and thus as a debit item, the interruption of the colonial trade merely curtailed the scale of a debit balance misleadingly added by the colonial trade. Therefore during the war the error of this allocation of commercial services in the balances was partially eliminated, leaving France with the highly favorable balances it customarily enjoyed in trade with European regions alone. In peacetime, in contrast, the trade surplus is understated by the data gathered in the eighteenth century for the reason already mentioned—that peacetime balances include a large entry for commercial services supplied the colonies but entered in the balances under imports rather than exports and thus as a debit rather than a credit.

The French balance of trade was, except when war curtailed colonial trade, even more favorable than is suggested by Chart 4.2. The 1:2 ratio of French to Antilles prices that prevailed in 1729-1730 was preserved through the eighteenth century. Although this is a rule-of-thumb measure, one that undoubtedly suffered some variations, it can be used in conjunction with evidence from the balances to reestimate France's peacetime trade surplus. In Table 4.4, data from Table 4.1 are recalculated by reversing the flows provided in the balances for peacetime trade with the colonies. According to this interpretation, the imports more closely capture the value of French exports to the colonies because they subsume French commercial services, those mentioned above (which, as noted, nearly matched the value of the cargoes) plus a very approximate addition for the value of expertise, information, and good will provided by French merchants, which is otherwise included in the profits of this trade. This recalculation, however rough, comes closer than the balances

[49] Carrière, *Négociants marseillais*, I, 496ff. and 543ff.

TABLE 4.4
Reestimated French Trade Balances, 1740-1765
(in millions of constant l.t.)

	uncorrected balance	reestimated balance
1740	45	91
1741	48	82
1742	48	90
1743	46	95
1744	42	war—no change
1745	54	
1746	57	
1747	49	
1748	40	
1749	39	99
1750	41	101
1751	55	92
1752	58	85
1753	61	136
1754	61	134
1755	33	106
1756	74	war—no change
1757	36	
1758	46	
1759	57	
1760	50	
1761	35	
1762	45	
1763	59	85
1764	69	152
1765	78	161

SOURCES: Table 4.1; Romano, "Documenti," 1,291; and explanations in the text of the present volume.

themselves to estimating the scale of the French trade surplus. Thus it, rather than the data from the *états*, suggests the magnitude of the favorable balance that France enjoyed, the balance that must be explained.

During 1749-1763 France had a current account surplus of around 1,181 million l.t. rather than the 750 million that would be inferred from the *états*.[50] Thus France could afford a much larger capital account outflow without facing any long-run bullion losses. The judgment reached in the previous chapter—that war tended to alter the composition of the French money supply as specie flowing

[50] For reasons already given, the recalculation should be suspended in peacetime.

abroad to pay troops and for other purposes was replaced by credit instruments issued to pay for the war—can now be modified. War brought a sudden increase in current account credits as calculated incorrectly by the French, and therefore war seemed to create the possibility of making large transfers abroad without running any risk of specie shortage. In reality, however, war curtailed French income from invisibles since it diminished the supply of commercial services to the colonies and increased French purchases of commercial services in Europe. Still, war left France with a surplus balance on current account, which eased the payment of subsidies to allies and the support of troops operating abroad. The recalculation of the French trade balances reduces further the possibility that war depleted France's specie stock, because it shows that the peacetime current account surplus in visibles was significantly larger than realized by French statisticians. Not having found quantities for all these variables, it is unwise to pretend to have measured the net flow of specie. The most plausible judgment seems to be that war occasioned a marked slowdown in bullion imports and thus in *new* supplies of precious metals that might have gone to the mints. The coin stock may nevertheless have retained prewar levels or even grown slightly.

WAR AND THE INTERNAL ECONOMY

Our attention has been focused on the costs of war for the international economy. This is appropriate because even though the French commercial sector contributed only a small part of national economic activity, it was not only the most dynamic sector but also the part of the economy believed to have been most open to effects from war. In agriculture and manufacturing the Seven Years War was not a significant event, and was less so as French trade contacts with Europe—to which agricultural and manufactured goods were shipped—expanded during the war to compensate for the British blockage of overseas routes. The absence of more than localized harvest crises—along the Channel coast in 1755-1756 and in Burgundy in 1762—indicates at least that war in the old regime style had no simple and straightforward effect on agriculture. Because French agriculture was prosperous during this war, so also was manufacturing. Labrousse detects a depression at the conclusion of the conflict, signalled by low wheat prices.[51] But the mechanism behind this putative depression is not described, and it is difficult to see why unusually good harvests should be held to promote economic depression. The king's role as a provider of outdoor relief in the enlarged wartime militia and coast guard should have heightened demand for both food and industrial goods. Not all industries prospered during the war. Rouen linen output fell off during 1755-1759, and Labrousse associates this with war.[52] But output revived vigorously from 1760 to the end of the war and beyond so that it is difficult to see why the earlier decline should be linked to war. Furthermore, Rouen woollens, which were for the most part exported, do not show any responsiveness to war in either their short-run or long-run cycles. Markovitch believes that the causes of fluctuations are changes in factor costs and demand, which he does not associate with war.[53] Some import- and export-dependent industries—cotton and, in Montpellier, verdigris—suffered to the extent that war curtailed trade contacts.[54] But these were small industries indeed in eighteenth-century France.

By all testimony eighteenth-century conflicts cost France dearly in ships lost to enemy naval vessels and privateers and in ships laid up because of the nearly prohibitive risks of wartime activity, risks reflected in insurance rates. Here, therefore, is one significant segment of the economy harmed by war. To some degree, French merchants turned to alternative routes during war.[55] But shipping activity fell chiefly into the hands of neutrals. Thus French ships not taken by privateers early on were usually laid up in port or sold to neutral shippers on unfavorable terms.

Recent research has uncovered information about ship longevity, which allows some tentative steps toward an evaluation of how much war cost the French commercial fleet. The life spans assigned to larger vessels, which accounted for most of the goods carried in

[51] Ernest Labrousse, "Les ruptures périodiques de la prospérité: Les crises économiques du XVIIIe siècle," in Braudel and Labrousse, eds., *Histoire économique*, II, 556-57.

[52] *Ibid.*, 548 and 556.

[53] Tihomir J. Markovitch, *Histoire des industries françaises: Les industries lainières de Colbert à la Révolution* (Geneva, 1976), 33 and 35.

[54] Reed Benhamou, "Verdigris and the Entrepreneuse," *Technology and Culture*, 25, no. 2 (Apr. 1984), 171-81.

[55] Carrière, *Négociants marseillais*, I, 543ff.

international maritime trade, average some fifteen years.[56] The full
life of these vessels was not at risk since at the beginning of conflict
the fleet would have used up part of its useful life, presumably about
half of it. Thus a conflict like the Seven Years War, which lasted for
about half the useful life of a large merchant vessel, cost the French
commercial fleet most of the capital stock in vessels that existed at
the beginning of war. To this serious effect must be added the curtailment of ship construction during war. Against these effects
stands the rise of ship construction—one of the "éléments moteurs"
of French trade—toward the end of the war.[57] Thus for the important ship-building industry, war acted both to erode the capital stock
and to stimulate fresh building of the comparatively inexpensive
wooden vessels used in overseas trade.

CONCLUSION

"I had a much better opinion of the Country of France this time
[1763] than the last [1751]."[58] Thus the actor David Garrick described his reaction to the roads, the state of cultivation, and the
conditions of life in general in France immediately after the Seven
Years War. Garrick cannot be trusted, of course, since his impressions have behind them no systematic comparison. But his opinion
agrees with what we can now reconstruct about the trend of material
prosperity in the old regime. France began the Seven Years War at
a peak in its economic well being. In the short run the war took a
light toll on the economy, so that we must suppose also that France
emerged from the war still enjoying this unaccustomed boom.

The measurement of war costs has been influenced unduly by
conclusions drawn from trade statistics expressed in current livres,
which inflate apparent losses, and by a tendency to compare wartime trade curtailed by British naval activity to prewar and postwar

[56] T.J.A. Le Goff and Jean Meyer, "Les constructions navales en France pendant la
seconde moitié du XVIII⁵ siècle," *Annales E.S.C.*, 26, no. 1 (Jan.-Feb. 1971), 185. In
the Indies trade, large vessels lasted an average of eight to ten years. Villiers, *Le
commerce colonial atlantique*, 134 and 136. *Id.*, p. 135, gives data indicating the average age
of vessels of the colonial fleet in Nantes in 1779: 4.4 years (figuring at mid-years).

[57] Carrière, *Négociants marseillais*, I, 488. The quote is from Le Goff and Meyer,
"Les constructions navales," 173.

[58] George Winchester Stone, ed., *The Journal of David Garrick describing his Visit to
France and Italy in 1763* (New York, 1939), 4.

periods of compensatory shipping. The prevailing interpretation overlooks the capability of merchants to foresee war, watching signs supplied by the warring states themselves, and thereby to diminish its costs. The most impressive thing that French merchants could do was foresee war well enough to stockpile the goods—colonial food-stuffs—most likely to be cut off. How much more profitable it is to anticipate war when transactions costs—especially insurance rates—are low rather than when they are high.

War certainly added to the costs of doing business. It brought heavy losses in capital goods, ships, it added transactions costs, and it compounded the speculative element in trade. But these are not effects that warrant the adjectives so often used to describe the commercial effects of war: brutal, disastrous, brutally disruptive. Even in trade, the loss leader in war, old regime conflicts had comparatively mild short-term effects.

FINANCING THE WAR

On verra les dépenses militaires s'accroître sans mesure.
C'est une suite nécessaire du système général des
puissances de l'Europe.[1]

A N irony charges the history of the old regime. War was the chief
business of government in that time. Yet revenues were inadequate to pay for this chief business. They were enough to pay for
peace, which in the eighteenth century included the cost of the
peacetime army and navy. And most of the time, up to 1756 at least,
they were enough to pay also for the accumulating costs of prior
wars, which took the form of debts. But they were not enough to pay
for a continuing succession of new wars. The irony is that states
which made war the principal business of government did not find
a way to fund the continuing series of conflicts so that the organism—the warring state—could survive in the long run.

In France every war brought additions to the debt because every
war demanded more expenditures than could be raised from existing taxes plus the new levies that were politically feasible. This is a
banal fact. What is not banal is the measure of the addition to the
debt, and the government's plan for absorbing the new debt
charges. How much more indebtedness might be tolerated without
counterproductive financial, economic, and political effects? How
should policy respond to each new postwar financial situation? The
history of the modern French monarchy is a history of wars that did
not cost too much interspersed with wars that did cost too much.
The War of the League of Augsburg (1688-1697) and the War of
Austrian Succession (1740-1748) were major conflicts that did not
cost too much. The Thirty Years War (for France, 1631-1648) and
the War of Spanish Succession (1701-1714) were major conflicts
that did cost too much. The monarchy dealt with these excess costs
by repudiation, although different repudiations were handled in

---

[1] [Mathon de la Cour], *Collection de comptes-rendus* . . . (Lausanne, 1788), 226.

different ways. Turning once again to the accounts, to the style of financial history that Clamageran followed but Marion did not, let us study the costs of the Seven Years War. Should this war join other conflicts that did not cost too much, or those that did? How did the financial authorities propose to deal with the costs of this war?

WAR COSTS

What do the accounts reveal? First, it is necessary to survey the characteristics of the sources, which are substitutes for the official accounts destroyed by fires in the archives. Mathon de la Cour, who collected such data for some twenty-five years beginning in 1761, provides this scheme:

1) *Les comptes effectifs*, or final accounts (usually called the *états au vrai*). These are audited statements, but because of many obstacles and uncertainties, they are unavailable when they would be most useful. They are seldom consulted because the financial authorities are more concerned with the future than the past several years distant and overlook how much the past can reveal about the future.

2) *Les comptes de prévoyance*, a projection of revenues and expenditures. These are merely a design and may be altered by events. Often they anticipate surpluses when the final accounts show deficits. This tendency is one of the leading causes of the growth of the debt.

3) *Les comptes d'une année commune*, or income and expenditure averages. The great usefulness of these accounts is diminished by the unavailability of final accounts until many years have passed.

4) *Les comptes des recettes et dépenses ordinaires*, which are based in part on final accounts and in part on estimates. When new measures are introduced, the estimates about them may be seriously in error. Furthermore, the ordinary account is incomplete; it excludes extraordinary revenues and expenditures.[2]

To these should be added a fifth category of preliminary retrospective accounts, struck at the end of the fiscal year (when closely

[2] *Ibid.*, vii-x, paraphrasing and summarizing. Mathon de la Cour provides these observations to prepare the reader for the different types of documents to be encountered in his collection and to allow judgments about reliability. But he does not reveal to which of the four categories each document belongs. These issues are discussed further in James C. Riley, "French Finances, 1727-1768," forthcoming, *Journal of Modern History* (1987).

associated with the *comtes de prévoyance* for the following fiscal year) or in following months.[3] Archives outside France yield a selection of these documents, gathered through fiscal espionage and other means. Together with documents in French archives and Mathon de la Cour's collection, the new sources make it possible to reconstruct the accounts.

Historians have wished for access to the final accounts, which seem to have been destroyed or which, several years behind, were never constructed. But let us not deceive ourselves about what they would reveal. The final revenue accounts would differ from the preliminary retrospective accounts in a minor way even in years in which expectations about revenues were not met because of severe economic distress. The king allowed remissions, some in prospect and some after the fact. Every year also there were shortages—*non-valeurs*—that had to be written off. But these sums, which can be examined for years like 1740 when the harvest fell below expectations, will not make a large difference in the information available to us and to the financial authorities themselves. They will be partially offset by the *revenants-bons*, savings in various forms, from expenditures ordered but not executed and deaths among pension holders and life annuity nominees.[4] The expenditure accounts present larger problems, for some agencies on occasion spent more than had been authorized. Instances of this will enter the discussion that follows. But even the scale of these discrepancies will be small in comparison to the sums at issue—on the order of 10 percent or less of preliminary expenditure accounts, which include extraordinary revenues.

It is necessary only to acknowledge the bias in the available documents. They tend to overstate revenues and understate expenditures. Thus the size of deficits that they project and the story they tell about the growth of the debt will err on the side of caution. In reality the financial problem was somewhat larger than what will be claimed here. Furthermore, it is documents of this kind, not final accounts, that informed financial authorities and prompted them to

[3] On the basis of the documents available to me, it appears that in war the financial authorities compiled income and expenditure averages—*les comptes d'une année commune*—whereas in peace they compiled separate annual preliminary statements.

[4] And of course there will be larger discrepancies if the final accounts arrange revenues and expenditures in a different chronological scheme than do the preliminary accounts. But discrepancies such as these must be worked out by historians.

propose policies, reforms, plans to cover deficits, and otherwise to administer the financial business of the realm. Thus, in their own way, these documents are more revealing than the final accounts would be, for they allow us to infer why the authorities made the proposals and took the actions that they did.[5]

Revenues and Expenditures

Most of the information available about both revenues and expenditures during the war appears in the form of Mathon de la Cour's category 3—income and expenditure averages. Revenue information is given in five categories:

1) ordinary revenues
2) revenues alienated for a limited time
3) revenues alienated in perpetuity (a rubric admitted to be archaic)
4) *affaires extraordinaires*
5) private (chiefly church and seigneurial) revenues (*affaires particulières*)

The documents report gradually rising revenue and expenditure averages as these amounts increased over time. They also project these amounts backward over time so that the late war averages exceed early war figures. To adjust for this, different versions of this same basic document are dated to the year of compilation when possible, which is determined by internal evidence, specifically statements about deficits or surpluses in the ordinary account, and the averages are presented as revenue and expenditure figures for that year. Information about the ordinary transactions of the monarchy is supplemented by lists of the *affaires extraordinaires* of the war years. Each document follows a set format, to the extent even that manuscripts written in different years reproduce some explanatory notes word for word and that there is in most entries little change from year to year.

The documents of principal use in this search appear in nearly

---

[5] They are also more revealing than the *états de prévoyance* and *arrangements*, discussed by Michel Morineau, "Budgets de l'état et gestion des finances royales en France au dix-huitième siècle," *Revue historique*, 264, no. 2 (1980), 289-336, because those documents tended to underestimate expenditures, as Mathon observed.

identical form in several archives inside and outside France. In London Adam Smith acquired two *états*, which are preserved with his bookplate and bound with John Holker's *Mémoire instructif sur la fabrique*.[6] In Brussels Austro-Belgian authorities also owned *états*, which were confiscated by the French during the Revolution and returned after the Congress of Vienna.[7] In the Dutch Republic the foreign office and the States General obtained these documents, as did also a large number of British authorities, some clearly through espionage. Both the Bibliothèque de l'Arsenal in Paris, the library built from books and manuscripts owned by the marquis d'Argenson by his son, the marquis de Paulmy, and the Haus-, Hof- und Staatsarchiv in Vienna hold more documents, as do also the Bibliothèque Mazarine, the Bibliothèque Nationale, and other depositories outside France. Other sources reveal that the French government sometimes supplied other powers, including Spain and Prussia, with copies of model financial documents.[8] But the wide spread of these manuscripts indicates that friendly, neutral, and enemy states alike were able to acquire *états*.

These documents make it possible to provide a partial table of revenues and expenditures during the war. Because the monarchy preferred predictable to maximum yields, individual levies raised approximately the same sum from year to year, a point made by Morineau.[9] Table 5.1 presents subtotals for revenues, leaving out the categories *affaires extraordinaires* and *affaires particulières* and combining revenues assigned before reaching the treasury with revenues passing through the treasury.[10] In this part of finances, the

[6] (Paris, 1764).

[7] They bear the estampille of the Bibliothèque Nationale, Paris.

[8] Algemeen Rijksarchief, The Hague, Legatiearchief, Eerste Afdeling, Frankrijk, 784; Public Record Office, London, SP 9, 86; British Library, Manuscript Department, Additional Mss. 25597, 38335, 38339, 38468, 40759, and Stowe Papers 86 and 87; and Kungliga Biblioteket, Stockholm, Manuscript Department, Engeströmska Samling C.XIV.1.24.

[9] Morineau, "Budgets de l'état," 292.

[10] Items included in each category are indicated by [Mathon de la Cour], *Comptes-rendus*, 3-18. The "revenus royaux destinés et aliénés à perpétuité" were not all in fact alienated in perpetuity; some were sold for specific periods. Items in this category include the *droits* of the courts which provided judicial officials with compensation (27 million) and the municipalities' half of 18 million livres collected under the king's authority but split with the cities. This designation also includes the list of other royal taxes in *id.*, 16-18. The data in the first column combine the so-called net revenues, revenues actually spent from the royal treasury, with revenues assigned before

TABLE 5.1
Revenues and Overheads, 1755-1765
(in millions of livres tournois)

	ordinary revenues	revenues with limited duration	overhead and "revenues alienated in perpetuity"	subtotal
1755	—	—	—	—
1756	—	—	—	—
1757	237.8	34.9	94.2	366.9
1758[b]	236.0	37.1	92.2	365.3
1759	239.5[a]	—	—	—
1760	—	—	—	—
1761	265.6	37.1	94.4	397.1
1762	—	—	—	—
1763	263.4	56.4[c]	105.6	425.4
1764	265.4	56.3[c]	106.3	428.0
1765	270.7	62.6[c]	110.3	443.6

Sources: Bibliothèque Mazarine, Paris, 2825 (1761); Bibliothèque Nationale, Paris, ms fr. 14081 (1761); University Library, London, Palæography Room, 127(2) (1757 and 1765); Koninklijke Bibliotheek, Brussels, Manuscript Department, 10744 (1765); British Library, London, Manuscript Department, Additional Mss., 38468, folios 121ff. (1763), Bibliothèque de l'Arsenal, Paris, 4062 (1764) and 4066A (1764); Haus-, Hof- und Staatsarchiv, Vienna, Bohm-Supplement, Frankreich, 960-W922 (1764); and [Mathon de la Cour], *Collection de comptes-rendus . . .* (Lausanne, 1788), 3-46.

[a] Based on Silhouette's September 1759 accounts ([Mathon de la Cour], 46), excluding the *vingtièmes*.

[b] Evidently a prospective account, since it includes *affaires extraordinaires* only through 1757.

[c] Includes revenues from two *vingtièmes*.

reaching the treasury. See Chapter 2. Table 5.1 does not include the *affaires particulières*, some fees and levies paid the church, seigneurs, the hôpitaux généraux, the poor, the hôtels dieu, provincial governors general, and officers of justice. For 1765 the total of these was 51.7 million, of which 26.2 million, raised as surcharges on existing taxes and to sustain the administrative system, might be included in the figure for total central government taxation. University Library, London, Palæography Room, 127(2); and on 1758, [Mathon de la Cour], *Comptes-rendus*, 24-26. Notice the effect of averaging: the 1758 accounts report entries nearly identical to the 1761 accounts. This same pattern shows up in the ordinary expenditures. Bibliothèque Nationale, Joly de Fleury, 1432, furnishes a prospective account for 1760 based on 1759 revenues, but it is not reported here because part of the accounting is of revenues by type and part of revenues by region of assessment. Dating has been done using internal evidence, chiefly in the form of references to deficits in the ordinary account and the years of *affaires extraordinaires* covered by each *état*. This table differs from information in Riley, "French Finances," because it adds sums not part of revenues paid to the treasury (chiefly the third column).

revenues more or less matched expenditures. Table 5.2 gives a
breakdown of expenditures in these categories.[11]

TABLE 5.2
Expenditures, 1755–1765
(in millions of l.t.)

	ordinary expenditures	expenditures earmarked from revenues with limited duration	expenditures on "revenues alienated in perpetuity"	subtotal	(deficit) or surplus
1755	—	—	—	—	—
1756	—	—	—	—	—
1757	—	—	—	—	—
1758	237.1	37.1	92.2	366.4	(1.1)
1759	—	—	—	—	—
1760	—	—	—	—	—
1761	237.1	37.1	94.4	368.6	28.5
1762	—	—	—	—	—
1763	280.2	56.4	105.6	442.2	(16.8)
1764	268.4	56.3	106.3	431.3	(3.3)
1765	273.7	62.6	110.3	446.6	(3.0)

SOURCES: See previous table.

The Extraordinary Account

It is obvious that no war could be fought on the ordinary account.
In financial terms France fought its wars as *affaires extraordinaires.*[12]
A list of these revenues was compiled during the war. Table 5.3 ar-
ranges those data into four categories, adding information from
Clamageran and Marion. The last column provides the key series.[13]
The Seven Years War seems to have cost some 1,325 million livres,
or about 189 million a year in addition to the ordinary costs of government, in which some economies were made for the sake of the
conflict, and in addition to "off budget" spending via short-term

[11] Haus-, Hof- und Staatsarchiv, Vienna, Böhm-Supplement, Frankreich, 960-
W922, gives an alternate figure (104.3 million) for 1764 expenditures from revenues
alienated in perpetuity and an incorrectly added total for earmarked expenditures.

[12] In military expenditures a distinction was made between the small *ordinaire des
guerres* and the large *extraordinaire des guerres*, which grew larger still in wartime. Lee
Kennett, *The French Armies in the Seven Years' War* (Durham, N.C., 1967), 90-91.

[13] These data are apparently for the calendar rather than the fiscal year but, lack-

borrowing. To add short-term borrowing would push the annual total of extraordinary spending above 200 million, perhaps to 225 million. Aggregate spending during the seven years of war totalled more than 4 billion l.t.[14]

The extraordinary revenues were allocated to the army and the navy, fortifications and war equipment, subsidies to allies, and the increasing burden of debt service.[15] A distribution of spending does not appear in these documents, but another source reveals the growth of allocations to the navy (Table 5.4).[16] The deficit that these accounts reveals formed one of many occasions for the issue of short-term credit instruments, which the ministry of the marine put into circulation to anticipate budgeted spending and to cover unbudgeted spending. Other ministries also overspent, and financed this by issuing short-term paper.[17] In 1758, to take only one year, France spent just over 200 million to meet budgeted extraordinary military, naval, and colonial expenses.[18] Each year the new loans added to the cost of debt service so that by 1758 France was certainly

---

ing the full accounts, it is not clear when authorities entered the expectation of these revenues. Some items do not easily fit into these categories. In August 1758 the price of tobacco under the monopoly was increased by 20 percent for ten years, and the farmers advanced 30 million on that. Bibliothèque de l'Arsenal, Paris, 4062, pp. 26ff. and 55-57, also reports surcharges on certain farms, and adds these to the totals at a rate of 7.44 million a year. But it also furnishes data about rebates on other farms, indicating that the net addition to revenues over the period 1756-1762 was 9.38 million. I have not included this figure because I do not know how to date this complex transaction.

[14] Bibliothèque de l'Arsenal, 4062, p. 62, gives a figure of 4.16 billion, but this overstates the revenues (by using late war average figures) and some extraordinary income (by failing to delete rebates to some farms and by overstating General Farm lease advances in 1762) while omitting other extraordinary revenues. Haus-, Hof- und Staatsarchiv, Böhm 960-W922, p. 116, citing a translation of David Hume's *Political Essays*, concurs, giving a figure of over 200 million a year in war spending, which is the amount given by the translator's additions to David Hume, *Essais sur le commerce* . . . (Paris, 1767), 175. The translator may have been Mademoiselle de la Chaux.

[15] [Mathon de la Cour], *Comptes-rendus*, 22.

[16] Henri Legohérel, *Les trésoriers généraux de la marine (1517-1788)* (Paris, [1965]), discusses variations in series due to whether the accounts were prospective, preliminary retrospective, or final, and gives other series.

[17] These sums, which show up in the figures for accumulated floating or short-term debt at the end of the war, do not, however, approximate the level of funded extraordinary spending.

[18] J[ean]-J[ules] Clamageran, *Histoire de l'impôt en France* (3 vols.; Paris, 1867-1876), III, 358-59.

TABLE 5.3
Extraordinary Revenues, 1756-1762
(in millions of l.t.)

	credit (long-term only)		finance on offices	tax increases[a]		church grants; leases and taxes alienated[c]	total
	loans	advances from farms		general	second vingtième estimated[b]		
1756	32[d]	46	0	0	0	43	121
1757	136	0	0	0	21.3	0	157.3
1758	132.2[ef]	30	26.9	0	21.3	8.7	219.1
1759	96.3[f]	72[g]	8	3.7[h]	21.3	24	225.3
1760	130	0	0[j]	102.6[i]	21.3	0	253.9
1761	80.5[kf]	0	25.8	76	21.3	0	203.6
1762	6	27[l]	0	76	21.3	15	145.3
TOTALS	613	175	60.7	258.3	127.8	90.7	1,325.5

SOURCES: University Library, London, 127(2); J[ean]-J[ules] Clamageran, *Histoire de l'impôt en France* (3 vols.; Paris, 1867-1876), III, 32-33, 353, 355, 368-69, and Marcel Marion, *Histoire financière de la France depuis 1715* (5 vols.; Paris, 1927-1928), I, 472-73.

a Not included in Tables 5.1 and 5.2

b Revenues from the second *vingtième* are estimated on the basis of Silhouette's report on 1759 income, in [Mathon de la Cour], 46. Another source, Bibliothèque Nationale, Joly de Fleury, 577. folio 124, reports a smaller sum (19.8 million) for proceeds in c. 1763. The second *vingtième* went into effect on October 1, 1756, thus at the beginning of the 1757 fiscal year. A breakdown of all elements in the 72.3 million tax increase included in the fourth column is unavailable, and it may be that the figures for 1760-1762 include the second *vingtième*. In 1763-1765 revenues from the second *vingtième* show up in Table 5.1 in the second column.

c Includes grants from the church for remission of the *vingtième*.

d Clamageran also lists a perpetual annuity loan for 36 million, but cites a source that contains no mention of it.

e Clamageran gives the life annuity loan at a principal of 36 million rather than 45 million, and Marion, I, 472, gives the total as 39 million. Clamageran and Marion, I, 185 and 472, both give the total of the April 1758 loan at 80 million rather than the 40 million recorded in University Library, London, 127(2) with the addition composed of subscriptions in outstanding paper, here excluded.

f Marion's subscription totals are used in place of the authorized loan totals. Clamageran lists the December 1759 tontine at 30 rather than 60 million, as indicated in University Library, London, 127(2). Marion, I, 190n3, and 472, lists a February 1759 tontine with a principal of 46.83 or 46.87 million.

g In theory a public loan partially transforming the General Farm into a joint-stock company, but in practice an additional advance from the farmers

h An extraordinary grant decreed in August 1759 to be paid by certain municipalities for ten years. Different documents give different totals for proceeds ranging from 3.46 to 3.69 million, and Clamageran, III, 334-35, draws information from later records on financial flows.

i Clamageran lists an additional 40 million, which appears to be covered by a smaller sum (25.8 million) under 1761 in University Library, London, 127(2).

j The extraordinary grant first collected in 1759 is omitted from the 1760 list in University Library, London, 127(2) but included in Bibliothèque de l'Arsenal, 4062, as an addition after the fact. I have omitted it because of uncertainty about whether the amount reported for 1759 covers the 1760 fiscal year contribution. Includes prepayment for the continuation until 1782 of certain taxes levied in Paris

k Clamageran lists the life annuity loans of this year at 40 rather than 50 million, but leaves open the possibility of further emissions. Marion lists them at 43.5 million. A loan from the generalities, mentioned in Bibliothèque Nationale, ms. fr. 7748, folio 24, is included.

l Including a net additional advance from the farmers general of 20 million.

TABLE 5.4
Naval Spending, 1755-1764
(in millions of l.t.)

	ordinary	extraordinary	secret	total projected spending	actual spending
1755	14.9	16.3	.1	31.3	34.5
1756	14.9	25.0	.1	40.0	49.3
1757	14.9	24.0	.1	39.0	60.3
1758	14.8	27.4	.2	42.4	55.3
1759	14.8	41.9	.2	56.9	77.0
1760	14.8	8.7	.2	23.7	33.8
1761	12.0	18.0	.2	30.2	—[a]
1762	17.6	6.7	.2	24.5	—[a]
1763	18.8	1.1	.2	20.1	—[a]
1764	15.8	.3	.2	16.3	—[a]

SOURCES: *Etat sommaire des Archives de la Marine antérieures à la Révolution* (Paris, 1898), 616-17; and Henri Legohérel, *Les trésoriers généraux de la marine (1517-1788)* (Paris, [1965]), 177ff., esp. 186.
[a] *Not available.*

spending 100 million in that direction. In each year of the conflict Louis XV also ordered subsidies for French allies and states he wished to influence.[19] War could cost as much again as peace.

Table 5.3 shows how the war was financed (excepting only the rather small matter of economies in ordinary spending, such as by the court, and the larger item of spending covered by short-term credit).[20] The 1,325 million livres was raised in the following manner:

credit	788.0 million	59 percent
offices	60.7	5
tax increases	386.1	29
other	90.7	7
	1,325.5	100

Three-fifths of the total came from credit—and more than three-

[19] Archives Nationales, Paris, 2AQ9, papiers des banquiers Laborde, includes some information on subsidies.

[20] This table gives a retrospective list of extraordinary revenues, after reducing loans to known subscription levels. Silhouette discussed the problem of subscription shortfalls with the king in September 1759. [Mathon de la Cour], *Comptes-rendus*, 33.

fifths if we take the view, as eighteenth-century financial authorities did, that the *finance* behind offices constituted part of the state debt. France paid for the war by borrowing.[21]

The reasons for this preference for borrowing over taxing are not difficult to find. We know already of the aversion the French felt for taxes. The remonstrances of the parlements—the parlement of Paris remonstrated fifteen times in the 1750s and twenty-five times in the 1760s, and the king held six *lits de justice* in these two decades—signs of an emerging struggle between the king and the law courts, articulate this loathing,[22] as does also the opposition that greeted Séchelles' plan to augment the *taille*.[23] A memorandum written during or immediately after the war underscores the intensity of this struggle and reveals how difficult it was to raise taxes even by 29 percent of extraordinary spending.[24] This memorandum, an *état* for the war years joined "avec des observations politiques et intéressantes . . . sur la multiplicité onéreuse des Impôts," constitutes a general attack on the taxes. Its anonymous author denounced not merely the financiers and tax farmers but the weight of the taxes in general. "L'agriculture, les arts, le commerce tout gémit dans l'accablement" because of the weight of the taxes.[25] The people have been reduced to the last misery. The taxes have reached so high a level that they are counterproductive—new levies produce smaller rather than larger overall yields.[26]

This is hyperbole. The document combines information about the budget with an interpretation that does not follow from that information. The second *vingtième* had, it is true, returned a smaller sum than the first, but it also carried more exclusions. Only the 1758

[21] William J. McGill, *Maria Theresa* (New York, 1972), 126, maintains that Austria also financed two-thirds of its much smaller part of the war by borrowing. Also P.G.M. Dickson, *The Financial Revolution in England* (New York, 1967), 10, on Britain.

[22] E.g., Bibliothèque Nationale, Joly de Fleury, 1446, folio 37, on the remonstrances of the parlement of Lorraine, in Jan. 1761, against the third *vingtième*. Dale K. Van Kley, *The Damiens Affair and the Unravelling of the "Ancien Régime," 1750-1770* (Princeton, 1984), 100, counts the remonstrances and *lits*, which concerned religious and constitutional as well as fiscal issues, but mostly fiscal issues.

[23] René-Louis de Voyer d'Argenson, *Journal et mémoires*, ed. by E.J.B. Rathery (9 vols.; Paris, 1859-1867), IX, 145-46.

[24] Bibliothèque de l'Arsenal, 4066B, dated by the references to specific tax increases. Another copy may be found in University Library, London, 127(2).

[25] Bibliothèque de l'Arsenal, 4066B, p. 210.

[26] *Ibid.*, pp. 213, 228, and 229ff.

increase in the cost of tobacco sold under the General Farm monopoly had produced lower revenues, which may be explained by smuggling rather than by diminished consumption. There can be no question that other added levies continued to deliver larger yields (in nominal values). Nor does the author provide any evidence of the pitiable economic plight to which, in his view, the entire country (barring only the financiers and tax farmers) had been reduced. He is content to proclaim "une vérité constante." If the interpretation is suspect, the passion is undeniable. Here is someone who believed, as strongly as language permitted him to express, that the taxes were excessive to the point at which they threatened even "la liberté légitime des Sujets."[27] (We can now detect at least two ingredients in the eighteenth-century French view of basic liberties: the right to maintain the secrecy of household finances, and the right to pay taxes at a level modest enough not to compromise economic activity.)

A measured version of the same case appears in a memoir prepared in September 1764 by the parlement of Brittany: "On ne peut s'empêcher de reconnoitre ces deux vérités: la première, que les peuples payent trop d'Impositions; la seconde, qu'il n'est pas proposable de diminuer les revenus du Roy."[28] Here too sentiment is in conflict with reality. The Seven Years War had done little more than restore the level of taxes that had prevailed in the last conflict. Between 1744 and 1749 ordinary and temporary tax revenues ranged from 269.3 to 289.7 million, including the *dixième* reduced during 1750 to a *vingtième*.[29] At the end of the Seven Years War (1764) this same category of revenues, which is the total sum moving through the central accounts, reached 321.7 million, an increase of 11 percent over 1749. But prices had risen by 14 percent.[30] Taxation was not much heavier during the Seven Years War than during the War of Austrian Succession. What is more, taxes had expanded during the War of Austrian Succession at a rate about twice as high as dur-

[27] *Ibid.*, pp. 227 and 229.

[28] Bibliothèque Nationale, Joly de Fleury, 1432, folios 167ff., the quote from folio 167.

[29] Algemeen Rijksarchief, Legatie, 787-88.

[30] Ernest Labrousse, "Les 'bon prix' agricoles du XVIIIᵉ siècle," in Fernand Braudel and Ernest Labrousse, eds., *Histoire économique et sociale de la France* (Paris, 1970), II, 387, using thirteen-year averages centered on 1749 and 1764.

ing the Seven Years War.[31] Assessments increased during the Seven
Years War, but not to the degree asserted by the critics. Indeed,
what is striking is that the costs of the war grew much more rapidly
than did the taxes. France tried to fight the conflict of 1756-1763 by
adding to the taxes at no higher rate than had been done for the
conflict of 1741-1748.

War and the National Product

War brought an expansion in the portion of national income
claimed by the public sector, but during 1756-1763 the expansion
occurred chiefly in non-tax revenues. At the peak of the previous
conflict, 1744-1749, non-tax revenues averaged less than half of the
affaires extraordinaires. In the Seven Years War, in contrast, between
three-fifths and two-thirds of additional spending was funded by
credit.

What part of national product was required to fight these mid-
century wars? Table 5.5, column 3, suggests that the approximate
part of agricultural and manufacturing output raised in taxes contracted somewhat between 1744 and 1765, falling from 9-11 percent to 9 percent.[32] Ordinary peacetime spending, represented by
1752 and 1765, totalled about 9 percent of output.[33] In war this figure peaked at 15 percent or slightly more.[34] That is, war required a
large change in the distribution of national product and income,
and the Seven Years War required a still larger redistribution than
had the War of Austrian Succession. The war of 1756-1763 did not

[31] From 210.0 million in 1739 to 289.7 million in 1748, or by 38 percent, as compared to a growth from 262.4 million in 1752 to 321.7 million in 1764, an increase of
23 percent.

[32] Since some of the *affaires extraordinaires* of 1744 were new taxes and taxes alienated for an advance, this comparison actually understates the decline. This table includes ordinary revenues, temporary taxes, and extraordinary revenues, and omits
revenues alienated in perpetuity, which include overhead, because information on
these items is incomplete or unavailable in a consistent form. Thus it differs from a
similar table in Riley, "French Finances, 1727-1768," in which non-tax revenues are
omitted and in which also tax revenues are averaged over several years.

[33] Compare with [Jean-Baptiste Naveau], *Le financier citoyen* (2 vols.; [Paris], 1757),
II, 77, who estimated French agricultural and manufacturing output at only 2 billion,
of which 15 percent was paid in taxes at his lower estimate of taxes.

[34] Other items, overhead and revenues alienated in perpetuity, added another 3 to
6 percent.

TABLE 5.5
Central Government Revenues as a Percentage of Output
(in millions of current l.t.)

	output	ordinary and temporary revenues	ratio, col. 2/col. 1	affaires extraordinaires	total, cols. 2 + 4	ratio, col. 5/col. 1
1744	2,500-3,000	270	9-11%	63	333	11-13%
1748	2,600-3,000	290	10-11	89	379	13-15
1752	2,700-3,100	262	8-10	0	262	8-10
1758	2,900-3,200	273	9	219	492	15-17
1761	3,100-3,300	303	9-10	204	506	15-16
1765	3,600-3,700	333	9	0	333	9

SOURCES: Algemeen Rijksarchief, The Hague, Legatiearchief, Eerste Afdeling, Frankrijk, 784 and 787-88; [Mathon de la Cour], Comptes-rendus, 6-10, Bibliothèque Mazarine, 2825; University Library, London, 127(2); and Table 5.3. On how the output estimates were made, see n. 90 in Chapter 2 of this volume.

break sharply with previous experience in this measure, and it did not bring the public revenues up to the high proportion of output suggested by the physiocrats to be appropriate: 20 percent.[35] It did, however, break with prior experience in two important ways, war costs and the program for financing the conflict.

Rising Cost of War

In January 1751 someone with inside knowledge about the French financial administration, Daniel Trudaine, an *intendant des finances*, composed a plan to increase the revenues in the event of another war.[36] That year, with the halving of the *dixième*, the revenues had fallen to some 263 million,[37] an amount potentially adequate to allow a slow retirement of the debt but not large enough to pay for another conflict. Trudaine proposed that a new war be financed by increased taxation and showed how 90 million l.t. might be added to the revenues. Most of this addition would come from the restoration of the *dixième*, to be assessed on clergy and laity, and from the recovery of taxes established for temporary terms (twelve to fifteen years) in the previous war and sold for cash up front. Of course these levies, for the most part excises on goods moving into Paris, were collected in any event by the people who had bought these rights from the king. But Trudaine looked forward to the time when their proceeds might flow each year into the royal treasury. In this memoir a renewal of war was expected to augment spending to some 294 million a year. But since the plan for additional tax revenues could add 90 million or more, bringing revenues up to 350 or 360 million, war spending might be extended further still. Clearly the monarchy could afford another conflict.

This is a revealing document for what it says about the anticipated annual costs of a new conflict. The previous war had cost 90 to 100 million a year, summing expenditures over and beyond ordinary revenues from 1741 through 1749. Thus Trudaine would prepare France financially to fight another war on the same scale. But the

[35] Anon., "Considérations sur les finances & le commerce de France," *Journal de commerce et d'agriculture* (Brussels) (Feb. 1761), 13 and 14. The argument is continued in later numbers.

[36] Haus-, Hof- und Staatsarchiv, Böhm 992-W939; and British Library, Additional Mss. 35498, folios 20v-52v; and 38331, folios 146-152v.

[37] Algemeen Rijksarchief, Legatie, 783 and 789.

Seven Years War did not preserve the ceiling on war spending in effect during the 1740s. By 1757 extraordinary war spending exceeded 150 million and was continuing to rise. Silhouette, who uncovered the truly serious proportions of this problem in 1759, asserted that the war could not be financed without some 217 million in supplementary revenues in addition to the ordinary revenues and the two *vingtièmes* in force.[38] Estimates presented here indicate that the war added an annual average of 189 million to expenditures, which might be as high as 225 million if all short-term borrowing were added in. A large inflation in war costs had occurred, one for which French authorities were unprepared. The annual cost of the 1756-1763 war, which was a worldwide conflict, exceeded the annual cost of the War of Austrian Succession, which was chiefly a European conflict, by over 100 percent.

War Finance

France elected to finance the Seven Years War not in the fashion ordinarily associated with old regime monarchies—involuntary taxes, requisitions, or forced loans—but by a resort to voluntary lending (Table 5.6). In 1756 financial authorities believed the conflict could

TABLE 5.6
Extraordinary Revenue Policy during the War

	credit	other
1756	64%	36%
1757	86	14
1758	86	14
1759	78	22
1760	51	49
1761	52	48
1762	23	77

SOURCE: Table 5.3.

be paid for without increasing taxes. The king and his ministers seem to have had high hopes for the war and France's ability to fight it, in part because the first fiscal year of the conflict, October 1, 1755–September 30, 1756, coincided with an unusually rich windfall from tax lease renewals and a resumption of the clergy's grants

[38] [Mathon de la Cour], *Comptes-rendus*, 35.

paid in lieu of the *vingtième*.[39] In October 1755 the several tax farms and the clergy furnished an additional 79 million over and above ordinary revenues. Together with a life annuity loan opened in the same month, and the prolongation in December of taxes on wood and charcoal in Paris, which together brought in 42 million, the windfall covered war costs until March 1757. Then France turned to loans on the open market. In them the role of the much celebrated court bankers—who, like the farmers general and the receivers, helped tide the treasury over between expenditures and revenues—was less important than that of the borrowing administration centered on the controller general.

The credit policy was the creation of three controllers general who served briefly: Jean Moreau de Séchelles, who succeeded Machault on July 30, 1754; François Marie Peyrenc de Moras, who succeeded Séchelles on April 24, 1756; and Jean Nicholas de Boullongne, who succeeded Moras on August 25, 1757. Boullongne was replaced on March 4, 1759, by Etienne de Silhouette, who served for eight months and seventeen days (until replaced on November 21, 1759, by Henri Bertin). Silhouette has been depicted, accurately enough, by Mathon de la Cour:

> On lui connoissoit de l'esprit, de l'honnêteté, beaucoup de vues et d'excellentes intentions: mais il n'avoit ni l'adresse ordinaire aux courtisans, ni même, il faut l'avouer, toute la prudence nécessaire à l'homme d'état. Il voyoit bien, et il étoit moins propre à l'exécution, parce qu'il avoit, comme presque tous les esprits systématiques, plus étudié les hommes dans les livres et dans son cabinet, que dans la société et dans les vrais rapports qui les lient, et que, par cette raison, il ne savoit ni prévoir les obstacles, ni les vaincre.[40]

In his brief tenure Silhouette emerged as a caricature of the reforming minister of finances. He saw a version of the problem of a rich

---

[39] During 1750-1755 the church did not pay its customary grant for exemption from the *vingtième*. In 1756 payment began again, according to prior arrangement, and the king assumed some 60 million in church debts. Haus-, Hof- und Staatsarchiv, Böhm 992-W939. The British spy Michael Hatton reported in March 1755, quoting Louis XV, that the French king was not worried about financing a war. British Library, Egmont 3465, folio 42, Hatton to the Earl of Holdernesse, Mar. 26, 1755.

[40] [Mathon de la Cour], *Comptes-rendus*, 28. Maurice Guillaumat-Vallet, *Le contrôleur-général Silhouette et ses réformes en matière financière* (Paris, 1914), 3 and *passim*, esp.

land providing the king with insufficient revenues, and proposed a reform. In September 1759, in a memoir read to the king in a common meeting of the royal councils, Silhouette explained his program. It was a long session, for the memoir totalled some 4,500 words. One can imagine how difficult it was to listen attentively.

In office for half a year, Silhouette believed he had seen the problem. Expedients will no longer suffice. "Les emprunts multipliés, & le haut intérêt auquel l'argent a été porté, ont averti le public des détresses de l'Etat. Toute opération de crédit ne produiroit aujourd'hui que le funeste effet de dévoiler son impuissance aux ennemis & de rendre la paix plus difficile." There is no choice but to augment revenues.[41] Such a measure will pay part of the costs of the war, bring a surplus in peacetime revenues large enough to amortize the debt and thereby "procurer au peuple un soulagement réel & solide," and reestablish government credit.[42] Even Silhouette, who saw the need to increase taxes, recognized that the war would have to be fought at least in part on credit. But the crying problem of the moment arose from the decision to enter the war without a large tax increase. Paraphrasing Silhouette, the king's wish not to tax more heavily has led him to rely on credit, which is now exhausted. At the moment it is impossible to meet expenses without issuing short-term paper, which, because it is discounted so heavily, leads the suppliers to raise prices on what they furnish. To bring the point home, Silhouette told the king and the councils a story from French history. In 1672 Colbert favored taxes and the parlement loans. "M. de Colbert fit de vains efforts pour dissuader les magistrats, & finit par leur dire qu'ils répondroient devant Dieu du mal qu'ils faisoient au Roi & à l'Etat. . . ."[43] What was left unsaid is what exactly was the evil that followed the rejection of Colbert's advice.

87ff.; and [François Véron Duverger de Forbonnais], *Lettre d'un banquier à son correspondant de province* (Paris, 1759), give a more favorable picture. Silhouette's collaborators included Forbonnais and Jacob Nicolas Moreau, on whom see Moreau, *Mes Souvenirs*, ed. by Camille Hermelin (2 vols.; Paris, 1898-1901).

Honnêteté, probity, does not preclude at least the accusation of dishonesty, or rather of taking advantage of an office to line one's pockets. Lord Holdernesse's dispatches (British Library, Additional Mss. 6818, folios 92-95, Mar. 14, 1760) maintain that Silhouette made 50,000 l.t. while in office.

[41] [Mathon de la Cour], *Comptes-rendus*, 29, reproducing on pp. 29-45 Silhouette's memoir, which is the basis for the discussion that follows.

[42] *Ibid.*, 30.

[43] *Ibid.*, 31. Northamptonshire Record Office, Northampton, England, Fitzwilliam

Silhouette told the tale of financial woe with considerable drama, insofar as stories about numbers ever have drama, that is. For 1759, of which the fiscal year would close at the end of September, Silhouette predicted revenues of 286.6 million, expenditures of 503.8 million, and a deficit of 217.2 million. His predecessor, Boullongne, by omitting some expenses and projecting the immediate subscription of loans, had forecast a deficit of only 133 million. The situation was much worse, although Silhouette's rhetoric (more than his figures) leads to this conclusion. Silhouette portrayed the bottom line as the anticipation of future revenues: having found the *recettes générales* (that is, principally the *taille* and *capitation* revenues) for 1759 and part of 1760 consumed in anticipation, he had had no choice but to issue more *rescriptions*—short-term credit instruments issued in anticipation of revenues—on the revenues of 1760. The receivers general and the farmers general had also advanced money beyond the ordinary course of things. Together with spending arrears, these amounted to some 150 million over and above the anticipation of a full year's (1760) *recettes générales*. Every year for the remainder of the war it would be necessary to supplement revenues by about the same sum needed this year, 217 million. Silhouette foresaw a situation in which, when peace arrived, all the revenues would have been consumed in anticipation.

New loans seemed impossible because existing issues had not yet been filled, because prices on government securities were well below par, because with war specie had to be exported, and because some of the new loans had been issued without having specific revenue allotted to them for service and retirement. The public could see that without augmentation the revenues would not suffice to pay the debts. Like other eighteenth-century financial analysts, Silhouette drew back from the inflation of credit. The signs of an exhaustion of credit markets were signs of the need to alter policy.

Here is an innovation of two parts: a conservative approach on the part of government to monetary creation, and an unusually cautious view of credit. Earlier French governments had been willing to add directly to the money stock as a way of financing wars or, earlier still, to manipulate the money stock in order to increase seigniorage

Manuscripts, A.xxxii.22, gives some detail on Silhouette's projections of revenues and expenditures for 1759.

revenues. But Silhouette, like his predecessors in the War of Austrian Succession and the Seven Years War, drew back from such a step while, in the same breath, lamenting the tendency of war to draw specie abroad.[44] That is, men like Silhouette complained about the shrinkage of the money stock that war brought, while they also declined to restore the money thus drained in an intentional manner. (Silhouette did not see the *rescriptions* and other short-term credit instruments as money.)

The second element of innovation was a desire to preserve the sanctity of government credit. Previous governments had repudiated parts of their liabilities, but the mid-eighteenth-century financial authorities were loath to consider any repudiation not linked directly to overcharging by suppliers or fraud. Thus they continued to negotiate, or order, reductions on bills presented by war suppliers, but they declined to adopt other measures to reduce debt service costs. Silhouette had asserted this conservative policy in 1747,[45] well before he gained power or a position from which he might influence those with power. What was lacking in Silhouette's analysis was any recognition that a conservative monetary policy and the strict preservation of government credit had their own costs, which might exceed their benefits.

What was Silhouette's plan? It was to tax the rich. The king had already economized and set himself up as a model. The people of the countryside and all the other classes except the rich already paid too much in taxation. But "la prodigalité et le luxe . . . regnent encore dans les villes."[46] Therefore new taxes had to be levied on gold and silver plate and jewelry to be joined with inducements to convert plate into coin; on luxury items (e.g., domestic servants, carriages, silks); and on celibacy. But the principal reform that Silhouette projected was a *subvention proportionnelle*, a levy of 10 percent on certain property, payable half in cash and half in kind. "[O]n a pré-

[44] Pierre Clément and Alfred Lemoine, *M. de Silhouette, Bouret et les derniers fermiers généraux* (Paris, 1872), 63-64, relate that Silhouette rejected a plan submitted by the intendant of Flanders and Artois to issue *billets de circulation* to augment the money stock.

[45] Guillaumat-Vallet, *Silhouette,* 13.

[46] [Mathon de la Cour], *Comptes-rendus,* 38. Silhouette seems to have drawn most of the plan from Rousseau's 1755 article in the *Encyclopédie.* Jean Jacques Rousseau, "Political Economy," in Roger D. Masters, ed., *On the Social Contract,* trans. by Judith R. Masters (New York, 1978).

féré des voies de perception désirées depuis long-temps par les peuples, & dont l'essai, s'il réussit, conduira réellement à la réforme
d'abus qui contribuent à la surcharge [on other groups] autant &
peut-être plus que le fonds même de l'imposition."[47] Like so many
controllers general, Silhouette dreamed of a taxation "vraiment
juste & proportionnelle."[48] But these levies, and certain measures
designed to recall taxes previously alienated, would raise only some
48 million when the deficit was much larger.

Silhouette proposed also to create new honors (hereditary patents
of master status in gilds of commerce and artisanship), and offices
(receivers of *rentes*). He wished also to farm the new tax on carriages.
Together these measures would, he believed, raise a once-only figure of some 45 million (including an advance of 30 to 36 million for
the fifteen-year farm on carriages). After these programs had been
introduced, the lenders would see that their investments were secure and would subscribe outstanding loans to the full. The new
measures would produce 93 million, and the unfilled loans for the
second half of 1759, 60 million more. Supposing that peace would
be made in 1760, France would emerge from the war with an annual
surplus of 23 million, which would suffice to service subsequent
loans and pay off the anticipations. What is more, by 1769 the state
would be free to spend 43 million a year in debt repayment. The
people would be happy and prosperous.

It is difficult to see at once the full absurdity of this plan. One can
understand why the king ordered parts of it adopted in a *lit de justice*
on September 20, then had second thoughts, and withdrew the order. Silhouette may have had some reason to believe that the taxes
he proposed would produce the yields he suggested. He did not, in
his address to the king, discuss evidence. But his case is unpersua-
sive enough without reference to the reliability of these beliefs. Silhouette proposed to augment taxes by 48 million at a time when he
believed that annual war costs exceeded tax revenues (ordinary revenues plus the *vingtième*) by more than 200 million a year. And he
proposed to do this by taxing the people who sat on the king's councils and otherwise occupied positions of influence in the French government. That is, he proposed to abrogate the concept of taxation
paid in service, and to levy only taxes in cash (and kind).

[47] [Mathon de la Cour], *Comptes-rendus*, 39.
[48] *Ibid.*, 40.

Both the memoir and the response it received are unusually revealing. Let us notice first what Silhouette proposed indirectly—that the war should end in 1760. We cannot hold Silhouette or any other controller general responsible for failing to make this point in a less oblique way, or for the decision to continue the war. The task of the financial authorities was not to decide whether war could be afforded, but to explain how it could be funded.

What raised a cry of opposition to Silhouette's plan of reform was the opportunity it presented for the personnel of the parlements, the courtiers and ministers, and influential people in general to ally against the truly hapless Silhouette, who suffered the indignity of seeing his name pass into the vocabulary as a word designating the mere outline of a thing, superficial and empty.[49] That is neither surprising nor revealing. What is revealing is the list of assumptions and claims in the memoir that did not rouse any opposition, that represented orthodox opinion in 1759. In the first place, Silhouette believed taxation was so heavy that it forced the economy to languish.[50] Second, he believed that self-amortizing loans were preferable to perpetual annuities (that is, annuities whose redemption depends upon action by the state). Third, he believed that the anticipation of revenues had reached a critical point. Fourth, he rejected the short-term expedients used to finance the prior years of conflict but designed a group of measures whose effect depended upon a quick end to the war. Fifth, he believed that credit markets could be replenished if only lenders were reassured.

Each of these beliefs is in error, although the errors differ in gravity. About the first, taxation was increasing, but the economy was growing. About the second point, Silhouette, like so many other French financial authorities, saw the essential issue to lie in the amortization schedule rather than in the cost of servicing loans. Thus he did not call attention to the fact that the new life annuity loans and lotteries paid yields more than twice as high as the old life annuities, and that the government had already exhausted some of the possibilities of borrowing money by paying lenders much higher yields than could be obtained elsewhere. About point three, the ac-

[49] Moreau, *Mes souvenirs*, I, 60n1, explains that Silhouette "s'amusait à couvrir les murs de son château de ces dessins qui représentent un profil tracé d'après l'ombre d'un visage. De là le nom de leur auteur donné à ces sortes de dessins."

[50] [Mathon de la Cour], *Comptes-rendus*, 32 and 37.

cumulation of *rescriptions* had reached the levels Silhouette indicated. But this is not merely a sign that extraordinary revenues are flowing in more slowly than extraordinary expenditures are flowing out. It is an inevitable consequence of any rapid increase in the extraordinary account. War brings immediate spending needs that are funded by long-term credit, which is anticipated by short-term credit. One may decry the costliness of such procedures, but every country faces them. The growth of anticipations is first a signal of war itself and only secondarily of a financial pinch. Of course, Silhouette's diagnosis is accurate also. By 1759 the war had produced a financial pinch, and the government was exploiting short-term credit opportunities because it could not raise enough in long-term loans and had not yet resolved to augment taxes.

On point four, Silhouette failed to see the possibility that the desperate problems he detected in 1759-1760 might merely prefigure more severe problems should the war continue beyond 1760. And, on the last point, Silhouette imagined the existence of plentiful supplies of credit flowing forth, or not, merely on grounds of whether lenders believed in the long-run ability of the government to service its loans from existing revenues. There is much sense in this, if the public knows the scale of revenues and service charges. But these were matters of secrecy in old regime France. Even Silhouette's address to the king did not set them forth. (Thus foreign powers knew more about the finances than did the French people.) Silhouette's lack of realism on this point reveals his profound ignorance of finance. We can recognize the political naiveté and the courage of appealing to the rich to approve higher taxes without first securing the king's commitment. What we must also recognize is the simple-mindedness of the financial thought in this document, the simple-mindedness in terms of informed thinking in the eighteenth century.

Silhouette also confused the issue of money supply with the issue of credit costs, which, it must be admitted, was a common point of confusion. In his judgment money was tight because specie was flowing abroad, because loans had been issued too frequently, and because the public had lost confidence in the government's long-run ability to service its loans.[51] Credit costs may have been high, but money was not tight. Comparatively small wartime specie exports

[51] *Ibid.*, 36.

must be compared to quite large issues of money substitutes—the *rescriptions* are an example even if Silhouette did not see that.[52] Overall, the war brought a substantial but undetected increase in the money stock, together with a shift in its composition toward paper and a redistribution toward higher denominations most useable in restricted ways. Not all paper issued by the government was readily convertible into specie, and much of it was in denominations too large to be used in retail exchanges or for salary and wage payments. Nevertheless, this paper added to the money stock, if in a way that made high denomination means of payment in particular more common. What is not clear, on available evidence, is by how much the remaining specie stock plus the discounted specie value of new paper (plus all other monetary instruments) exceeded the prewar money stock.

And Silhouette failed to detect a transformation of extraordinary importance: war altered the nature of credit transactions. With every conflict, the French treasury, in peacetime a supplier of investment capital to capital markets, became a net borrower. In some conflicts the additions to the debt were small and could be accommodated with little change in existing credit terms. In the Seven Years War, however, France sought to borrow on an unprecedented scale.

Borrowing is financed from savings. In the eighteenth century French borrowers called on the savings of compatriots and foreigners alike. We do not know either the level of savings at home or the net flow of savings from abroad. But we know something about priorities: savers preferred to invest in what historians term proprietary or lineage wealth, wealth that could be handed down intact to later generations.[53] Such wealth took the form of land, dowries protected from consumption of the capital, offices, and some government securities. We presume also that many in the populace could not afford to save, and that a small part of the population provided most of the demand for these goods. And the sense of the

[52] Silhouette did not see, as Claude Dupin had argued in 1745 (*Œconomiques* [Paris, 1913 reprint], I, 138ff), that these credit instruments were money substitutes. He continued to define money in terms of specie.

[53] George V. Taylor, "Noncapitalist Wealth and the Origins of the French Revolution," *American Historical Review*, 72, no. 2 (Jan. 1967), 469-96; and Ralph E. Giesey, "Rules of Inheritance and Strategies of Mobility in Prerevolutionary France," *American Historical Review*, 82, no. 2 (Apr. 1977), 271-89.

scholarly literature is that the annual level of savings was not high. Perhaps it approached or exceeded 5 percent of national income. Whatever the case, a flow of savings into government loans on the scale required by the Seven Years War certainly demanded special inducements.

As Table 5.3 has established, somewhere between three-fifths and two-thirds of extraordinary spending during the war was financed by credit. The central government and its agents, including the farmers general, sought to borrow about 121 million l.t. a year in long-term loans during 1756-1762.[54] As a portion of estimated national output, public sector spending increased by more than half between 1752 and 1761—from 8-10 to 15-16 percent—and most of that increase came in the form of loans. Before the war the government, servicing and retiring loans, put 50 to 75 million a year into the hands of potential savers and lenders, and in most years borrowed little or nothing of that back. During the Seven Years War this contribution toward savings grew, but so did the demand for credit. Each year the treasury, by 1758 allotting at least 100 million to debt service, borrowed more than it put into the pockets of lenders (although the difference is difficult to establish because we lack running totals on debt service and any idea of what part of payments to lenders was available once again as credit). In addition to long-term borrowing, the government and its financiers sought short-term credit at a rate of perhaps 20 million a year. All of a sudden, the central government attempted to borrow each year about 5 percent of national agricultural and manufacturing output.[55] But the most significant feature of this demand was the treasury's shift from being a large net peacetime contributor to private savings, via interest payments that exceeded new borrowing, to being a large net wartime consumer of investment capital on French markets. Every war, but in particular this expensive conflict financed via credit, put extraordinary pressure on the capital markets. What is astonishing is that the markets could adjust as well as they did, meeting this demand, although of course at rising costs.

To his credit, Silhouette saw the need to increase taxes. But he proposed a peculiar assortment of levies that, moreover, would not

[54] That is, 788 plus 60.7 million divided by 7. See above, this chapter.

[55] This sum, 121 million plus 20 million, as a proportion of an output of some 3,000 million (see Table 5.5).

have raised enough money. In the final analysis, his goal was to raise enough from taxes and the sale of honors and offices to pry open the purses of lenders so that the war could continue to be financed by credit. The annual sum of these additional revenues, 48 million, amounted to less than the unfilled part of loans for the second half of 1759 alone, 60 million. As Dufort de Lagraulet, who probably hoped to take Silhouette's place, observed: "Toutes les opérations dernières annoncent beaucoup de charges sur les peuples, et peu de ressources dans les produits."[56]

Silhouette's plan is worth exploring because it represents not the worst form of French financial policy and insider thinking about finance, which tended to neglect the economic and financial consequences of fiscal decisions, and sometimes to recommend plans so absurd that they were seen even by inexpert observers to be ridiculous. Silhouette represents instead the reformist school, or rather one of the many of these schools. The notion of taxing the rich and curtailing tax avoidance is a recurrent feature of reformist thought. The shortcomings in this plan (aside from its political naiveté) are not peculiar to Silhouette. They are typical of ministerial thought, and a consequence of the French practice of staffing the financial ministry with people whose backgrounds and training had not prepared them to grapple successfully with public finance. Moreau de Séchelles, Peyrenc de Moras, Boullongne, and Silhouette (like Machault before them and Bertin after them) were jurists whose careers had begun as counseillers to the Parlements of Paris or Metz, or, in the case of Bertin, to the Grand Conseil. Silhouette had some exposure to banking and finance. He was the son of a *receveur des tailles*, and is said to have spent a year in London with a banker named Bénézet.[57] But neither he nor the others understood finance. Once in office they had to devote their time to mastering the intricate financial system in place in old regime France, a system that has so baffled historians that it is said to have been "muddled" and is likened to an "opium den."[58] Thus the archives are generous in

[56] Dufort de Lagraulet, "Observations sur les opérations de finance," Bibliothèque Mazarine, 2767, folio 41v.

[57] Clamageran, *Histoire de l'impôt*, III, 338-39.

[58] Respectively, John F. Bosher's review of Orville T. Murphy, *Charles Gravier, comte de Vergennes* in the *Journal of Modern History*, 56, no. 1 (Mar. 1984), 157; and George V. Taylor's review of John F. Bosher, *French Finances, 1770-1795* in the *Journal of Economic History*, 31, no. 4 (Dec. 1971), 949.

supplying introductory memorandums, presumably requested by new ministers. These French Catholics in the ministries did not have the opportunity to study money and finance, to learn about the often Protestant and alien world of banking described by Herbert Lüthy,[59] or the still largely theoretical world of monetary economics described by the eighteenth-century merchant Richard Cantillon.[60] Even the farmers general, if we judge from the contents of their personal libraries, read little or nothing on trade and finance, preferring history and literature.[61]

What is more, the long tenures of men with principal roles in the financial administration, even if with different formal titles, Fleury (1726-1743) and Machault (1745-1754), gave way to short tenures in office, a scheme which lasted until the end of the war and which forms an abrupt contrast with the apprenticeship time of bankers and financiers and with the tenure of French kings. In 1761 France began a second century in which the land was ruled by only two men, Louis XIV and Louis XV. Other than financial ministers might also come and go. But their tasks neither stirred the public imagination—they did not grapple each day with the forces of evil and deceit—nor figured so importantly in the survival of this organism, the warring state.

CONCLUSION

France could not afford in 1755 to fight the Seven Years War. But that fact, grasped by financial authorities in the midst of the war although not perhaps by the king, is a banal feature of old regime government finance. The monarchies, empires, and republics of Europe seldom could afford to fight their wars, but they fought them nevertheless. What removes this fact from the realm of things

[59] Herbert Luthy, *La banque protestante en France de la révocation de l'édit de Nantes à la Révolution* (2 vols.; Paris, 1959-1961). Forbonnais, Silhouette's adviser, made a point of the need to improve the economic and financial training of men of affairs. [François Véron Duverger de Forbonnais], *Mémoires et considérations sur le commerce et les finances d'Espagne . . .* (2 vols.; Amsterdam, 1764), II, pt. 2, 279, in a book first published in 1753.

[60] Richard Cantillon, *Essai sur la nature du commerce en général*, ed. and trans. by Henry Higgs (New York, 1964 reprint), written between 1730 and 1734, and first published in 1755.

[61] Yves Durand, *Finance et mécénat: les fermiers généraux au XVIIIᵉ siècle* (n.p., 1976), 270.

banal is the unforeseen costliness of the war. In 1751 Trudaine had
believed it reasonable to project that the next war would cost about
as much as the last war. But the next war cost more than twice as
much, on an annual basis, as the last war, some 189 to 225 million a
year instead of 90 to 100 million. The principal issue before us is not
the war, but the way in which the war was financed. France elected
to fund the Seven Years War by credit rather than by taxes. Only
after having nearly exhausted credit resources did the king order
substantial tax increases. Even Louis XV, secretive and timid, im-
perious but vacillating, was a political animal as well as an absolutist
monarch, and that becomes evident nowhere more starkly than in
his deferral of the inevitably unpopular tax increases.

New documents bring to light the costs of this war, insofar as
those were understood at the time. Undoubtedly the final audited
accounts, which have been destroyed or lost, would tell a slightly different story. They would certainly tell the story in figures exact to
the sou and denier. The more precise information they would provide would tell a harsher version of the story of deficits in the extraordinary account. But we are dealing with an extraordinary account of considerably more than 1,000 million l.t. so that it is
unnecessary to insist on too fine a point. Spending at the wartime
level—over 237 million in ordinary revenues plus some 37 million
in revenues of limited duration, 94 million in so-called revenues alienated in perpetuity, and an average of 189 million in extraordinary revenues—totalled nearly 560 million a year, a figure that still
does not include all government costs.[62]

The French believed that they paid an unreasonable burden of
taxes. Who is to say that their judgment was in error? Perhaps they
did pay more than the level optimally suited to growth in the agrarian economy of the middle eighteenth century. If we cannot determine that level today, how can we expect to determine it for an era
about which our statistical knowledge is defective? Presumably
agrarian economies using traditional technologies possess, in the
aggregate, a smaller ceiling to which public sector spending may rise
without harmful effects. In any event, the taxes did not become
more burdensome, as the rhetoric would lead us to believe, and
French arguments about the levels of taxation—which maintained

[62] It excludes, for example, the costs of the judicial courts, which since 1744 had
been sustained entirely by fees charged litigants.

that as much as one-third of income was taken in taxes—exaggerated shamefully. Furthermore, the part of national income or output taken in central government revenues seems to have declined between 1744 and 1765. The point is this: the French may have been overtaxed, as they said they were and as all people are wont to say is true. But the tax burden was neither as great as the critics claimed nor, in constant values or as a proportion of output, growing. The tax increases introduced by Fleury and Machault were not sustained by Machault's immediate successors except temporarily, in wartime levies.

The belief that his subjects were already overtaxed encouraged Louis XV to finance the war through credit. To manage an unprecedented series of loans, the king turned to a succession of controllers general. Each man came to this office without prior training in finance, and each gives no evidence of having known more than should have been learned from the management of family assets. Each remained in office for too short a period to become acquainted with the complexities of public finance. Each proposed his own solution to the increasingly grave financial problem. And each left office having contributed to the precariousness of the king's and the nation's finances, and having contributed also, we may speculate, to the king's confusion. It is difficult enough to understand finance if taught by a knowledgeable instructor. How much more difficult it must be for a man of average or less intelligence to learn anything from advisers who themselves do not grasp the issues clearly or well and who hold differing opinions about them.

In such circumstances who is to be blamed for the unwise policies that were adopted? Every individual and each group bears some responsibility. The king failed to demand more of his appointees and failed to heed his great-grandfather's advice: that he had loved war too much. The ministers themselves bear responsibility for failing to refuse commissions for which they were not competent and for promoting unworkable reforms. The articulate taxpayers bear the responsibility of complaining too bitterly about their burden and thus of limiting the freedom of action of their leaders. Let the burden rest among all these groups. We need only recall that the responsibility is borne by those who lost much in the subsequent fall of the monarchy as well as by those who gained. And neither saw the consequences of their actions.

CHAPTER 6

THE DEBT

*Enfin se libérer avec toute justice & toute décence des
dettes contractées jusqu'à ce jour, mais n'en plus faire de
nouvelles. . .*[1]

C ONVENTIONAL judgments about the defects in the finances
of old regime France need to be modified. The heart of the
problem lay not with the defects customarily identified: the inefficiency and costliness of the tax system (a motor for the greed of the
traitant), or tax avoidance linked to a social hierarchy founded on
privilege (a motor for social ambition in general). Nor did it lie, as
Michel Morineau has argued, with war.[2] Of course it is true that
inefficiency, privilege, and a taste for war were major problems. But
these characteristics stood at the heart of this government and society. To identify them as basic problems of the old regime is to call
for the transformation of the old regime and to beg the question of
how this regime ever got started and how it lasted as long as it did.
The strength of the old regime is to be found in its capacity, despite
inefficiencies and the fiscal costs of privilege, to augment the royal
revenues and for so long to prevent the debt from overtaking resources. During the eighteenth century, as is now apparent, the
long-run peacetime growth of the revenues was suspended at a critical moment, at the conclusion of the War of Austrian Succession.
At the same time, the financial authorities introduced new standards of fiscal behavior. They resolved that they would neither manipulate the money stock nor toy with the sanctity of public credit.
Everything was to be preserved as it was. These were the innova-
tions that undermined the royal finances. These were the innova-
tions that made the Seven Years War not merely a war that cost too
much but also a war whose excessive costs would burden the mon-

---

[1] [Nicolas Baudeau], *Idées d'un citoyen sur l'administration des finances du roi* (Amsterdam, 1763), 2.

[2] Michel Morineau, "Budgets de l'état et gestion des finances royales en France au
dix-huitième siècle," *Revue historique*, 264, no. 2 (1980), 316-17.

archy beyond recovery. To see why this is so, it is necessary to look more closely at the French debt and its management.

One of the accusations against the old regime monarchy arises from its tendency to resort to large financial write-offs, a tendency repeatedly evident in the seventeenth century and last seen, before the collapse of the monarchy, in the period between 1715 and 1725. State bankruptcies are generally disapproved, and historians talk knowingly of the instability that such measures reveal. They say that it is a sign of growth toward political maturity that the eighteenth-century French monarchy did not, after the Law system, indulge in large write-offs, only in small. Like historians, the eighteenth-century monarchy came to be persuaded of the undesirability of large financial write-offs. Moreover, it was eighteenth-century critics who first levelled the accusations about privilege and inefficiency that constitute the main themes of the conventional case against the financial policy followed by the monarchy: it is a good thing that debts were no longer repudiated in a big way, but a bad thing (for the monarchy) that so much of what the people paid, or should have paid, was lost before reaching the royal treasury.

If it is wise to concede the principle that large financial write-offs are disruptive, it is necessary also to recognize that failing to indulge in them may be yet costlier and more disruptive. Let us not be unduly influenced by the charges made by eighteenth-century critics of financial policy, or by what only appear to be profound truths. Let us take up Mathon de la Cour's advice and bring under scrutiny the information we have about the royal accounts in order that we may expose those popular ideas that are ill informed and unjust.[3] And let us look at how the other states of Europe managed their debts, to see whether France, in introducing a strict and conservative policy of monetary creation and debt management, deviated from practice elsewhere.

Debt Management

French financial authorities often found it necessary to borrow.[4] A

[3] [Mathon de la Cour], *Collection de comptes-rendus* . . . (Lausanne, 1788), iv. C.-J. Mathon de la Cour, who was guillotined in 1793, wrote learned analyses on many of the questions about which eighteenth-century readers were most curious, such as wet nursing, compound interest, bread costs, and patriotism. He also edited the *Journal de Lyon*.

[4] We can, however, reject Geoffrey Parker's claim ("The Emergence of Modern Fi-

manuscript in the Bibliothèque de l'Arsenal, which reconstructs revenues and expenditures during 1712, 1722, 1734, 1739, and 1740, reveals deficits in 1712 and 1722 and surpluses in the other years. But the deficits were larger than the surpluses, so for these five years, which include years of peace and war, deficits totalled nearly 25 million.[5] Moreover, revenues included credit. That France often borrowed makes it typical among eighteenth-century states, which found expenditures rising ahead of revenues and which preferred to borrow rather than to accumulate war chests, as France had done in the era of Henri IV and Sully but as Prussia alone still did.[6] In France at the middle of the eighteenth century the debt still included liabilities dating from the reign of Louis XIV, which had ended in 1715, this despite the massive write-offs of the regency (1715-1723). Since most of the eighteenth century was an era of price inflation, rising nominal expenditures did not always mean rising real expenditures. But revenues often evaded the effects of inflation so that they rose more slowly, creating deficits. And among the structural causes of deficits, it is necessary to mention a second time the tendency of public authorities to allow the range and costs of their ambitions to grow. Even under Louis XV, who to present-day eyes possessed so few admirable traits, the French state experienced significant growth and took on a number of new responsibilities.

What is more important than the act of borrowing is the manner. In a period in which other states were changing loan formats and practices, France also was adopting reforms. Elsewhere the reforms brought less expensive modes of borrowing in something that can be categorized as a financial revolution. The revolution had two forms, one Dutch and the other Swedish. The Dutch form introduced a shift away from amortization-plus-interest loans (such as

nance in Europe, 1500-1730," in Carlo M. Cipolla, ed., *The Fontana Economic History of Europe* [n.p., 1974], II, 575) that the only surpluses between 1610 and 1789 are to be found during 1662-1671.

[5] Bibliothèque de l'Arsenal, Paris, 4489, folio 74, summarizing accounts discussed in previous folios. This document combines material recorded at very different periods. The *états* in Det Kongelige Bibliotek, Copenhagen, Manuscript Department, Ny kgl. S. 495(c) and (d), provide more complete information on final revenues and expenditures in these and other years.

[6] James C. Riley, *International Government Finance and the Amsterdam Capital Market, 1740-1815* (Cambridge, 1980), 101-118.

the life annuity) and toward interest-only loans (such as the perpetual annuity). Such loans increased the amount of indebtedness that could be carried from the same level of expenditures because they eliminated or reduced allocations for the repayment of principal, and they did this at a time when nominal interest rates were falling. During periods of inflation the price trend acts as a tax on holders of government securities; and Dutch credit policy, introduced during the seventeenth-century deflation when it was difficult to afford to retire debts, took full advantage of eighteenth-century inflation. The Dutch debt, which to a far greater extent even than the French debt had been amassed during the seventeenth century, would be "repaid" by the erosion of its value rather than by the retirement of principal.

Swedish policy took a different path, one that appealed to states lacking well-developed capital markets and internal credit resources sufficient to cover government deficits. Unable to borrow through the sale of interest-bearing securities, these states turned, as France did under John Law, to paper currency issues. Such a means of covering deficits was cost-free in financial terms—it involved no service payments and nearly insignificant material and labor costs—but not in economic terms, for it could promote inflation, even hyperinflation. Both the Dutch and the Swedish modes of financial reform increased the government's ability to spend. The economic rationale that informed them posited that an enlarged money stock, which each policy fostered in its own way, would act as an economic motor, fostering prosperity and taxability.[7]

---

[7] This section draws on ibid., *passim*, esp. 119-94. Examples of this rationale may be found in Claude Dupin, *Œconomiques* (Paris, 1913 reprint), I, 138-43; and Bibliothèque Nationale, Paris, Joly de Fleury, 1079, no. 23. Actual economic consequences are more difficult to specify. Mercantilist thought about the benefits of increasing the money stock share much with present-day monetarist theory, which recommends a controlled and gradual increase in the money stock as a means of fostering growth without inviting excessive inflation. Mercantilist thought did not distinguish a boundary between moderate and excessive monetary growth, and where mercantilist policies were followed, especially in Sweden, it is possible to find periods of economic turmoil caused by this monetary policy. Less can be said, however, about the economic consequences of a shift from debt amortizations to interest-only debt servicing, that is, the financial revolution in its Dutch form (which was adopted also by Britain). If lenders were predominantly wealthy, and if their propensity to save was influenced by the reduction in income following an end to amortization payments, then one might postulate a large decline in savings levels and thus in the capacity of

France also reorganized its debt. In 1721, in the aftermath of the Mississippi Bubble collapse and during a decade of extraordinarily low interest rates, the perpetual annuity yield was cut in half—thus to the 32.7 million paid in 1722 (Table 6.1). The sum of *rentes* paid

TABLE 6.1
Expenditures on Loan Service
(millions of l.t.)

	1712	*1722*	*1734*	*1739*	*1740*[b]
Perpetual annuities	65.4	32.7	30.5	29.2	28.5
Life annuities	—[a]	34.1	29.0	22.1	20.4
TOTALS	65.4	66.8	59.5	51.3	48.9
Percentage for perpetual annuities	100[a]	49	51	57	58

SOURCE: Bibliothèque de l'Arsenal, Paris, 4489, folios 65v and 66r.
[a] The life annuity loans of 1702 and 1704 and the tontines are omitted without explanation.
[b] For 1740 these figures are prospective rather than retrospective, since internal evidence indicates that the document was drafted during the financial year 1740.

each year thereafter to service the interest-only loans declined gradually as some contracts were ceded to the king.[8] What is especially worth noticing here is the degree to which the settlement of the Law system involved a conversion of the debt to lower yields. Other states, including the Dutch Republic in the 1670s and the Dutch Admiralties in 1738, and Britain in 1717, again between 1727 and 1730, and from 1749, had discerned the secular trend of nominal interest rates, which was downward, in keeping with the secular deflation of prices from the middle to the end of the seventeenth century, and they converted debt liabilities to lower yields. In France nominal interest rates also declined; they were unusually low during the 1720s, as creditors, threatened by an explosion in the monetary stock under Law, sought to persuade debtors not to pay off debts in devalued currency.[9] In effect, therefore, the royal purse benefited

the economy to finance capital improvements, such as in mining or commerce, or to finance government borrowing.
[8] For example, in 1727 and 1730 perpetual annuities were ceded in connection with the creation of new offices paid for partly in cash and partly in securities.
[9] This trend is not evident in Chart 1.2 above or Table 6.2 below, but does appear from authorities cited in n. 59, Chapter 1.

from a massive write-down of both the scale of the debt and the cost of servicing it, a write-down obscured in Table 6.1 by the omission in the sources of certain information from before 1722.

At the same time, France continued to reduce the silver equivalent of its money of account, the livre tournois. Imagine a land in which the money stock consists of gold and silver coins carrying names but no designations of value in the money of account, livres tournois. Once that picture exists, it is easy to step further to imagine a land in which the money of account value of each coin can be altered at will, as long as the sovereign possesses the rights of minting coins, called seigniorage, and can induce or compel people to respond to decrees changing the official value of coins (whose precious metal content may also be revised through reminting). Between 1690 and 1726 French authorities repeatedly ordered changes in the gold and silver equivalent of the livre tournois, the money of account. To consider only the case of silver, which is the more important because of the greater use of silver coins in payments, the equivalent of the livre in grams of fine silver declined from 8.33 grams in 1689 to 4.45 grams from the end of 1726 onward. In this way, old debts were transformed into cheaper liabilities to any degree that the debt could be evaluated in foreign currencies (and thus in terms of international financial flows and France's large and continuing surplus on current account).[10] Of course, the taxpayer (as opposed to the merchant or banker) hardly noticed the transition from a livre equivalent to 8.33 grams of silver to one equivalent to 4.45 grams because the taxes were collected in the money of account, not in silver weights. In terms of silver, the scaling down of the livre cost the government revenues, but the government too paid its liabilities in the money of account. After 1726, when the silver equivalent was stabilized, to be preserved with only negligible changes until well into the twentieth century, any retirement of debt would occur at values that were significantly lower in international terms. To the degree that the debt was owned by the French, retirements remained a domestic transaction. Where a large savings to the treasury is evident is from its capacity after 1726 to augment revenues.

After 1726 the financial authorities settled down to a period of gradual debt retirement, which is evident from Table 6.1. Liabilities

[10] See Chapter 1.

scaled down in a large way in 1721 were gradually diminished, for the most part by the death of nominees in life annuity loans, and thus the extinction of the principal behind those advances.[11] The habit of earlier monarchs of financing deficits by creating offices to sell, or by forcing current officeholders to pay a larger *finance*, gave way under Louis XV to greater reliance on voluntary loans. In the process the monarchy turned less and less often to an exploitation of the dependent position of the officers, which took the form of arbitrary reductions in the *gages* or returns paid on the *finance* or purchase price of offices,[12] and turned more and more to voluntary loans. In the meantime certain characteristic usages went unchanged. To finance the gap between revenues and expenditures, the ministries continued to employ tax farmers, receivers, and court bankers—Jean Paris de Montmartel, later Jean Joseph Laborde and Beaujon, Goossens—to provide short-term credit.[13] The controllers general handled the larger and more important long-term credit program.

When Machault came to the controller general's post in 1745, he revived that fiercely sincere but short-lived conviction in the urgency of debt reimbursement which strikes financial authorities from time to time, and which had last struck French authorities in 1725.[14] Marion writes of "le culte de l'amortissement"[15] that seized

[11] In the settlement of the Law system the *billets de banque* were reimbursed in life annuities bearing a *rente* of 4 percent. Between 1720 and 1724, 400 million were issued, more or less at the customary rate of twice the level of long-term annuities because interest rates were then so low. Some additions to this part of the debt occurred also in the tontines created in 1733 and 1734 to help finance the fight against Spain and Sardinia in the War of Polish Succession, and because the royal lottery begun in 1727 to help retire the perpetual annuity debt paid prizes in life annuities.

[12] E.g., in 1744 a 20.6 million augmentation of the *finance* on certain offices was adopted, with a yield of 5 percent. To fund the 1.03 million more in *gages*, all *offices gagés* were required from 1747 and 1748 to pay 10 percent surcharges on both the *capitation* and the *dixième*. Algemeen Rijksarchief, The Hague, Legatiearchief, Eerste Afdeling, Frankrijk, 776.

[13] See Yves-René Durand, "Mémoires de Jean-Joseph de Laborde, banquier de la cour et fermier général," *Annuaire-Bulletin de la Société de l'histoire de France* (1968-1969), esp. 92-98.

[14] Bibliothèque Nationale, Joly de Fleury, 1432, folio 181v. Also Marcel Marion, *Machault d'Arnouville: Etude sur l'histoire du contrôle général des finances de 1749 à 1754* (Paris, 1891), 367-68; and Henri de Jouvencel, *Le contrôleur général des finances sous l'ancien régime* (Paris, 1901), 159-60.

[15] Marion, *Machault*, 368. Also Maurice Morel, "Les caisses d'amortissement au XVIIIᵉ siècle," *Revue historique de droit français et étranger*, 4th ser., 5 (1926), 476-500, esp. 482.

everyone at mid-century, a cult to which belonged the tax farmer Naveau,[16] the economic writer Forbonnais,[17] the ambitious promoter Dufort de Lagraulet,[18] and many others. But there is more to this than a conviction that the debt had to be repaid, which is not an extraordinary sentiment. At the center of the world of French financial management the authorities were swept up in an intensification of caution. They were loath to consider any proposal that added to the risks of monetary or fiscal distress. Dufort, who wished to join this world, expressed the feeling in 1759: "j'ai pour principe que toute opération de finance qui fomentera les convulsions de la bourse sera toujours nuisible à l'Etat."[19] Imagine a financial policy so steady that it leaves no repercussions on the bourse, where government and private securities are exchanged, and which exists, as a location for speculation, only if prices fluctuate.

Machault could not act immediately on the central feature of this program of caution, amortization of the debt, because of the War of Austrian Succession. But at the conclusion of that conflict he designed an ambitious program of debt conversion and reimbursement. All the world has applauded this program, but unjustly.

Machault urged the adoption of four measures: 1) retrenchments of some 10 million livres a year; 2) the allocation of revenues totalling nearly 36 million a year, provided principally from the continuation of the *dixième* in peacetime as a *vingtième*, to a *caisse d'amortissement*; 3) a low interest loan of 12 million, arranged at the end of 1753, to cover the net deficit of 1750-1753;[20] and 4) the conversion of the debt to life annuities.[21] Historians have applauded this design

[16] [Jean-Baptiste Naveau], *Le financier citoyen* (2 vols.; [Paris], 1757), I, 413-14 and 423-24, and II, 76-77 and *passim*.

[17] [François Véron Duverger de Forbonnais], *Mémoires et considérations sur le commerce et les finances d'Espagne . . .* (2 vols.; Amsterdam, 1764), II, pt. 2, 72-80 (first published in 1753).

[18] An obscure individual who left a long series of manuscripts available now in the Bibliothèque Mazarine, Paris, 2767, Dufort may be the individual mentioned unfavorably in J. N. Dufort de Cheverny, *Mémoires sur les règnes de Louis XV et Louis XVI et sur la Révolution*, ed. by Robert de Crèvecoeur (2 vols.; Paris, 1886), I, 12-13 and 254.

[19] Bibliothèque Mazarine, 2767, folio 16r. I do not know anything about who read Dufort's memorandums, but it is worth noting that already in October 1759 he urged the nullification of Silhouette's tax reform program (folio 42v).

[20] Secured on revenues from the farm of gunpowder and saltpeter taxes, this loan paid less than 5 percent interest. Algemeen Rijksarchief, The Hague, Archief Fagel, 1566.

[21] Machault wanted to begin retiring both the interest-bearing and the non-interest-bearing debt, the latter composed of venal offices in the judiciary that he deemed

to pay off the debt, but the central element of the project, and its principal defect, lies in the idea of repressing the perpetual annuities by converting them, during a twenty-year transition period, into life annuities.[22]

Why is this so? Machault wanted to reimburse the perpetual annuities, which typically paid a yield of 5 percent, with life annuities, which, in the loans issued since 1737, had typically paid a yield of 10 percent. At a time when interest rates were falling, Machault proposed to *increase* the interest paid on the debt. To explain the intricacies of this, it is necessary to explore both the prevailing interest rate and the portion of the *rente* in a life annuity that may be considered interest.

As has been remarked already, French law prohibited charging interest in private transactions in most of the realm. But the government was not bound by this law, and private individuals evaded it by charging *rente* rather than interest. As a handy way of construing the principal behind outstanding debts, because the laws on private contracts set a maximum *rente* level of 5 percent, and perhaps for other reasons too, French authorities considered 5 percent to be the customary yield of interest-only loans, like the perpetual annuities. They set the yield of the life annuities at twice that level, accepting an old rule-of-thumb device. Thus the authorities assumed that public sector interest rates in France were invariable in the short and medium run, at 5 percent, and that a doubling of this return provided a fair yield for life annuity contracts. Neither assumption was justified. Private sector rates varied considerably in the short and long run, and in the 1750s were lower than at any time since the 1720s. They may have been no more than 3 percent for certain transactions, and many authorities mention private sector rates of 3 to 4 percent.[23]

---

unnecessary and of 185.76 million in arrears on the payment of salaries and pensions. See Algemeen Rijksarchief, Fagel, 1567 on this item, and 1566 on Machault's plan in general. Also Algemeen Rijksarchief, Legatie, 788, pp. 58-59; and Bibliothèque de l'Arsenal, 4063, pp. 151ff.

[22] Algemeen Rijksarchief, Legatie, 786, pp. 68-69; and 779.

[23] Emmanuel Le Roy Ladurie, *Les paysans de Languedoc* (2 vols.; Paris, 1966), II, 1,024-1,025; Anon., "Lettre d'un Hollandois . . . ," *Journal de commerce* (Brussels) (Jan. 1759), 117; Marion, *Machault*, 385-87; and [Simon] Clicquot [de] Blervache, *Dissertations sur les effets que produit le taux de l'intérest de l'argent, sur le commerce et l'agriculture* (Amiens, 1755), 52n.

Table 6.2 attempts to estimate the difference between yields in the private and public sectors using the assumption made by public authorities—that 5 percent was an appropriate yield—and one sample of interest charged in *rentes constituées*.[24] It suggests that in the 1740s and 1750s public loans offered a 1.8 to 2 percent premium in nominal yield over private sector loans, a premium higher than that given earlier or later. That is, private sector interest rates were declining, but the financial authorities, led by Machault, continued to regard 5 percent as an appropriate return from old and new government perpetual annuities. Even though observers of government practice judged the appeal of royal issues in comparison to returns in the private sector of French capital markets,[25] and therefore did not demand a fixed rate, merely a certain differential between the two, the financial authorities adhered to the 5 percent convention.

TABLE 6.2

Private and Public Sector Interest Rates in France, 1720-1769

	nominal rates		decennial average expected rate of inflation	real rates	
	private	public		private	public
1720-1729	3.6	5	—	—	—
1730-1739	3.5	5	—	—	—
1740-1749	3.2	5	1.4	1.8	3.6
1750-1759	3.0	5	0.4	2.6	4.6
1760-1769	4.3	5	1.8	2.5	3.2

SOURCE: Table 1.3.

Today we possess a different view of price change than prevailed in the eighteenth century. Our view is informed not only by impressionistic testimony but also by official measurements. In the eighteenth century impressions counted more, and few people made an attempt to measure price change. Thus it is this difference in nom-

[24] Public sector rates are assumed to have remained at 5 percent, the yield most often stated to be in use in new loans and the rate used in official calculations. Price changes, calculated on an annual basis from data supplied by Ernest Labrousse, "Les 'bon prix' agricoles du XVIIIᵉ siècle," in Fernand Braudel and Ernest Labrousse, eds., *Histoire économique et sociale de la France* (Paris, 1970), II, 387, are decennial averages of the expected rate of inflation, which is defined as the average price change experience in the prior three years.

[25] E.g., Algemeen Rijksarchief, Fagel, 1566, Dec. 1753, on the 12 million l.t. loan.

inal rates that people noticed first. Nevertheless, the French were
alive to the existence of a price trend, even if they lacked the statistical tools to measure it. It is not clear how this appreciation expressed itself in portfolio management, but the sources leave us in
no doubt that many people sensed the difference between nominal
and real yields. If we add our way of measuring this difference to
the analysis, we see that there too the large gap between private and
public sector yields was preserved. Real yields on perpetual annuities peaked in the 1750s, at which time the treasury was paying a real
return of 4.6 percent, exceptionally generous by eighteenth-century standards. And the treasury was paying this yield on the *cheap-
est* portion of the debt.

This was the best of all possible moments for a reduction in the
yield of French securities, in duplication of what other powers had
done and of what France itself had done in the Law settlement. The
War of Austrian Succession had ended, thus France had made the
customary shift from net consumer to net supplier of investment
capital to the markets. The real interest rate peaked between 1750
and 1756. A conversion at this moment would have brought large
savings in debt service, savings that might have been applied to a far
more rapid reimbursement of the debt than Machault's plan allowed. A reduction of the standard yield from 5 to 4 percent, which
would have left French annuities at a premium over both the *rentes
constituées* of the private sector and the yield of Dutch and British
government loans, would nevertheless have saved the treasury 20
percent or more of the approximately 70 million paid in 1753 in
debt service. Then and at other times such a conversion operation
was proposed, and discussed in council, but not adopted.[26] Nor did
the authorities take up any of the proposals to follow a Swedish style
response of converting debt into paper currency. In 1747 one Gou-

[26] E.g., by Dufort de Lagraulet in 1754 (Bibliothèque Mazarine, 2767, folio 85r).
Anon., "Lettre d'un Hollandois . . . ," 117, remarked upon the opportunity and supposed that it had been missed because the government was reluctant to offer to reimburse all notes for fear that too many holders would opt for reimbursement rather
than conversion. Also the translator of David Hume, *Essais sur le commerce . . .* (Paris,
1767), 121-23. It is worth noticing that the *pays d'état* usually paid 5 percent for wartime loans and converted these to 4 percent yields in peace, when interest rates fell.
Marcel Marion, *Histoire financière de la France* (5 vols.; Paris, 1927-1928), I, 47-48. In
1763 the Danish minister reported court discussion of an interest reduction. Rigsar-
kivet, Copenhagen, Ges. Arkiv, Frankrig B, 855, May 13, 1763.

vion Darmentiers suggested that the perpetual annuities be transformed into *contrats mobiliers* paying 5 percent interest and circulating in the same manner as specie; and in 1745 Claude Dupin, a tax receiver and farmer general, recommended a simple conversion of part of the debt into paper currency, a suggestion made also by the physiocrat Nicolas Baudeau and chevalier de Forbin, a mathematician, soldier, and military theorist.[27] But neither form appealed to the authorities. Moreover, Machault's program, which shifted emphasis toward voluntary loans and away from the exploitation of officeholders, sacrificed the *gages* of 4 percent or less paid venal officers for open market loans paying 5 to 10 percent. Thus, while other governments shifted away from interest-plus-amortization toward interest-only loans, or toward answering the mercantilist's cry for an enlarged money supply by issuing fiat money, France moved in the opposite direction.

What, more exactly, were the additional costs involved in this shift from perpetual to life annuities? The life annuities paid yields ranging from the denier 25, or 4 percent, on Law system settlements to the denier 12 (8.33 percent) on prizes from the royal lotteries and to the denier 10 (10 percent) on loans issued from 1737 to 1751.[28] It is appropriate, of course, that the interest-plus-amortization loan yields should have been higher than the interest-only yields. But how much higher?

Other governments, in particular central and municipal authorities in the Dutch Republic and Britain, stopped issuing life annuity and tontine loans because they learned in the latter decades of the seventeenth century that even when returns were scaled down to adjust for the youthful age of nominees—the nominee is the person at whose death the principal was extinguished—traditional yields had been excessively generous.[29] They learned this because they were instructed by probabilists in a new mathematical technology, mathematical expectation. Using compound interest tables and evi-

[27] Bibliothèque Nationale, Joly de Fleury, 1079, no. 23; [Dupin], *Œconomiques*, I, 138-43; [Gaspard François Anne de] F[orbin], *Système d'imposition et de liquidation de dettes d'état . . .* (n.p., 1763), 105ff.; and [Baudeau], *Idées d'un citoyen*, 106-123.

[28] Bibliothèque de l'Arsenal, 4489; and, on the yield of 1737 and 1739 loans, Marion, *Histoire financière*, I, 472.

[29] The section that follows draws on George Alter and James C. Riley, "How to Bet on Lives: A Guide to Life Contingent Contracts in Early Modern Europe," forthcoming, *Research in Economic History* (1986).

dence about life expectation, Johan de Witt in the 1670s and Edmund Halley in the 1690s calculated what the fair yield of a life annuity should be when ordinary loans were paying a certain interest rate and when nominees of different ages were selected. De Witt recognized that for various reasons, lenders would not be willing to invest in a completely "fair" life annuity and would demand a slight premium to invest in such loans. But the life annuities that Dutch authorities issued usually paid twice the yield of perpetual annuities, a premium far in excess of what lenders required. Thus in 1671 De Witt urged that the yield in life annuity loans be reduced. In practice such a reduction was difficult to accomplish because lenders were accustomed to high yields, did not fully understand this arcane and intricate mathematics, and preferred to lend in perpetual annuities rather than reduced-yield life annuities. As a result in the Dutch Republic, and somewhat later in Britain, the life annuity and tontine format went out of use.

French financial authorities were inept in mathematics and failed to learn what Dutch and British predecessors had about the actual costs of life annuity loans. Drawn almost exclusively from the ranks of men trained in law, and thus from a pool of people who had little or no training in the mathematics of probability and who, moreover, were not adept in banking and finance, French officials did not have access even to the kind of secondhand information about such issues that undoubtedly guided most borrowers and lenders, who also did not know probability but who heard about how experts applied their insights.

Both this ineptness and the potentially low interest rates available to the government are evident in a loan format used by the monarchy between 1742 and 1751. In those years five *rentes passagères* were created, *rentes passagères* being loans in which the service was distributed between interest and amortization. Thus in 1746 a 12 million l.t. loan was issued for a term of fifteen years, to be retired by annual payments of 600,000 l.t. plus an equal sum for interest. Financial authorities claimed that the first four of these issues paid 5 percent yields, and the last 3 percent—another sign of the favorable opportunity around 1750 for low yield loans.[30] These figures they derived apparently by dividing the first year's interest payment by the amount of the loan. In fact, however, the self-extinguishing

[30] Algemeen Rijksarchief, Legatie, 784.

character of these loans requires a slightly more complex computation to figure the interest rate. From the perspective of the government these loans actually paid the following yields:

creation	stated yield	actual yield
1742	5 percent	5.6 percent
1746	5	5.6
1747	5	5.6
1749	5	4.7
1751	3	negligible

The deviations are not large, especially in cumulative terms. But they demonstrate unfamiliarity with the mathematics of finance in what is a comparatively simple problem that merchants and bankers regularly faced, the problem of calculating interest on a diminishing balance, and which merchants and bankers solved (if they could not make the calculations themselves) by referring to financial manuals.[31] In the case of the life annuities, the same ineptness produced large and costly errors.

What gives these errors away to us, and might be expected to have given them away to the financial authorities, was the very public taste for life annuities upon which the authorities remarked,[32] a taste that shows up in the rapid subscription of these loans.[33] Even if they could not usually repeat the mathematical procedures followed by De Witt, Halley, and most recently, in 1746, by the French probabilist Antoine Deparcieux in *Essai sur les probabilités de la durée de la vie humaine*, investors could detect the superior yield of the life annuity loans.

Calculating how much of the *rente* in a life annuity is interest and how much the amortization of principal requires some assumptions about life expectation. Alter and Riley have tested and applied a model table of life expectation to estimate these values, finding that, consciously or unconsciously, authorities assumed unrealistically low life expectancies. By predicting low values for the number of

[31] This situation also trapped J[ean]-J[ules] Clamageran, *Histoire de l'impôt en France* (3 vols.; Paris, 1867-1876), III, 319, into arguing that the slow placement of the 1751 issue is a sign of the government's weak credit. It is instead a consequence of the negligible yield.

[32] Algemeen Rijksarchief, Fagel, 1571, p. 47.

[33] Bibliothèque de l'Arsenal, 4063, p. 123, compares the early subscription record of two December 1746 loans with the July 1747 life annuity.

years that nominees would survive, the authorities inferred that a fair return would consist of a *rente* twice the level of the prevailing interest rate, 5 percent. Thus France continued, in all nine life annuity loans issued between 1737 and 1751, to use the rule-of-thumb for setting life annuity yields that De Witt had rejected in 1671.[34]

In fact the annual *rente* did not need to be doubled. If the treasury was correct in assuming that an interest-only loan would have cost 5 percent, then a life annuity yield of some 6.3 percent would have provided a fair return to investors—that is, would have paid 5 percent interest plus amortization at realistic life expectancies.[35] A small additional yield would compensate investors for the risk that individual nominees would die young, a cost that by itself should have made the life annuity format unattractive to France. Even taking this into account, the treasury paid in life annuity loans a yield about a half greater than necessary, 10 percent rather than slightly more than 6.3 percent, providing lenders with windfall earnings.[36] In this way French officials vastly increased the cost of servicing the debt without adding a sou to redemption, since none of the excess in any way reduced the size of the government's liability.[37] This is the defect in Machault's plan, and the reason that this plan should be condemned rather than applauded.

[34] Earlier French life annuities paid lower nominal returns but were bound up with the settlement of the Law system. Their actual returns are difficult to calculate because it is difficult to fix the value of the paper taken in exchange for new life annuities during 1720-1724.

[35] Since the expected utility of a large pay-off will, in proportion, be less than the expected utility of a small pay-off, and because lenders will be more sensitive to the risks of nominee death than will borrowers, investors will have been (and were) risk averse, demanding somewhat higher yields than those associated with a "fair wager" in which buyer and seller would break even.

[36] This calculation uses Alter and Riley, "How to Bet on Lives," table A7b, and assumes an average age of all nominees of seventeen, which is a high figure based upon the average ages of nominees in a 1771 loan rather than upon the lower average age of nominees in other loans. This rather high average age figure has the effect of reducing my estimate of the size of error made by French authorities.

[37] Nor did this policy achieve any of the economic benefits associated with mercantilist financial policy. The life annuity contracts were not readily negotiable, because tied to the life expectation of the nominee, and thus did not add as effectively to the money stock as did perpetual annuity notes. France's money stock expanded during this period—the 1720s, 1730s, and 1740s—but for other reasons. Hypothetically, the government's unwitting decision to pay an excessive interest in life annuities shifted income from taxpayers in general to the rich, and thus into the hands of people likelier to save and invest. It is possible, therefore, that this program contributed to

The Scale of the Debt

The French debt was unnecessarily costly to service. But how large was it on the eve of the Seven Years War? One of the manuscripts found in The Hague gives a summary of crown/state debts as of January 1, 1753, and other sources provide additional information.[38] Table 6.3 summarizes this document.[39]

This is one way to present the debt, and is a version faithful to a narrow view of the magnitude of the long-term debt. It recognizes

TABLE 6.3
The French Debt as of January 1, 1753
(in millions of l.t.)

	interest	principal
Perpetual annuities	26.15	523.0
31,000 Compagnie des Indes shares sustained by the king	2.48[a]	49.6
Royal debt to Compagnie des Indes	2.35	47.0
Charges et offices comptables	10.0	200.0
Rentes passagères	—[b]	—[c]
Life annuities	—[b]	—[c]
TOTALS	40.98	819.6[d]

SOURCE: Algemeen Rijksarchief, The Hague, Legatiearchief, Eerste Afdeling, Frankrijk, 784.
[a] Dividend.
[b] The amount given in the schedule combines interest and amortization.
[c] No principal was calculated for the *rentes passagères* or life annuities
[d] Excluding the principal of the life annuities and *rentes passagères*

French economic growth, and especially to commercial, mining, and industrial expansion, which required investments in capital equipment. It may also have tended to reduce interest rates in the private sector.

[38] Algemeen Rijksarchief, Legatie, 784. Also Legatie, 783; and Fagel, 1567 and 1571. According to these sources, royal debt *états* had been prepared each year since 1740 in which any change occurred.

[39] The royal debt to the Compagnie des Indes charged to the company before 1752 was assumed by the king. Algemeen Rijksarchief, Fagel, 1571: "La Compagnie des Indes est le Roi . . . ," which reflects the role of the company and its predecessors in borrowing from the public to lend to the king. These figures reflect earlier reductions in debt principal, such as the 1721 consolidation that lowered the reimbursement value of perpetual annuities by half. In the standard form, applied in 1721 and at other times, the yield was reduced. Then the government applied the standard 5 percent rate to revalue the principal, cutting it in half and restoring the original yield. The documents refer sometimes to crown and at other times to state debts. Fagel, 1571, p. 138, provides a distinction according to which some debts concerned the king directly and others were owed by the state.

the annual interest-plus-amortization payments on the life annuities, 19.54 million, and *rentes passagères*, 8 million, which increased annual service to a figure of 68.52 million, or 58.52 million excluding the small body of offices included here. But some categories of debt are omitted from this schedule; they appear in Table 6.4. Taking this larger view, therefore, the long-term debt of the state early in 1753 totalled not 820 million but more than 1,200 million, excluding still the unpaid balance on life annuities and *rentes passagères* and a large portion of the venal offices. The annual charges totalled not 70 but some 85 million (including life annuity *rentes*). To this debt might be added 185 million in arrears and a number of other items, which would increase the total to 2,200 million or more.[40] Machault was concerned enough about the magnitude of the debt to introduce an amortization plan and to speak encouragingly of eventual repayment. He could find grounds for optimism in his ability to fund the amortization plan with revenues from the *vingtième*. His aim was to pay off the entire debt during fifty to sixty years.[41] It was, as we have seen, a plan arising out of ignorance of high finance. It was also an uncommonly naive proposal. On what grounds could anyone in the old regime assume fifty to sixty years of peace?

The Debt After the Seven Years War

France emerged from the War of Spanish Succession in 1714 with an enormous debt, some 2,600 million l.t.[42] In a population of 23 million or fewer, the debt amounted to more than 113 l.t. for every individual in the kingdom. At that level it came to a sum strikingly close to the estimate for annual French national income in the first

[40] Other sources (e.g., Algemeen Rijksarchief, Fagel, 1567) estimate the debt at a higher figure by failing to discount debts contracted by Louis XIV or by including items not listed here: temporary expenses of 720,000 a year linked to the 1745 lottery; loans of the Compagnie des Indes in 1747, 1749, and 1751 to build vessels and fortifications and to retire some older debts; an estimated total of 890 million for the value of royal and sovereign court offices not counted as part of the state debt, and since 1744 compensated wholly by fees charged litigants; an estimated 50 million in non-hereditary offices; and the parts of debts of the *pays d'état* and municipalities not linked to central government finance.

[41] Algemeen Rijksarchief, Fagel, 1566.

[42] Koninklijke Bibliotheek, Brussels, Manuscript Department, 15723, folios 284r-285v, a manuscript owned by S.N.H. Linguet. Clamageran, *Histoire de l'impôt*, III, 119, prefers a figure of 1,936 million.

TABLE 6.4
Additional Debt Items
(in millions of l.t.)

	interest	principal
1748 lottery loan, funded by a surcharge on the *capitation*	1.3	20.0
1749 lottery loan, funded by General Farm revenues	.863	15.0
Debts of the *pays d'état* in perpetual annuities, as of 1750	9.06	181.2
Debts of the *pays d'état* in life annuities, as of 1750	—[a]	—[b]
Debts of the *pays conquis* in life annuities, as of 1750	—[c]	—[b]
Debts of municipalities contracted on behalf of royal finances, as of 1750	.729	14.584
Unsalaried offices, as of 1750	0	60.0
Offices in the *pays d'état*, municipalities, police, and otherwise, some salaried and some not, as of 1750	3.0	100.0
TOTALS	14.956	390.78

SOURCE: See note 38.

[a] 1.56 million, combining interest and amortization.

[b] No total given for life annuities.

[c] .094 million, combining interest and amortization. Totals for 1750 are used when information for 1753 is lacking. There was in these categories little or no change in the intervening period.

decade of the eighteenth century—2,700 million or about 125 l.t. per capita.[43] For an agrarian economy with limited opportunities to expand public or government revenues, this was a burden that could not be tolerated.

Two policy decisions brought an immediate reduction in the debt. A third development, over which French authorities exercised little or no intentional control, brought a long-run decline in its scale. The first of these three interventions is well known. The Law system, which was intended to permit a reimbursement of the debt, transformed it into a speculative commodity and thoroughly confused the issue of legitimacy in royal liabilities. Because Law's plan did not work, and as a consequence of the confusion it brought, authorities in the regency ordered a general scaling down of a substantial part of the debt. This scaling down took the form of halving the

[43] See above, Chapter 1.

yield on government securities, which has already been discussed. This measure had the additional effect of leaving in confusion the question of valuing the debt. Unofficially the principal was also re-aligned, so that after restoring the standard 5 percent yield, it too was halved.[44] The second measure of policy took the form of a re-duction in the silver and gold equivalents of the livre tournois.

Together, these two measures and the increase of revenues after 1715 brought the debt to a manageable level. In following decades France made some progress in paying off outstanding securities, and more progress still by servicing the life annuities, whose nomi-nees died in growing numbers. But by and large the debt of 1726 was the debt that France carried into the War of Austrian Succes-sion.

The third inroad into the debt came via inflation. In the 1720s France left behind a period of secular price stability (amidst short-run instability) and entered a long period of inflation. Inflation did not directly affect the nominal amount of the debt, but it did reduce its real value. Thus creditors received interest payments that grad-ually diminished in purchasing power, as did also the principal it-self. Since price changes increased government revenues, inflation promoted a general reduction in the scale of accumulated debts. Thus inflation served both to create deficits, because expenditures rose more rapidly than revenues, and to reduce the real burden of the debt. In order to measure the scale of debts over time, it will be necessary to consider price changes.

After the conclusion of the War of Austrian Succession, at the be-ginning of the calendar year 1753, the debt totalled between 850 and 2,200 million, depending on how one chooses to construe dif-ficult matters (but still omitting a figure for the principal of life an-nuity and tontine loans). Everyone who looks at the French debt sees it differently. In order to compare it over time, certain compro-

---

[44] Thereafter, officials reveal their confusion by valuing the debt sometimes at its original nominal amount but reduced yield (2.5 percent) and sometimes at its halved nominal amount after recalculating from the yield figured at 5 rather than 2.5 per-cent. Later reimbursement procedures adhered to the unofficial halving of princi-pal, thus it seems wise to construe the eighteenth-century debt in these terms. E.g., the amortizations of the 1750s, as discussed in the *états* compiled during the Seven Years War: Bibliothèque Mazarine, 2825; Bibliothèque de l'Arsenal, 4062; and Uni-versity Library, London, Palæography Room, 127(2).

mises are necessary. The largest of these involves the matter of offices. Pierre Goubert and David Bien have both argued that the offices which Louis XIV and Louis XV sold constitute a French version of the creation of a public debt. The *gages* paid on these offices thus consist not of salary but interest, which could be reduced.[45] How is this portion of the debt to be valued, at the sale price of offices or at the values implied by treasury assessments? The information is simply inadequate to the task. But it has already been established that less and less emphasis was placed on the creation of new offices or the expansion of *finance* in old offices from the 1740s onward. During the Seven Years War only 5 percent of the *affaires extraordinaires* took the form of new or higher *finance*. Thus the portion of the debt consisting of loans-as-offices stabilized after the early years of the reign of Louis XV, forming a more or less constant amount according to the treasury valuation (but not according to market values, which rose).

This stabilization simplifies the issue of comparing the debt over time, for it makes it possible to set aside the debt in *finance* and to concentrate on the part of the debt composed of negotiable securities. In 1753 France owed 850 million plus the principal behind the life annuities and tontines (Table 6.5). This part of the debt cost

TABLE 6.5
The Debt in 1753
(in millions of l.t.)

	principal	interest	other service[a]
Central government liabilities in loans	654.6	33.1	27.5
Local and provincial government liabilities in loans	195.8	9.8	0
TOTALS	850.4	42.9	27.5

SOURCE: See Table 6.3.
[a] The "other service" column covers payments on self-amortizing loans, chiefly the life annuities.

[45] Pierre Goubert, *L'ancien régime: Les pouvoirs* (Paris, 1973), 142; and David D. Bien, "The *secrétaires du roi*: Absolutism, Corps, and Privilege under the Ancien Régime," in Ernst Hinrichs et al., eds., *Vom Ancien Régime zur Französischen Revolution* (Göttingen, 1978), 159ff. The *gages* fell from 10 percent in 1672 to about 2 percent in the 1720s.

70.4 million to service, or 30 percent of ordinary revenues.[46] In addition, the arrears amounted to some 185 million, representing *gages* and pensions paid late since many years but not bearing any interest. To arrive at a comprehensive figure for this part of the debt, it is necessary also to estimate the unpaid balance of life annuity and tontine loans. Eighteenth-century authorities usually did this by adopting a multiplier, such as ten.[47] To repeat that procedure is to introduce an unnecessary distortion. The French life annuity loans were not opened steadily during the century, but came instead in clusters. Thus the extinction of their nominees was not distributed evenly over time, as the use of a single multiplier would suggest.

According to a calculation explained in Appendix 2, the principal of the life annuity/tontine portion of the debt amounted in 1753 to at least 325 million, and in 1764 to at least 520 million. By that latter date other portions of the debt-in-securities totalled 1,800 million, distributed as explained in Table 6.6.[48] Thus bringing these estimates together, it appears that the monarchy's debt in 1764 amounted to more than 2,300 million l.t., including interest-bearing securities but excluding the *finance* of offices, the debts of the Com-

[46] Algemeen Rijksarchief, Legatie, 779: 232.5 million.

[47] E.g., in Bibliothèque Nationale, Joly de Fleury, 1432, folio 173v.

[48] Rounding from sums in the source, which has been used by others, e.g., J.-M. Gorges, *La dette publique: Histoire de la rente française* (Paris, 1884). [Mathon de la Cour], *Comptes-rendus*, 49, questions the exactness of the document he reproduces on p. 51 listing the debt by categories. His grounds are the failure of the document to set the *dettes des départements* at a figure as high as that given in a 1768 calculation—more than 400 million. Thus the figures reported here may understate the short-term debt, given here as the *dettes des départements* plus the anticipations, together 314 million.

The document reproduced by Mathon de la Cour divides the perpetual annuity debt into categories set by the original interest level, from 1 to 5 percent. Thus old distinctions about the nominal value are reasserted, with the most significant of these relating to 2.5 percent notes. The principal is calculated according to both a standard 5 percent yield and the estimated cost of reimbursement, which approximately splits the difference between the original nominal value of notes and the par value estimated at a standard 5 percent yield. The lower figure, in the first column, is the more important. Haus-, Hof- und Staatsarchiv, Vienna, Böhm Supplement, Frankreich, Böhm 960-W922, lists the *effets publics* in circulation toward the end of the 1760s. Northamptonshire Record Office, Northampton, England, Fitzwilliam Manuscripts, A.xxxii.21, reports that Laverdy drafted a calculation of the debt in December 1763 which showed a total of 2.131 billion, with interest charges of 151.5 million a year. No detail is given, so there is no way to compare elements with Mathon de la Cour's version.

TABLE 6.6
The Debt in 1764
(in millions of l.t.)

	principal calculated at 5 percent yield	principal calculated at estimated reimbursement cost	interest
Perpetual annuities	1,095.6	1,348.3	55.9
Advances from the General Farm	115.0	115.0	5.2
Debts of:			
pays d'état	59.8	59.8	3.0
départements	234.0	234.0	9.4
clergy	100.0	100.0	5.0
municipalities	120.0	120.0	6.0
Anticipations	80.0	80.0	4.0
Subtotals	1,804.5	2,057.1	88.5
Life annuities and tontines	520.0		
TOTAL	2,324.5		

SOURCE: [Mathon de la Cour], *Collection de comptes-rendus* . . . (Lausanne, 1788), 51.

pagnie des Indes, and a number of lesser figures which cannot be included for various reasons.[49] Other arrears, which Mathon de la Cour identified with the life annuity loans, had also grown, and in 1764 they totalled 53.1 million l.t.[50] Together the short and long-term debt and the interest and non-interest-bearing debt—but only the debt-in-securities—amounted to about 2,350 million l.t., a sum not much less than the debt total of 1715.[51] The overall debt, adding

[49] E.g., life annuity lotteries before 1755 are excluded because of incomplete information.

[50] [Mathon de la Cour], *Comptes-rendus*, 51.

[51] Mathon prefers the higher total reached by valuing the perpetual annuities at their estimated reimbursement cost, thus 1,057 million (offices excluded), plus my estimate of the life annuity principal (520 million), or 2,577 million. Another source, a memoir from the parlement of Bordeaux to the king proposing a tax on interest paid on government securities, gives another view of the perpetual and life annuity part of the debt. It divides the perpetual annuity portion into interest categories, values them at their full nominal value, and gives a total of 2,100 million (not 2,200 million, as stated in the document, which contains a misprint of 600 million rather than 500 million for the estimate of 4 percent annuities). The life annuity debt is then set at ten times the amount of annual service, or a further 300 million. These totals also are unrealistically high for the perpetual annuity portion of the debt and too low for the unretired principal of the life annuity portion. Bibliothèque Nationale, Joly de Fleury, 1432, folios 167r-179r. (My judgment about the misprint is based on the total

especially the value of offices, would be much larger still. By the late 1760s, when a comprehensive list is first available, debt service (which was principally the payment of interest) required some 196 million l.t. a year—more than 60 percent of expenditures and double the proportion of 1753.[52]

In 1764 the debt-in-securities totalled nearly two-thirds of agricultural and manufacturing output, estimated at 3,500 to 3,600 million l.t.[53] What is more striking still is the increase of the debt in real terms. In 1753 France owed, in this part of its liabilities, something in excess of 1,360 million.[54] Prices did not rise significantly until after 1765, so no adjustment for inflation is necessary.[55] In 1764 prices the 1753 debt-in-securities still amounted to 1,360 million. Thus, in constant as well as current prices, the 2,350 million l.t. debt-in-securities had grown in thirteen years by nearly 1,000 million l.t.[56]

The "Prepaid" Repudiation

Interest rates in sixteenth- and seventeenth-century government loans seem in retrospect to have been extraordinarily high. Their levels, up to or even beyond 20 percent for loans opened by France, the Dutch Republic, and Britain, are not justified by price trends or market inefficiencies. Even when the price trend was inflationary,

---

of this column of figures and the interest multiplier for the 4 percent entry.)

[52] Haus-, Hof- und Staatsarchiv, Bohm 960-W922, as follows:

perpetual annuities	90 million
life annuities	64
rescriptions	30
other	12
TOTAL	196 million

This life annuity total probably includes the loans of 1766 and 1768, which brought in 104.6 million and therefore added over 10 million to service. (This figure indicates that my estimate of the outstanding life annuity/tontine principal in 1764 is conservative, since some of that part of the debt, which I estimate at 520 million, paid a yield less than 10 percent.) It is important to notice that the debt service paid from ordinary revenues was declining, while overall debt service was growing rapidly, and more rapidly than suggested by Morineau, "Budgets de l'état," 308.

[53] See Chapter 2 for an explanation of the method of estimation.

[54] That is, 850 million from Table 6.5 plus 325 million for the life annuity/tontine debt plus 185 million in arrears.

[55] See Table 1.2.

[56] Other parts of the debt, chiefly the *finance* of offices, had not changed much.

its secular rate was not high enough to warrant such yields. Nor can the defects of markets account for a large part of these returns, for high rates were demanded in areas like the Dutch Republic where capital markets were well developed as well as in regions where markets were slower to develop. Investors demanded these high yields because they would not supply governments with credit without charging a premium for the risks involved. Thus lenders were paid in advance for the risk of default, which they knew from experience was a real risk.

During the seventeenth century government policy began to shift away from intermittent defaults toward policies that sought to eliminate this risk premium. The Dutch Republic and Britain both completed this transformation before the 1720s, so that lenders no longer identified their securities with risks high enough to require a sizeable premium. Thereafter changes in nominal interest rates in their loans may be identified with shifts in the demand for credit, price changes, and remaining market inefficiencies, of which few can be identified in financial markets.[57] In France the desire to make such a transformation came somewhat later. There the public debt had first been built to a sizeable level through the sale of venal offices, a mode that sometimes involved costly grants of privilege to officers but that also provided the monarchy with a captive group of creditors who could be pushed around. During the reign of Louis XIV the debt shifted toward a debt-in-securities, a transformation continued under Louis XV. But the monarchy continued to pay high yields on loans whenever credit was raised under voluntary subscription. These yields are all the more worthy of note in a period of secular deflation, such as the early decades of the reign of Louis XIV were. Thus real yields, and the risk premium earned by lenders, were high. That such a premium, with its effective prepayment of default, was necessary became evident last in the Law system, which was settled by a large write-off of royal indebtedness. This write-off was by no means devoid of costs for lenders and for the economy. But to a large extent it too had been prepaid.

In the decades that followed French financial authorities began to

[57] Larry Neal, "The Stock Markets of the Eighteenth Century in London and Amsterdam: How Efficient Were They?" unpublished paper; and Philip Mirowski, "Does Present Value Theory Explain Asset Pricing in Eighteenth Century England?" unpublished paper.

rethink policy. As their predecessors had believed, so they too were convinced of the usefulness of paying off the royal debt. In the 1720s and 1730s Fleury introduced some unsuccessful efforts to fund a regular amortization program and pioneered a successful program of gradual debt repayment. What especially appealed to Fleury was the public's taste for life annuity loans, which he regarded as self-extinguishing and thus secure from the temptation present in perpetual annuity loans of borrowing more and more without ever living up to provisions for retirement.

What had appealed to Fleury more in principle than in practice became for Machault a matter of government policy. Machault introduced an ambitious program for converting the so-called perpetual into a self-extinguishing debt by substituting life annuities for perpetual annuities. In the process, he preserved the yield on life annuities that Fleury had established, a yield nearly or fully twice the level customarily paid in perpetual annuities, without (as we have seen) noticing that the difference was composed mostly of interest rather than of amortization payments. Like his predecessors and successors, Machault understood finance by means of maxims and aphorisms, such as the tirelessly iterated "les finances sont les nerfs de l'état." How curious it is that statesmen and commentators, from Richelieu and before to Turgot and after, continued to repeat this adage without spending the time necessary to inform themselves about finance.

Did Machault's reform and other measures that increased the yield to investors in the debt amount to an eighteenth-century prepayment of a debt write-off? Why, if a default was paid in advance, did the financial authorities elect not to adopt it? Fleury and Machault, two controllers general who served for lengthy periods, reversed the trend of the yield paid on French securities, which had fallen, reestablishing a large premium between the rate that market conditions indicate needed to be paid and the rate that was actually paid. Yet the full scale of this premium arose not on the entire debt, but only on the most rapidly growing part of it, the life annuity loans. Machault's *rentes passagères* reveal that the financial authorities could design a self-amortizing annuity that paid interest at a rate no greater than the conventional perpetual annuity (even if they did not fully understand how to distinguish interest from amortization payments in such loans). But as established above, the life

annuity loans paid yields generally half again higher than those offered in perpetual annuities, with the difference making up a premium for investors in this type of paper.[58] Thus, for example, the
combined life annuity issue of late 1757 for 60 million was serviced
with an annual payment of 6 million when 3.8 million would have
sufficed to pay interest and amortization on the terms established by
the borrowing authorities.

It cannot be said that this bonus was a risk premium demanded
by lenders, for up to 1759 investors signalled their willingness to
lend on life annuities at 10 percent or perpetual annuities at 5 percent. Of course, they bought the life annuities more eagerly. But the
point is that they continued to buy the perpetual annuities paying a
much lower yield. Apparently the financial authorities, Fleury and
Machault and their successors, failed to see that a prepayment toward default was underway, failed to notice that the aggressive demand among investors for life annuity paper constituted something
more than a taste preference.

Thus they failed to observe significant signs on the financial markets. In 1758 Boullongne did not notice, or did not understand the
significance of, heavy buying from abroad. A retired Dutch military
officer, Johan van Tuyll van Serooskerken, bought 316,000 l.t. in
the loan of April 1758, and other foreigners, from Genoa, Geneva,
Amsterdam, The Hague, Haarlem, even the enemy capitals London and Berlin, joined him.[59] At home Van Tuyll might have gotten
2.5 percent. Buying these *rentes*, on which subscriptions could be
paid half in discounted paper issued in 1720 and half in cash,
brought 5.3 percent or more.[60] Thus this investor's premium for
buying French over Dutch paper was nearly 3 percent, half again
more than an anonymous writer in the *Journal de commerce* said in
January 1759 was necessary.[61] To give one more example of an obvious sign that French authorities missed, the *Annual Register* re-

[58] See above, this chapter.

[59] Archives Nationales, Paris, P 6303, lists subscriptions. Also Minutier central des
notaires de Paris, e.g. Etude LXXXIV, 456, on foreign subscriptions in the wartime
life annuity loans through the Paris bankers Christophe Jean Baur, Pierre François
Goossens, and J. B. van den Yver.

[60] This assumes that the old 2.5 percent paper was discounted to 50 percent—that
is, to the point at which new buyers would have earned the standard yield of 5 percent.

[61] See n. 23, this chapter.

ported early in 1763 that gold could scarcely be found in London because the Dutch, who had for decades bought heavily in British paper, were taking advantage of high yields in French securities.[62] The French controllers general Bertin and Laverdy might have seen in this an opportunity to reduce the yield on French paper toward the return then paid on the British 3 percent consolidated annuities, 3.4 percent.[63]

According to Marion's report of subscription records, the life annuity loans of 1737-1761 brought in 239 million l.t.[64] Calculating an amortization schedule, as applied in the *rentes passagères*, each year's payment in excess of the necessary interest might have been used to retire securities, thereby economizing on interest payments for following years as the principal was gradually repaid. At the yield actually paid, retirement in full would have occurred early in the fifteenth year of the loan.[65] In short, the life annuity loans were an exceptional bargain for investors because they paid a large dividend that had nothing to do with any additional risk of default.

If this were the only part of the debt in which such a measure occurred, it would not constitute an excessive burden. But the inattentiveness to large issues in finance that prevailed here prevailed elsewhere too. During war, yields on royal securities traditionally increased as government shifted from a net supplier to a net consumer of investment capital. For public officials and many observers, this situation created a feeling that lenders, especially lenders providing short-term credit, like arms suppliers, were taking advan-

[62] *Annual Register* (London), 1763, pt. 1, 78. Also *Gazette van Antwerpen*, 1763 numbers, which follow closely discussions in France about fiscal reforms, suggesting that Antwerp, a center of foreign investment, also had extensive holdings in French paper. On foreign holdings in the French debt in the 1740s and 1750s, see Herbert Lüthy, *La banque protestante en France de la révocation de l'édit de Nantes à la Révolution* (2 vols.; Paris, 1959-1961), II, 238.
[63] Cornelius Walford, *The Insurance Cyclopædia* . . . (5 vols.; New York, 1871-1878), II, 47, provides a table of annual average prices.
[64] Marion, *Histoire financière*, I, 472-73.
[65] Assuming an interest rate of 5 percent, and calculated using an income stream formula:

$$n = \frac{[\text{Log } H - \text{Log }(H - Pi)]}{\text{Log }(1 + i)}$$

where n = the number of years to extinction, P = the amount of the loan, H = the expected average annual net income, and i = the interest rate.

tage of the situation. A partial default was justified, and at the end of the War of Polish Succession the authorities had written off part of the claims of arms suppliers.[66] During the Seven Years War, payments were suspended in 1759 and 1760 on two leading instruments of short-term credit, the *billets* issued by the farmers general and the *rescriptions* of the receivers general. But these were resumed in 1761, with the unpaid interest being added to the sum of the debt. Thus no default occurred on this paper (although there were some write-downs after the war, for example on the Canada debt).[67] What is more, while other European governments continued their programs of debt conversion to lower yields, French authorities elected instead to preserve customary yields, even to the point of rejecting appeals for a tax on the interest paid in government loans. By 1764 the burden of the debt was so great that France shifted from being a large to a small net supplier of investment capital in peacetime. Neither the debt nor its yield would be written down to a point at which the traditional peacetime role of the royal treasury in French capital markets could be resumed.

Both because all government securities paid an exceptionally generous premium over private sector loans in the 1740s and 1750s, and because the life annuities paid a still larger premium, the eighteenth-century French government unwittingly prepaid another large debt write-down. Neither investors nor financial authorities would have tolerated a default of the type involved in the Law system, or any other overt and arbitrary write-off. But the authorities had access to several techniques in use in other states reputed to have stronger credit-worthiness, techniques proposed by French reformers and discussed at court. These included an interest reduction such as through a conversion operation, a partial debt repayment in paper currency, or a tax on debt service. Any one of them would have substantially reduced the scale and burden of the debt. As used in other states, these techniques preserved government credit-worthiness in an age of unusually large public debts. In

[66] Algemeen Rijksarchief, Legatie, 776, p. 56, the interest requested by suppliers on advances made during the war.

[67] J. F. Bosher, "The French Government's Motives in the *Affaire du Canada*, 1761-1763," *English Historical Review*, 96, no. 378 (Jan. 1981), 70 and 77, in which France recognized only 37.6 of 90 million issued in paper.

France, where fiscal policy was too cautious to enact any of these measures, the failure of enactment and the inauguration of a policy of inflexible caution had the paradoxical effect of undermining credit-worthiness.

CONCLUSION

Of all the options before financial authorities at the middle of the eighteenth century, the easiest to adopt was a revised program of debt management. A long-run trend of declining nominal interest rates persisted to the middle of the eighteenth century before being reversed during the Seven Years War. What is more, inflation in the 1730s and 1740s had eroded the real yield of public and private sector securities without creating a strong demand among lenders for higher rates. By the early 1750s the government could borrow at the lowest nominal and real yields experienced in the eighteenth century (excepting only the 1720s, a period of serious monetary confusion). French authorities faced the opportunity—an opportunity pointed out to them by some reform proposals submitted during the 1740s and 1750s—to reduce the costs of the debt and to adopt either a Dutch or a Swedish strategy of debt management. But the authorities were inept. They contented themselves with maxims and aphorisms whose financial and economic implications they did not understand.

What is most astonishing about the intensification of caution—this risk aversion in finance—to which the authorities submitted in the 1750s is that it coincided with a risk-loving attitude in economic policy. At the same time that the ministers rejected advice about the reformulation of fiscal and financial policy, they took steps to free the trade in France's most important product, grain. Hesitantly in 1754 and with force in 1763 the authorities introduced this first high-risk experiment in a nearly unregulated trade in basic foodstuffs,[68] an experiment that ended in a failure consisting of broad popular misery.

The financial authorities did not possess an understanding of fi-

---

[68] Steven L. Kaplan, *Bread, Politics and Political Economy in the Reign of Louis XV* (2 vols.; The Hague, 1976), I, 91 and 106. On the earlier phase, see J.K.J. Thomson, *Clermont-de-Lodève, 1633-1789: Fluctuations in the Prosperity of a Languedocian Cloth-Making Town* (Cambridge, 1982), 357ff.

nance sufficient to see the great costs of their program of converting perpetual to life annuities, and they did not understand how to make the calculations basic to financial policy. Led by Machault, they made the wrong decisions, decisions that misconstrued price trends and financial realities, decisions that counted upon the perpetuation of peace in an age of war. Moreover, the authorities suspended the peacetime augmentation of French taxation at a time when the economy continued to grow. Applauded for their desire to pay off the debt, the French controllers general should instead be condemned for increasing the scale of the debt and debt service far more than necessary.

When war began again in 1756 the financial authorities elected to attempt to finance it with credit rather than taxes. In consequence the debt, counting only that portion taking the form of securities, nearly doubled itself between 1753 and 1764, growing from 1,360 to 2,350 million. Once again, as in 1714, France emerged from a war that cost too much with a burden of debt that could not be borne.

CHAPTER 7

A CRISIS OF CONFIDENCE

Tout le monde se mêle à présent de vouloir être Réformateur.[1]

T*O* lose the war and win the peace (as English critics of Lord Bute's peace terms saw matters) was not to assuage a sense that much was badly wrong in France in 1763. What distinguishes this sense of misgiving from earlier criticisms of French institutions is its intensity and breadth at a time when many feared that all was lost, that France was "reduit à la dernière extrémité par les dépenses forcées qu'il a faites pour soutenir une guerre aussi malheureuse que longue."[2] In December 1760 Mirabeau, whose aim in *Théorie de l'impôt* was to proclaim the natural laws governing public finance, warned that bankruptcy of the state would be a watershed bringing dramatic change, perhaps even the destruction of the state.[3] The Seven Years War produced a crisis of confidence in which large numbers of royal servants, members of the liberal professions, merchants, landowners, economic theorists, and others expressed specific views on the shortcomings of French institutions, and expressed them not only as an application of Enlightenment images of ideal institutions to their own terrain but also from a pragmatic sense of the urgency of reform—and more the latter. The king too was a reformer. In the spring of 1763 he ordered an inquiry into the conditions of Paris cemeteries (March 23) with the aim of improving public hygiene,[4] authorized an appeal of the Toulouse parlement's decision in the Calas case (March) that led to a posthumous exoneration, and established the freedom of trade in grain within France

---

[1] *Journal encyclopédique*, Aug. 15, 1763, 149.

[2] Such feelings are ascribed in *Bien de l'état* (n.p., [1763]), 1; Sébastien Alexander Costé de Saint-Supplix, *Le consolateur, pour servir de réponse à la Théorie de l'impôt . . .* (Brussels, 1763), 9-10; and *Questions sur la Richesse de l'état* (n.p., [1763]), 1, from which the quote is drawn.

[3] [Victor de Riquetti de Mirabeau], *Théorie de l'impôt* (n.p., 1760), 50-51.

[4] Richard Allan Etlin, *The Cemetery and the City: Paris, 1744-1804* (Ph.D. dissertation, Princeton University, 1978), 63-64.

and authorized some exports (May 25) with the intention of fostering agriculture. Like his subjects, Louis was intrigued by the notion that discord between man and nature, which hindered the fulfillment of man, could be resolved by panaceas.

In this multifaceted effort to improve humankind, one line of inquiry is especially interesting. That is the debate on financial reform, which began in May.[5] Why was this debate so important? There are two reasons. Taking advantage of the failure of the authorities to interfere with the first pamphlet in the series, to arrest its author, who was quickly known, or the publisher and distributor, an outpouring of ideas followed.[6] One discovers in 1763 a brief but searching discussion that resembles, in its radical nature and in the content of reforms suggested and implied, the public discussion of reform in 1788 and 1789 on the eve of the Revolution, a rehearsal of open discussion about altering the most basic institutions and usages of the French polity and society. Since this debate provided a rare opportunity to express private views publicly, we may assume that a sense of the need for reform was felt keenly by many people at other times, before and after 1763.[7] What produced the debate of that year was no sudden realization that reform was needed, but a belief, created by the war's obvious intensification of France's fiscal dilemma, that the financial system urgently needed revamping. What the king knew in a general way, many other people knew in matters of detail. The existing system could not stand unreformed. In recapturing this belief we can see why the debate of 1763 is of such importance, and why its failure to lead to reform has such large significance for the subsequent history of the monarchy.

The second reason this debate is significant is that another form of it brought the king into confrontation with the parlements, provoking a great and climactic clash over the right to identify and sus-

[5] There was a debate—an exchange of books rather than pamphlets—over Mirabeau's anonymously published *Théorie de l'impôt*. See [Buchet du Pavillon], *Les finances considerées dans le droit naturel et politique des hommes, ou examen critique de la Théorie de l'impôt* (Amsterdam, 1762); *Mémoire contenant quelques changements à faire pour l'utilité de l'état* (n.p., [1762?]); and Saint-Supplix, *Le consolateur*. In light of frequent references before, during, and after the Seven Years War to Sully, Colbert, Vauban, Saint-Pierre, Montesquieu, and other writers on public finance, it is evident that many older ideas retained currency and influenced subsequent exchanges about reform.

[6] [Louis Petit de Bachaumont] et al., *Mémoires secrets pour servir à l'histoire de la République des lettres en France . . .* (36 vols.; London, 1781-1789), I, 243.

[7] Indeed there were later surfacings of this debate, in 1774 and the early 1780s.

tain or reform the basic laws of the realm. In recent years Louis XV had ruled, it often seemed, by *lit de justice*, by royal sessions with the parlements in which he played one of the last cards in his hand, issuing the order for the parlement to obey the king and to register a royal edict or declaration that it had resisted. The parlementaires wished to reassert ancient rights before a timid and secretive king who seemed weaker than he was. They also wished to adopt basic reforms, and not only financial reforms. The king, for his part, wanted to preserve the gains toward absolutism made by his great-grandfather, Louis XIV. He too wanted to enact reforms, and not always ones different from those in the minds of the parlementaires. The issue of the moment was not reform, but who would enact it.

PUBLIC DEBATE

About this debate we should notice first that it was more a controversy over the incidence of taxation (who shall pay the taxes?) and the mode of collection than about the economic consequences of certain types of taxes. Thus this debate shed temporarily the preoccupation of so many French reformers with internal and external tariffs and their constricting effects on trade. For a few weeks, if only a few weeks, attention fell directly on public finance.

The central figure in the debate was Roussel de la Tour, conseiller to the parlement of Paris and to the Chambre des Comptes.[8] Although his short pamphlet, *Richesse de l'état*—published anonymously in May on the eve of the *lit de justice* held on May 31 to compel the parlements to suppress the third *vingtième* (but to sustain the first and second), to continue the *dons gratuits* of the municipalities, to reestablish levies on *immeubles fictifs* (including venal offices and *rentes constituées*), and to accept a land cadastre[9]—provoked the debate, Roussel de la Tour did not remain a public figure. It is the ideas rather than the man that we can consider.

[8] See Louis Gabriel Michaud, ed., *Biographie universelle* . . . (new ed.; Paris, 1854-1865), XXXVI, 635-36. In 1762 and 1763 Roussel was also involved in drafting reports for the parlement of Paris on the expulsion of the Jesuits. Alexandre Cioranescu, *Bibliographie de la littérature française du dix-huitième siècle* (3 vols.; Paris, 1969), III, 1594.

[9] Bibliothèque Nationale, Paris, Collection Joly de Fleury, 577; *Déclaration du roi qui rétablit le centième denier sur les immeubles fictifs* (n.p., 1763); *Edit du roi qui ordonne le dé-*

"Chacun doit au bien public le tribut de ses réflexions."[10] But Roussel's reflections would not, he claimed, be the intricate proposals so common in his day. They would offer instead a prompt and efficacious remedy for the present crisis, a single reform that would at once enrich the king and succor the people. At the foundation of this proposal lies the notion that the rich can better afford taxes than the poor, and should therefore pay them. If France has 16 million inhabitants, as Roussel and most of his contemporaries believed, at least two million of them can afford to serve as *contribuables*. Yet the *aisance* of these two million will vary so that only a tax *par progression*—a *capitation* in the original form of 1695—would be equitable. Among twenty classes of 100,000 people each, the schedule of taxes listed in Table 7.1 should be decreed. This single levy will raise 698,366,666 l.t., enough to replace all but a few levies (import and export duties, the farms on the postal services and on tobacco, and certain other minor revenue sources). Together in the new system the king's revenues would amount to more than 740 million l.t. per annum. With such revenues the king could retire his debts, yet preserve the magnificence expected of a monarch. The people would be delivered from the multitude of taxes, yet pay less.

nombrement des bien-fonds du royaume . . . (n.p., 1763); Jules Flammermont, ed., *Remonstrances du parlement de Paris au XVIIIᵉ siècle* (3 vols.; Paris, 1888-1898), II, 322-39; on the anticipation of the *lit de justice* and of Roussel's pamphlet, E.-J.-F. Barbier, *Chronique de la régence et du règne de Louis XV (1718-1763); ou journal de Barbier* (8 vols.; Paris, 1857), VIII, 71-74; and on the date of publication, see Maurice Tourneux, ed., *Correspondance littéraire, philosophique et critique par Grimm* . . . (6 vols.; Paris, 1877-1882), V, 320. Barbier, *Journal*, VIII, 74, described some contents of *Richesse de l'état* under a different title on June 1, before the writer had any direct knowledge of the pamphlet. Barbier believed that copies had been sent to the parlement and the duc d'Orléans. [Bachaumont], *Mémoires secrets*, I, 225 and 230, reveals that the pamphlet was distributed gratis and in secret up to June 12 when it went on sale. The king also proposed to increase the levies of the General Farm, and announced a plan to value the principal of much of the debt at twenty years' purchase—that is, at a 5 percent yield.

[10] [Roussel de la Tour], *Richesse de l'état* (n.p., [1763]), 1 of the edition in sixteen pages, which will be quoted here. *Richesse de l'état* also appeared in 1763 in editions of eight, twenty-two, and thirty-one pages in different formats, and was followed by *Développement du plan intitulé Richesse de l'état* which appeared in editions of ten and twenty-two pages, of which the latter will be cited here. Roussel de la Tour is identified as the author of these pamphlets by Antoine Alexandre Barbier, *Dictionnaire des ouvrages anonymes* (3rd ed.; 7 vols.; Paris, 1964 reprint), IV, 366. In a 1775 revision of his ideas, Roussel, then *conseiller maître* in the Chambre des comptes and the Cour des aides, domaine et finances of the comté of Burgundy, allowed his name to appear on the title paper.

TABLE 7.1
Roussel's Schedule

class	daily tax share	annual tax share	number in class	total from class
1	2 l.t.	3, 0,10 l.t.	100,000	304,166 l.t.
2	3	4,11, 3	100,000	456,250
3	6	9, 2, 6	100,000	912,500
4	9	13,13, 9	100,000	1,368,750
5	1, 0	18, 5, 0	100,000	1,825,000
6	2, 0	36,10, 0	100,000	3,650,000
7	3, 0	54,15, 0	100,000	5,475,000
8	4, 0	73, 0, 0	100,000	7,300,000
9	8, 0	146, 0, 0	100,000	14,600,000
10	14, 0	255,10, 0	100,000	25,550,000
11	1, 5, 0	456, 5, 0	100,000	45,625,000
12	1,12, 0	584, 0, 0	100,000	58,400,000
13	1,13, 0	602, 5, 0	100,000	60,225,000
14	1,14, 0	620,10, 0	100,000	62,050,000
15	1,15, 0	638,15, 0	100,000	63,875,000
16	1,16, 0	657, 0, 0	100,000	65,700,000
17	1,17, 0	675, 5, 0	100,000	67,525,000
18	1,18, 0	693,10, 0	100,000	69,350,000
19	1,19, 0	711,15, 0	100,000	71,175,000
20	2, 0, 0	730, 0, 0	100,000	73,000,000
TOTALS			2,000,000	698,366,666 l.t.

SOURCE: [Roussel de la Tour], *Richesse de l'état* (n.p , [1763]), p 3 of 16 pp. ed.

A simple proposal, but what intricate simplicity! Roussel de la Tour would tax according to the ability to pay rather than according to *qualité*, and would thereby revolutionize a social system built patiently over the centuries on privilege, which expressed itself most usefully in tax avoidance. At one stroke he would demolish the practice of "paying" taxes in service. Roussel would also threaten the employment of all those officials, jurists, and lesser personnel who collected existing levies, arbitrated disputes over assessment and collection, and managed the transfer of funds to the treasury and to the financiers. In a phrase, Roussel could expect, even in naiveté, to rouse the antagonism of the most powerful and vocal interests of old regime France. In return for the revolution that he anticipated, he offered merely to provide the king with plentiful revenues and to relieve the largest part of the populace from any direct contribution. Vauban redux, but a more radical Vauban.

This was an appeal to those with no voice or, in the case of the king, with a voice unused. Yet Roussel saw a way to strengthen his hand. He described taxes which, even for the highest class, would be lighter than those paid by large merchants and which in general would relieve interior trade of taxation. To the grand officials of royal finances, the *trésoriers* and *receveurs*, he held out the promise of continued occupation in the new system with access to the larger sums that would flow through their hands into the treasury.[11] To the parlement of Paris he offered a plan consonant with the parlement's cry to the king that existing taxes could not continue to be increased, that loans offered no remedy, that unnecessary expenditures must be cut, taxes simplified, and collection overhead reduced. For Roussel, what he proposed was no more than a detailed version, a working out, of the principles laid down by the parlement. Refinements might be needed, and advance notice would have to be given to the employees of the existing collection apparatus. But this was a plan that would solve the financial crisis. "Puisse la France, renaître de ses propres ruines, effacer le passé, jouir du présent, assurer l'avenir, éteindre ses dettes, rétablir sa Culture, son Commerce & sa Marine, réparer ses pertes, rendre ses Peuples heureux & contens, & voir les Etrangers à l'envi s'empresser de venir partager notre félicité sous l'Empire d'un Roi plus que jamais puissant & redouté de ses enemis, précieux à ses Sujets, & déjà d'avance cher à la Postérité!"[12] "Tout le public l'a entre les mains, le peuple même raisonne en conséquence et en souhaite l'exécution." "Il paroît être, en général, le vœu de la nation."[13] Both the debate and its observers—Barbier and Bachaumont among others—experimented with the rhetoric of a revolution in sovereignty—"le vœu de la nation."

Aside from the appeal to *le bien commun*, an abstraction that in this instance could scarcely be expected to move an inarticulate mass of common taxpayers to applaud the proposal, Roussel's most telling argument was that his plan offered a way to close a vast gap between what the people paid in taxes and what the king received. In the first

---

[11] Uselessly, for "les financiers sont furieux contre ce projet. . . ." [Bachaumont], *Mémoires secrets*, I, 230.

[12] [Roussel de la Tour], *Développement du plan*, 22.

[13] Respectively, Barbier, *Journal*, VIII, 77; and [Bachaumont], *Mémoires secrets*, I, 230.

pamphlet he estimated revenues to the treasury in 1749 at 250 million l.t. and proposed to deliver 740 million. How could the tax burden, already allegedly onerous, be increased so much? In answer Roussel offered a principle—that in general assets, when leased, yield no more than a third of their actual product, with the rest consumed by the overhead of the lease. Since the king leased most of his revenues, it could be assumed that the people paid three times what the king received. Indeed, the people might pay 900 million, as some observers claimed. Perhaps 740 million was more than was needed, and certainly it would be too much in the long run, when the debt had been redeemed. But the schedule might be adapted to any desired revenue amount.

The most heavily taxed, who might object the most strongly, could console themselves with the opportunity to pass their levies along to others. As for those citizens whose *dignité*, grandeur, and opulence (Roussel avoided using the word "nobility") distinguished them from others, "on les entend déjà de toutes parts announcer que leur générosité ne peut se contenir dans des bornes aussi étroites, & qu'ils se taxeront eux-mêmes dix fois au delà."[14] These offers should be accepted, and used to relieve other citizens, with perhaps a new system of distinctions.[15]

That *Richesse de l'état* immediately provoked a public debate is attested by Roussel, who mentioned the lively discussion of his first pamphlet in *Développement du plan intitulé Richesse de l'état*, and claimed that seven-eighths of Paris supported his ideas. Other sources confirm this. Baron Grimm, who later described the debate as an insipid quarrel, opened his bulletin of July 1, 1763, with an extended discussion of *Richesse de l'état*, and in later bulletins returned to this issue.[16] So numerous were the responses that the editor of Grimm's correspondence, Jean Maurice Tourneux, described them as "ouvrages sans nombre." [17] The debate took two forms. In more than forty pamphlets supporters and opponents expressed their re-

[14] [Roussel de la Tour], *Développement du plan*, 11.

[15] This idea was followed up by the anonymous author of *L'Ordre du cens, ou les dons gratuits, nouveau plan sur les finances* . . . (n.p., [1763]).

[16] Tourneux, ed., *Correspondance littéraire*, V, 320-455 *passim*. Grimm's bulletins were dispatched every two weeks.

[17] *Ibid.*, V, 320n1. Various sources, including *ibid.*, V, 320-25, 352-53, 382-83, 392-93, 420-21, and 455; the *Journal œconomique* (Jan. 1764); and René Stourm, *Bibliographie historique des finances de la France au dix-huitième siècle* (Paris, 1895), 106n1, list contributions to this debate. Also [Bachaumont], *Mémoires secrets*, I, 233-67 *passim*; and

actions to Roussel's proposal and developed their own plans for financial reform. In private discussions, which now can be followed only in such sources as Grimm's correspondence, Bachaumont's secret memoirs, the journal of Barbier, in the critical discussion of current literature in periodicals like the *Journal encyclopédique*, and in public addresses such as a certain "Thomas" gave in eulogy of Sully before the Académie Française,[18] still more was said. For more than a month the discussion was impassioned.

From the first, Grimm was disdainful and skeptical. "Je ne crois pas qu'il y ait un pays au monde où l'on puisse se promettre de parler avec plus de succès de choses qu'on n'a jamais apprises, et sur lesquelles on n'a jamais réfléchi."[19] The craze (*engouement*) of favor for a specious plan depended on nothing more than the appeal of the low taxes it required. But were there two million who could afford to pay; and especially, were there one million who could pay the levies required of the higher ten classes in Roussel's schedule? What is more, how could the people pay so much less, yet the king take in so much more? In truth the tax had to fall exclusively on landowners, who alone possessed *richesse réelle*. And they would be wiped out. Thus Grimm set forth one line of criticism, a counterattack with strong physiocratic tones, but one grounded also in common sense skepticism about whether there were enough individuals in France able to pay these levies.

Against Roussel stood an imposing array, including Grimm, Voltaire, Du Pont de Nemours, Moreau, and, among authors who remain anonymous, the writer of *Questions sur la Richesse de l'état*.[20] On their side, Roussel's critics did not have a single vision of the reforms that should be adopted but had several visions. To follow the debate in the pamphlets rather than in Grimm's commentary is to discover three things: that the severity of the financial crisis was widely acknowledged, that most contributors shared Roussel's sense of the defects of the existing system, and that despite these fundamental

the collections of pamphlets in this debate: *Richesse de l'état, à laquelle on a ajouté les pièces qui ont paru pour & contre* (Amsterdam, 1764, and London, 1783).

[18] *Journal encyclopédique*, Aug. 30, 1763, 160.

[19] Tourneux, ed., *Correspondance littéraire*, V, 323, and to the same effect on p. 332.

[20] Voltaire's views are given in a letter to Du Pont de Nemours of Aug. 16, 1763. Eleutherian-Mills Historical Library, Papers of P. S. Du Pont de Nemours, Series A, Correspondence. See also Voltaire's correspondence on the debate in Theodore Besterman, ed., *Voltaire's Correspondence* (Geneva, 1953-1965), LII, 10,446-10,546 *passim*.

points of agreement—this unanimity of opinion about the need for and much of the necessary content of reform—the debate quickly became a cacophony of visions in which each contributor was more eager to show the shortcomings of rivals or to describe alternative reform plans than to extract from the debate some sense of the politically and financially possible path of reform. Even Roussel's supporters, Darigrand and many anonymous authors,[21] proposed revisions that complicated the issue of reform.

Among opponents, Jacob Nicolas Moreau, the principled anti-philosophe who supported the development of royal absolutism, expressed *Doutes modestes sur la Richesse de l'état*, provoking a debate within the debate.[22] Rather than a tax on wealth, Moreau preferred a levy on foodstuffs that would be hidden in their cost and would be paid in proportion to consumption. For Moreau the problem lay not with taxes so much as with the debt and the habit of fighting wars on credit. His sarcastic treatment of Roussel's ideas prompted a series of defenses and a general condemnation of Moreau for his own defense of the financiers, and probably also for his service as a propagandist for the government.

Du Pont de Nemours set forth his opposition in his first publication, one completed before he came into contact with the physiocrats, but a piece that nevertheless expresses some physiocratic ideas.[23] His case was that taxes fall ultimately on the propertied, from which he inferred that Roussel exaggerated the number of potential taxpayers by including merchants, artisans, and domestic servants who only appear to pay taxes. From Du Pont's autobiography we learn that he discussed Roussel's plan with his father's cook, a woman from Brie, and that later he walked from Paris to Nemours

[21] E.g., *Observations certaines sur les Doutes modestes d'un Quidam* . . . (n.p., [1763]; *L'Orage du 20 Juin 1763* (n.p., [1763]); *La boutte-selle* (n.p., [1763]); *Défense du véritable plan, intitulé: Richesse de l'état* . . . (n.p., 1763); and *Mes rêveries sur les doutes modestes, à l'occasion des Richesses de l'état* (n.p., [1763]).

[22] [Jacob Nicolas Moreau], *Doutes modestes sur la Richesse de l'état* . . . (Paris, 1763), reprinted at least three times. I worked from the twenty-one-page edition in 22 cm. Copies of Moreau's pamphlet were distributed by the controller general. Jean Egret, *Louis XV et l'opposition parlementaire, 1715-1774* (Paris, 1970), 95n15. Also for Moreau's views, [Jacob-Nicolas Moreau], *Entendons-nous, ou le radotage du vieux notaire; sur la Richesse de l'état* (n.p., [1763]). Grimm identifies Moreau as the author. Tourneux, ed., *Correspondance littéraire*, V, 336. This pamphlet may have been reissued in the 1780s. Also Jacob-Nicolas Moreau, *Mes souvenirs*, ed. by Camille Hermelin (2 vols.; Paris, 1898-1901), I, 64, 110, 119-20, and *passim*.

[23] *Réflexions sur les ressources actuelles* (n.p., [1763]).

to gather information, consulting laborers encountered on the road.[24] Armed with the expertise and insights of these people, Du Pont published in August a response to the critics of his first pamphlet, elaborating upon the paradox of a people paying less while the king received more and developing his ideas about the superiority of agriculture to commerce as a source of wealth. In Du Pont's view the debate had become less a discussion of how French finances might be reformed than an exchange over whether trade or agriculture promised the highest returns from encouragement.

Let us follow the debate not in attack and counterattack, but by looking for what it reveals about what the contributors knew of French finances and what they shared in recommendations about reform. Roussel, his supporters, and his opponents had at their disposal a modest collection of facts and impressions. The rich escaped taxation through privilege; the king's revenues were inadequate and were eaten away by the costs of collection. How much did collection cost? Roussel estimated the overhead at 500 million. Others suggested figures as high as 750 million and as low as 40 to 50 million.[25] About the level of revenues, most accepted Roussel's estimate of 1749 income to the treasury of 250 million and supposed the level of current revenues to be 250 to 350 million.[26] About what level of revenues would be needed to allow the debt to be repaid, the debaters had only the vaguest of ideas.

Roussel inferred something about the capacity of the people to pay taxes from the experience of a few landless *journaliers* and wine merchants. About the number of people capable of paying taxes, he worked from an assumption that the *taille* rolls contained more than

[24] Eleutherian-Mills Historical Library, Papers of P. S. Du Pont de Nemours, Autobiography, 27. In other respects, too, Du Pont was uninformed. He argued that the ideas in *Richesse de l'état* might be found in the *Testament politique* (Amsterdam, 1762), attributed sometimes to François Antoine Chevrier and sometimes to the maréchal de Belle-Isle. But there is in that book little that resembles Roussel's ideas, although some themes (e.g., the attack on the financiers) are in common with the 1763 debate.

[25] *Défense du véritable plan*, 13-14; and [Moreau], *Doutes modestes*, 8 in twenty-one-page edition. Also *Réponse à l'auteur de l'Anti-financier* (The Hague, 1764), 16, estimating the General Farm overhead at less than 10 percent of collections.

[26] [Gaspard François Anne de] F[orbin], *Système d'imposition et de liquidation de dettes d'état, établi par la raison* (n.p., 1763), 43, for the lowest estimate; *Défense du véritable plan* . . . , 20 in thirty-five-page edition; and *Lettre à M. S . . . sur un plan de réforme dans les finances* (n.p., [1763]), 15, for an estimate of 300 million; and Barbier, *Journal*, 76-77, for the higher figure.

6 million people, making 2 million taxpayers a conservative estimate. Others doubted these figures but could not replace them with
an accurate version of existing or potential taxpayers. About
France's current population, most debaters accepted Roussel's estimate of 16 million, a figure favored by the physiocrats who argued
the depopulation of the land since the seventeenth century. This ac-
ceptance is not surprising, since more reliable information on population level was only just becoming available.[27] But it is interesting,
since the low estimate preferred by the physiocrats carried with it a
condemnation of a French political performance that was alleged,
since about 1700, to have caused the population to shrink. Mirabeau
had made this case in *L'Ami des hommes*, thereby gaining the wrath of
critics who charged that he had undermined the French war effort.
Thus the debaters, few of whom would have allied themselves with
the physiocratic condemnation of the state, nevertheless accepted a
population figure that implied general disapproval of the reign of
Louis XV.

What we see in this hodgepodge of impressions, information, and
misinformation is an ignorance so fundamental as to undermine the
possibility of reform. The debaters knew some basic facts about the
finances—that the revenues had been about 250 million at the end
of the War of Austrian Succession and were about 300 million in
1763—but of other matters, such as the scale of overhead costs, they
had only the most confused notions. Nowhere does this show up
more forcefully than in the spread of estimates of the royal debt:
from 1.2 to 2.4 billion l.t.[28] Historians have judged Roussel's plan
impractical,[29] as indeed it was. The need for reform was urgent, as
nearly everyone sensed in 1763. But all the participants in this debate together lacked information of basic importance to any attempt
at reform.[30]

If the debaters lacked certain information, they nevertheless pos-

[27] James C. Riley, *Population Thought in the Age of the Demographic Revolution* (Durham, N.C., 1985), 44.
[28] *Prompte liquidation de toutes les dettes de l'état* . . . (n.p., [1763]), 5; F[orbin], *Système*,
57, 98, and 113; and *Mémoire sur la libération de l'état et le soulagement des peuples, présenté
par le parlement séant à Bordeaux* . . . (n.p., 1764), 2.
[29] E.g., Marcel Marion, *Histoire financière de la France* (5 vols.; Paris, 1927-1928),
I, 219.
[30] The need for basic information did not escape notice (e.g., *Lettre à M. S.* . . , 3-
4), but no number of calls for cadastres and censuses could produce such inquiries.

sessed a strong intuitive sense of the defects of the existing system. Like gamblers before the creation of a mathematics of expectation, they had played often enough with the system to infer its characteristics. What was this collective vision of the elements of the financial system most in need of reform? What did the articulate public believe most required reform? Not all the debaters made the same points; what follows is rather an assemblage of the most common themes.

In the first place, these critics shared a sense of the overwhelming and unnecessary intricacy of a tax system that had grown for centuries by accretions. "Une infinité d'impôts & de droits" demanded simplification through the creation of a single basic tax.[31] This idea, discussed earlier by economic theorists in Britain, Italy, and France, had been set forth at the beginning of the war by Clicquot de Blervache, in 1760 by Mirabeau and the parlement of Rouen, in 1761 and again in 1762 by Bellepierre de Neuve-Eglise, and in 1763 by the parlement of Bordeaux as well as by most of the contributors to this debate.[32] Yet what tax should be singled out? Should it be the physiocrats' land tax? (Imagine the delight of Baltic grain growers and Dutch shippers if the physiocrats had succeeded in levying a single tax on land in markets open to the importation of tax free grain.) Is it possible to discover one impost that would not be arbitrary in its assessment? Saint-Supplix stood out from the crowd in this debate in arguing that the taxes must be variegated in order to find a way to tax all citizens.[33]

As a corollary, critics of the existing tax system pointed to the collection apparatus, full of duplications of function, a source of reputedly enormous profits to a few, the cause of numerous legal disputes that took years to be settled if they could be settled at all. How many hirelings—100,000, 200,000, or more, an army of *commis*— were needed to collect the taxes? Darigrand, who was imprisoned in the Bastille along with his publisher for his invective, argued that

[31] The quote is drawn from *Défense du véritable plan*, 4. Also *Lettre d'un avocat de Paris à un de ses confrères en province* . . . (n.p., [1763]).

[32] [Mirabeau], *Théorie de l'impôt*; Bellepierre de Neuve-Eglise, *La pratique de l'impôt, ou vues d'un patriote* (2nd ed., Avignon, 1762) (first pub. 1761 under the title *Les vues d'un patriote*), 107; and Georges Weulersse, *Le mouvement physiocratique en France (de 1756 à 1770)* (2 vols.; Paris, 1910), II, 348 and 349.

[33] Saint-Supplix, *Le consolateur*, xlvii. Also *Le patriote financier, ou l'heureuse vérité* (n.p., [1763]).

there was no need for new taxes in the financial crisis of 1763, only for measures to recover what was lost in the collection. This he sought to demonstrate by following the progress of *droits d'aides* collected in his own canton of forty parishes to the treasury (and neglecting to notice that *charges* spent before reaching the central treasury nevertheless included legitimate and necessary payments on the king's behalf). Of 15,000 l.t. gathered, 12,000 left the canton for the *direction*, where 4,000 was absorbed by the *bureau général* and 8,000 forwarded to the *caisse* in Paris. There an additional 5,000 was siphoned off by the *régie*, leaving 3,000 for the royal treasury. Up to nineteen-twentieths of collections was lost in some instances, but Darigrand would settle for a general figure of four-fifths.[34] Moreover, the personnel of collection were exempt from taxes, although they were often most able to pay. By its attack on the collection apparatus, this debate helped fix in the public mind the image of waste and peculation: "ce colosse monstreux qui suffoque l'Etat"; "ces animaux voraces appellés Traitans," the "fléau des Financiers," who live among a people "inquiétés, chagrinés & tourmentés sans cesse pour la perception des Impôts."[35]

To some, the collection apparatus controverted notions of the liberties of Frenchmen, liberties that the parlements wished to safeguard. But this definition of liberties transcended the parlements' ambitions. Darigrand singled out the search of person and home executed by tax authorities and set forth a plan for a *capitation* assessed by taxpayers themselves.[36] To most observers, however, the existing system of collection and short-term credit usage was to be condemned not for its violations of basic liberties, but for its unnecessary costliness—to the people in extra levies and to the economy in a dampening effect on agriculture, industry, and trade. Some

[34] [Jean Baptiste Darigrand], *L'Anti-financier, ou relevé de quelques-unes des malversations dont se rendent journellement coupables les fermiers-généraux* . . . (Amsterdam, 1763), 59-60. Also, for a defense of the General Farm and a case that abuses were not its responsibility but the burden of a system of regional privileges and exclusions, see *Réponse à l'auteur de l'Anti-financier* ([1763]).

[35] The first quote is from [Nicolas Baudeau], *Idées d'un citoyen sur l'administration des finances du roi* (Amsterdam, 1763), 9; the next two are drawn from [Darigrand], *L'Anti-financier*, 2 and 57; and the last from *Mes rêveries sur les Doutes modestes, à l'occasion des Richesses de l'état, par M. B**** . . . , reprinted in *Richesse de l'état, à laquelle on a ajouté* . . . (Amsterdam, 1764), 103.

[36] [Darigrand], *L'Anti-financier*, 82 and *passim*.

critics argued that a major ill lay with "le défaut d'ordre et d'économie dans le paiement des dépenses du Roi."[37] But the principal
thrust of the attack aimed not at expenditures but at revenues, not
at the king's failings (which was of course dangerous territory) or
even at the obscurity of expenses on the royal household and pensions, but at the selfish failings of the king's agents. This was an un-
ambiguous appeal for absolutist intervention. Reform should be decreed.

In retrospect, with different ideas about accounting and account-
ability, we see in this debate a call for reform in the very area that
has so troubled historians seeking to reconstruct old regime French
finances—the payment of overhead costs of unknown scale off the
top. To the critics, it seemed that an unknown, and potentially immense, revenue was lost in the process of collection. Everyone worried about this issue in one way or another. Thus Baudeau, who, like
Darigrand, favored a uniform levy distributed among the thirty-two
generalities, would continue to employ the existing tax receivers but
would compensate them at a fixed rate rather than with a percentage of the money passing through their hands.[38] In other words,
Baudeau would take a step further toward the creation of a bureau-
cratic system of salaried administrators and a step away from venality. The reformers included those with misgivings about venality
in office and the limitations that venality put upon the authority of
the central government.

What makes this call for reform of the tax collection apparatus so
intriguing is the clash of interests within it. On the one hand, a
group of reformers from the parlements and from several other interest groups called for steps that would limit the authority of the
king by providing guarantees of basic principles and liberties,
among them the parlements' right of judicial review. On the other
hand, many of the same critics wished to transform the administrative apparatus of the state from venality to what we would now recognize as bureaucracy, from a system in which official functions
were leased to private entrepreneurs to one of salaried officialdom
subject to control from above. This is to say that they wished to en-

[37] [Baudeau], *Idées d'un citoyen*, 2.
[38] *Ibid.*, 23.

hance the authority of the king. Or perhaps they had in the back of their minds that the executive duties of government too would be redistributed.

Yet another corollary of the debaters' desire to simplify taxation is encountered by noticing something not present in the debate. This absent thing is the cry either to diminish expenditures or reduce the role of government spending in the economy. Certainly some people objected to excessive regulations, even to the regulation of trade at all, and some pointed to the need for continuous monitoring of expenditures. But the debaters focused on the inadequacy of revenues rather than on the excessive level of expenditures or a public sector grown too large. They foresaw an era of even vaster spending for at least as long a period as necessary to pay off the debt. And some held out the prospect of expanded spending on infrastructural improvements—roads, ports, bridges, training institutions—as visionary proposals about debt repayment released funds for other uses.

Finally, it is impossible to read this literature without recognizing in it a restatement of the principle of taxation in proportion to wealth.[39] As Forbin expressed this attitude in a book published in June, at the height of the debate, "chacun doit contribuer au payement des charges de l'Etat à proportion de son revenu ou de son gain."[40] This is not, it must be recognized at once, the idea of progressive taxation in which the percentage of the levy should rise with the wealth or income of the taxpayer. It is rather a proposal for a more or less neutral or flat tax—a single rate for all taxpayers so that the rich should pay more than the poor more or less in proportion to their greater riches. Opinion therefore still did not yet agree with Rousseau, who argued in an article published in the *Encyclopédie* in 1755 that taxation should not be strictly proportional to wealth but in proportion to the differences among taxpayers and the relative superfluity of their wealth.[41] Nevertheless, there was among the debaters nearly a consensus that the taxes should be paid in money. The rich should not escape their fair share of taxation. Exemptions

[39] Such a view is apparent also in earlier literature on financial reform. See, e.g., [Buchet du Pavillon], *Les finances considérées*, 107.

[40] F[orbin], *Système*, 6. The date of publication is inferred from [Bauchaumont], *Mémoires secrets*, I, 241, who mentions this book first on Jun. 30.

[41] Jean Jacques Rousseau, "Political Economy," in Roger D. Masters, *On the Social Contract*, trans. by Judith R. Masters (New York, 1978), 221 and 231-32.

for the nobility should end. The basis for them no longer existed, since the king paid for services and functions, such as the army, formerly supplied in kind.[42]

A consensus had arisen, at least among the debaters. It favored equality before the tax law, as monitored by the courts and expressed by agreement on two principles—all should pay the taxes, which was not a new idea, and all should pay them in cash, which was novel. By late August 1763, however, interest in the debate waned. The public was fatigued.[43] Darigrand revived the discussion briefly in December but was arrested in January 1764. Three months later Bachaumont said that the debate had passed like "une maladie épidémique."[44]

Why is this so? Why, if a consensus had been articulated, did the ministries, the parlements, and the king not seize upon it? The answer is that the consensus threatened, in a direct and immediate way, the very characteristics that made the old regime a distinct phase of social and political history. It threatened the pocketbooks of all who might have acted, even of the king, who was asked to risk a reform that would create an hiatus in revenues while it was introduced. It threatened, moreover, to remove the motor of the mechanism of the old regime, privilege, by withdrawing the right to give compensation for citizenship (the debaters described themselves as citizens and subjects) in the state in the form of service rather than cash. Bachaumont was correct. The debate was an epidemic, which no one in a position of power wanted to transform from theory and political maneuvering into practice. To enact the consensus on reform would have been to dismantle the old regime.

CONFRONTATION BETWEEN KING AND PARLEMENT

Beginning before the Seven Years War, with mounting aggressiveness during the conflict and in a grand clash of wills in 1763, the parlements of France, which were both judicial and administrative institutions, resisted the king's rule on finance and taxation. This resistance is part of a larger confrontation in which, on many matters

[42] *La taille réelle, lettre d'un avocat de Paris* (n.p., [1763]), 27; [Mirabeau], *Théorie de l'impôt*, 32.
[43] *Journal encyclopédique*, Aug. 15, 1763, p. 149.
[44] [Bachaumont], *Mémoires secrets*, II, 40.

of law, the parlements proclaimed their responsibility to speak for, defend the interests of, and introduce reforms on behalf of the nation. They set forth once again an old doctrine, that the power of the king is limited by certain basic laws and liberties; to the parlements belongs the responsibility of assuring adherence to these laws and liberties. In fiscal and financial policy, in that realm of issues where status and pride become confused and intensified by the self-interest of economic benefit, the king and the parlements struggled over political power and tax advantage.

The terms of the confrontation are explained in an usually long article published in January 1759 in the *Journal de commerce* of Brussels.[45] The anonymous author, a Francophile Netherlander, posed the issue of why British credit should be deemed superior to French. Investors living outside the two countries—in the Dutch Republic—were willing to lend to either, but in order to equalize the wartime flow of money France had to pay about 5 percent and Britain only 3 percent (and the Dutch Republic itself only 2.5 percent). It is said, the author wrote, that France warrants less confidence as a debtor, but in truth this is owing to prejudice rather than to a fair comparison of the two debtors. The leading reason usually given for this lesser degree of confidence is that France might repeat the debt reduction that settled the Law system. But those who say this overlook the fact that Britain did much the same thing at the same time in settling the South Sea Bubble.

Behind these prejudicial recollections, the author continued, lies a theory of rival state systems. Britain is preferred as a debtor because the British debt is said to be a state debt whereas the French is said to be a royal debt. In truth it is the nation that borrows in both lands (a point generally acknowledged in royal and public commentary in France). Just as the British parliament gives the seal of approval of the nation to a loan by adopting it, the French parlement acts on behalf of the nation by registering royal loan edicts. Just as parliament may decline to enact any measure deemed arbitrary, parlement may decline to register any royal act deemed unjust. No edict or declaration will possess the force of law until it has been registered.[46]

[45] "Lettre d'un Hollandois . . . crédit de la France . . . ," *Journal de commerce*, Jan. 1759, 71-136.
[46] The key passages appear in *ibid.*, 83-85.

These, then, were the issues. The parlements, led by the parlement of Paris, claimed the right to review royal decrees to determine whether they were in accord with tradition and law. This was a constitutional power, to which earlier kings had objected but failed to remove from the pretensions of the parlements. Instead they had turned to the *lit de justice*, a ceremony reminding the parlementaires that the right of judicial review was delegated and could be withdrawn, or to another means of forcing obedience. The confrontation of king and parlements during the Seven Years War raised the issue afresh because royal agents had to go to the parlements to register each new loan and each new taxation measure, for these measures specifically required parlementary action. Moreover, the eighteenth-century parlementaires had been gradually reviving assertions last made forcefully during the seventeenth-century revolt of the parlements and the nobility known as the Fronde. In 1732 the *Judicium Francorum* held that parlement was "la représentation de la monarchie tout entière."[47] The basis for this claim lay in the parlements' comparison of their functions and responsibilities with those of other institutions. As ancient as the monarchy, a permanent institution, and an institution possessing the people's confidence, the parlements claimed to represent the people. Such a concept of representation, so obviously different from the notion of selected representation, was founded on the parlements' claim to be the depository of the fundamental law, to be the only institution in France that could play such a role.[48]

Thus the twelve sovereign courts of France, each of which possessed the authority to review royal edicts, to raise its own objections or remonstrate, and in the end to register a law under its own conditions for its jurisdiction, would review legislation. The king did not dispute this authority, although Louis XV's great-grandfather, Louis XIV, had ordered the parlements to be silent. Two issues were at risk in the Seven Years War confrontation: Could the parlements revive their asserted right to reject royal edicts? Could the parlements initiate legislation? In the first of these the location of sovereignty was at issue, for although the formula used by the parle-

---

[47] Marcel Marion, *Dictionnaire des institutions de la France aux XVIIe et XVIIIe siècles* (Paris, 1923), 423.

[48] This is also the case that Darigrand made: "Actuellement la Nation n'a plus que vous, Nos seigneurs, pour représentans." *L'Anti-financier*, 5.

ments in remonstrances recognized the king as sovereign, the courts claimed that the final authority of law lay with them. In the second of these, the parlements were feeling their way toward a shift from a passive to an active role in legislation, especially in financial legislation, and in administration, overseeing financial and tax functions.

During the course of the eighteenth century, after the death of Louis XIV in 1715, the confrontation between the parlements and the king developed certain characteristics suggesting a sense of fair play. On the part of the parlements, the king's need for additional taxes in war was acknowledged, so that in 1733 and 1741 the extraordinary levy of a *dixième* was registered anew without difficulty. On the king's part, this informal adherence to rules required that he content himself with the ordinary taxes for peacetime revenues. In 1725 this agreement was temporarily abrogated when the king sought to levy a peacetime *cinquantième*, which, to be registered, required a *lit de justice*. But that measure was withdrawn in the following year.

This working agreement broke down at the end of the War of Austrian Succession, when Machault succeeded in carrying the *dixième*-halved-to-a-*vingtième* over into peace, a measure that coincided with the emergence in 1751 of serious conflict over the 1713 Bull Unigenitus, which asserted a theological position of strict orthodoxy that the parlements, centers of Jansenist and Gallican sentiment, opposed. (It is important to notice that the *gages* of the parlementaires were, beginning in the mid-1740s, no longer paid from central government revenues but directly from fees collected by the courts. Thus the parlementaires secured a financial freedom of action they had not earlier possessed.) This conflict ended in 1763 with the expulsion of the Jesuits, a considerable victory for the parlements.

When, in 1756, the king dispatched to the parlement of Paris the order for a second *vingtième*, the parlement resisted furiously, forcing Louis XV to hold a *lit de justice*. While this step compelled the parlement of Paris to submit, both the provincial parlements and the assemblies in the *pays d'état* took up the dispute. Their resistance led to a compromise according to which the *verificateurs* appointed under the terms of the 1749 continuation of the *vingtième* were expelled.[49] But the important point is that Machault had ended the era of fair play, freeing the parlementaires to assert themselves.

In 1756 not only the parlements but also the Cour des aides, in Paris an institution separate from the parlement possessing the authority to register royal edicts on certain issues, such as *taille* exemptions, put itself forth as a guardian of the interests of the people. Charged with handling judicial proceedings involving the *aides*, the *taille*, and some other taxes, the Cour des aides accepted the royal edict because of the urgency created by the war, and then, in September, drafted its remonstrances to the king.[50] Many issues troubled these magistrates—defects in the assessment of the first *vingtième*, which was not applied to the incomes of the farmers general, arbitrariness in the taxes in general, and the multiplicity of levies— but they drew the king's attention to one problem in particular. When would the first *vingtième* end? The king had ordered that the levy be continued for ten years after the peace, throughout to be used to retire debts from the last war. This was an unfixed period, since one did not know when the peace would occur (or whether the king would defer peace for some time after the conclusion of hostilities, as had happened before). Surely the magnitude of the debt was known, and from that could be inferred the term necessary to retire it. "Voilà, Sire, ce qui cause les plus vives alarmes de vos Peuples; l'idée de la perpétuité de l'impôt. . . ."[51] At the very beginning of the series of edicts that would be necessary to finance the Seven Years War, a series of edicts no different in nature from those necessary to arrange the finances of the War of Austrian Succession or the War of Polish Succession, the king was put on notice that the courts of the land and, so the parlementaires said, the people also demanded fundamental tax reforms. These reforms, the parlementaires said, would remove any threat that monarchical power should become despotic in finance.

In 1757 and 1758 pressure was kept on the ministers, and in 1759 open conflict reappeared. Silhouette's plan to tax the rich, which

[49] Egret, *Louis XV et l'opposition parlementaire*, 50 and 74-78.

[50] [Auger], ed., *Mémoires pour servir à l'histoire du droit public de la France en matières d'impôts . . .* (Brussels, 1779), 5-15. Also Marion, *Histoire financière*, I, 182ff., on other remonstrances of 1756-1757.

[51] [Auger], ed., *Mémoires*, 5.

has already been discussed, required a *lit de justice* in September. Again the Cour des aides also remonstrated, iterating the themes of 1756, including its cry for a general reform of the taxes. The judicial bodies, even one that was only beginning to assert its claim to the ancient permanence that qualified it too to represent the people, called for new legislation and offered to describe the contents of the new laws. And the Cour des comptes joined the struggle. "La guerre était donc déclarée entre la magistrature et le courageux ministre"[52] (which is Marion's view of the distribution of right and wrong).[53]

Silhouette's successor, Bertin, easily persuaded the king to withdraw the *subvention générale* only in February 1760 to induce him to adopt a third *vingtième* and a doubled *capitation* on all individuals not subject to the *taille*—the owners of non-taillable land and the residents of provinces where the *taille* was not assessed. It was the opposition of the parlementaires to the third *vingtième* that seems to have persuaded Marion that they had only their own selfish interests at heart.[54] This, in Marion's eyes the fairest of all old regime taxes, the courts resisted. The parlement of Paris declared its unwillingness to register the third *vingtième* without reform, and the parlement of Rouen denounced the taxes in general as arbitrary and tyrannical. Its magistrates iterated the responsibility of the courts as depository of the law and proclaimed the need for a national parlement—a parlement de France—to register fiscal laws. The magistrates of Rouen hoped to prohibit the collection of any taxes not freely registered. Louis XV held another *lit de justice* and summoned a selected group of parlementaires to Versailles to tell them: "Je suis votre maître. . . ; enregistrez mes édits sans délai. . . ."[55]

Each confrontation led the parlementaires into more assertive or

[52] Marion, *Histoire financière*, I, 196.
[53] Jean Egret offers a revisionist interpretation, arguing that the parlementaires often sought to protect other interests than their own. Egret, *Louis XV et l'opposition parlementaire, passim*, esp. 5-6. I find this argument not completely persuasive because the parlements analyzed the financial problem in terms of overhead costs and money squandered but not in terms of tax avoidance and privilege, issues striking closer to home. For Marion's case see Marcel Marion, *L'impôt sur le revenu au dix-huitième siècle principalement en Guyenne* (Toulouse, 1901), 169ff. Also R[obert] R. Palmer, *The Age of the Democratic Revolution* (2 vols.; Princeton, 1959-1961), I, 89-99, styling the longer conflict of 1763-1774 a "quasi-revolution."
[54] See his discussion in Marion, *Histoire financière*, I, 205ff.
[55] Quoted by *ibid.*, I, 208.

insolent language[56] and more radical claims about their authority and led the king into more severe measures of affirming royal authority. Here is the building of tension from which an open clash—a revolution—might be expected. Only the war, which the parlementaires did not want to risk being charged with having undermined, led the magistrates to submit. The climax came with peace, in 1763, when Bertin announced in April the need to prolong the first and second *vingtièmes* and the *dons gratuits* paid by the municipalities since 1759, to tax offices and *rentes*, and to conduct a land survey as the basis for general tax reform. In this series of edicts and declarations the parlements were challenged with both a new levy on their assets and the further prolongation of levies they had resisted in 1756.

In earlier remonstrances the courts had objected to general failings in the taxes—their arbitrariness and the number of disputes they occasioned (a strange protest from jurists, one that the magistrates may not have thoroughly thought through); their multiplicity and the desirability of fewer levies, even a single tax; and the suspicion raised by ignorance of the scale of the debt or the size of financial needs. Forced now to defend their own interests, the parlementaires elected to attack the financiers, to single out a segment of the system in far greater need of reform than the tax avoidance allowed owners of venal offices and *rentes*. In the remonstrances of November 21, 1763, the parlement of Aix pointed to a disproportion between the rewards received by the financiers and the services they provided.[57] No one except the financiers knew the scale of these rewards, but the parlementaires, like the writers of pamphlets, were persuaded that they were excessive. Like Darigrand, the parlementaires were also concerned about arbitrariness in the General Farm, about laws so variegated as to be obscure to payers and collectors alike, leading to the collection of revenues not due as well as to evasion.

One of the specific goals of the parlements was the regularization of the budget, an issue raised by the parlement of Rouen. Knowledge of the finances was too restricted; the accounts should be sent to the parlements. Each expenditure category should have specific

[56] See the views of the Cour des aides in a 1759 letter to the king, in [Auger], ed., *Mémoires*, 54.

[57] Egret, *Louis XV et l'opposition parlementaire*, 117.

revenues assigned to it in an inviolate system. Thus the magistrates of Rouen would expand the *charges* against central government revenues and make them the foundation for reform.[58] Before such a plentitude of ideas about reform, the king, who had at first resisted,[59] withdrew Bertin's April edicts, acknowledged the need for reform, called upon the parlements, the Cour des aides, and the Cour des comptes to suggest reform measures, and established a commission of jurists to collect and summarize these recommendations. At the same time, in November 1763, Louis XV renewed his order for a cadastre, ordered the continuation of the second *vingtième* until 1768, and initiated a five-year long investigation of the tax systems of Europe, headed by the *intendant des finances* Moreau de Beaumont.[60] He also dismissed Bertin, as a concession to the parlements, and appointed in his place Laverdy, a conseiller to the parlement of Paris and a well-known Jansenist.

Many of the parlements—Paris, Rouen, Aix, Metz, Dijon, Toulouse, Grenoble, Besançon, Bordeaux (especially Rouen, Toulouse, and Grenoble)—reacted in 1763.[61] In several provinces the magistrates threatened to arrest royal officials dispatched to enforce Bertin's measures. In Rouen, where opposition was most intense, where the magistrates spoke of "la Nation française dont le nom seul annonce la liberté qui lui est naturelle,"[62] and called (in 1760) for the convocation of the Estates General, registration was accomplished only under the threat that *lettres de cachet* would be issued, permitting the arrest of the jurists without the ordinary protections of French law. Even then only a rump of the parlement acquiesced, and the full body attempted to nullify registration.[63] Using the *mémoires* drafted by the magistrates in Aix, Paul Beik has described the

[58] *Ibid.*, 123-24.

[59] *Journal encyclopédique*, May 31, 1763, pp. 159 and 165-66; and [Auger], ed., *Mémoires*, 106.

[60] Peter Claus Hartmann, ed., *Das Steuersystem der europäischen Staaten am Ende des Ancien Régime* (Munich, 1979); and the first volume of [J. L. Moreau de Beaumont], *Mémoires concernant les impositions et droits* . . . (4 vols.; Paris, 1768-1769).

[61] Egret, *Louis XV et l'opposition parlementaire*, 148-54; Ernest D. Glasson, *Le parlement de Paris* (2 vols.; Paris, 1901), II, 281-87; and David Hudson, "The Parlementary Crisis of 1763 in France and its Consequences," *Canadian Journal of History*, 7, no. 2 (Sept. 1972), 97-117.

[62] Bibliothèque Nationale, Joly de Fleury, 577, folios 164-67, including the *Arrêt du parlement*, p. 2 for the quote.

[63] Paul H. Beik, *A Judgment of the Old Régime*, (New York, 1944), 49.

response of one parlement, a response that carried far beyond the issue of tax reform on which the king had solicited advice. This response, drawing heavily on Forbonnais' publications and on the worldly knowledge and insights of the magistrates, demonstrates the enormous complexity of even a superficial investigation of the taxes—an investigation, that is, which depended on these sources but did not consult the financial accounts, the actual condition of the economy, or the relationship between personal income and the taxes. (All these matters were commented upon, but from hypothetical rather than firsthand sources of information. The parlements asked to see the royal accounts, but were willing to explain the faults the accounts would reveal.) It also shows the vastness of the task the king had set for the tax reform commission. The magistrates of Aix planned an investigation of five parts, but seem to have lost their enthusiasm toward the end of the second, in 1766, when they had completed already fourteen manuscript volumes of prefatory material.[64] In March 1764, while these inquiries were underway and after Darigrand's brief revival of the public debate in December and January, the king forbade further publications on finance by writers "sans caractère," thus restricting the field to the parlementaires and other officials.[65]

The outcome of this confrontation between the parlements and the king, historians seem to agree unanimously,[66] was a parlementary victory, one of an exasperating series of victories leading to the temporary exile of the parlement of Paris in 1771. In 1763 the king dismissed Bertin, withdrew the April edicts, although in a coy way, and invited the courts to advise him on tax reform, thereby giving in to the parlement. This interpretation seems to me to misjudge the situation. What did the king want? Louis XV wanted to augment the ordinary peacetime revenues without revealing details on spending

[64] Ibid., 69-73.

[65] George T. Matthews, The Royal General Farms in Eighteenth-Century France (New York, 1958), 275n7, says that the farmers general persuaded the king to issue this edict. The debate did not stop, but for about a decade contributions to it appeared with little frequency and were often published abroad. E.g., [Jean François Le Vayer], Essai sur la possibilité d'un droit unique (London, 1764); and the republication of pamphlets from the debate in Richesse de l'état, à laquelle on a ajouté. . . .

[66] Beik, Judgment, passim, e.g., p. 55; Egret, Louis XV et l'opposition parlementaire, 156; Hudson, "Parlementary Crisis," 97 and 103; Marion, Histoire financière, I, 218; Palmer, Revolution, I, 92; and Steven L. Kaplan, Bread, Politics and Political Economy in the Reign of Louis XV (2 vols.; The Hague, 1976), 140.

or the debt, and he wanted to preserve the existing tax structure and its dual system of tax payments in service and cash.[67] He wanted also to maintain his inheritance of authority in the face of the parlementary challenge. What did the parlements want? They wished to overturn the existing tax system but lacked a specific plan for that. In any event, they would certainly diminish opportunities for financiers and tax farmers, augment their own authority in creating and modifying law as well as in settling disputes, and shift sovereignty away from the king.

The November 1763 modifications of the decrees of April preserved the peacetime *vingtième*, added a second *vingtième* in peace, and preserved the *dixième* surcharge first enacted during the War of Austrian Succession. They also retained the cadastre plan, which the king and the ministers saw as a step toward tax reform since it would provide information about the quantity and quality of all the land in France, that exempt from the *taille* (identified with privilege and tax avoidance) and that subject to it.[68] And in November the king inaugurated an investigation of tax systems in Europe, looking for alternatives to existing French practice. These modifications dropped the threat of a small tax on offices and *rentes constituées*, a tax directly offensive to the parlementaires, and seemed to open the way to parlementary involvement in tax reform. There are two ways to interpret this last part of the king's action. Did the king intend merely to engage the parlementaires in a long and fruitless discussion of the intricacies of tax reform? No better (or more modern) tactic can be imagined than to invite the magistrates to submit all their ideas to a commission while at the same time setting in train an international inquiry that would add to the multiplicity of views and recommendations. Or did the king intend to find a workable path for reform? The cadastre project, which could easily have been dropped, and the solicitation of ideas and models across a broad spectrum of French opinion and foreign practice, imply a search for a pragmatic reform grounded in specific and detailed knowledge

[67] See the royal response to the remonstrances of the parlement of Bordeaux in [Darigrand], *L'Anti-financier*, 94-100.

[68] In registering the November acts, however, the parlements added the proviso that the cadastre was not to lead to an end to the tax exemption of noble lands. The actual survey was postponed.

about the landed assets of the French (in a period in which the most progressive tax theorists focused their attention on land rather than manufacturing or commercial assets).

To speak of victory for the parlements in 1763 is to claim a triumph that was not won. The king gained more in 1763 than did the parlements, for he gained the continuation of extraordinary taxes into peace and he left unresolved the challenge to royal authority that the parlements had mounted. This is, of course, a short-run view. In the long run, since none of the visions of tax reform seen in 1763 was enacted, no one won.

THE LIBERTIES OF THE FRENCH

Several times now we have encountered this phrase, "the liberties of the French," which sounds so strange on the lips. Yet the literature of 1760-1763 is full of assertions about these liberties, as it is also full of rhetoric calling to mind words central to the Revolution: citoyen, égalité, liberté, patriotisme, la nation, "le vœu de la nation," "la Nation Française dont le nom seul annonce la liberté qui lui est naturelle."[69] Phrases so closely identified with the Revolution were used freely many decades before 1789. Two men who discussed what seemed to them to be basic principles—Mirabeau and Darigrand—were deprived of their freedom by being imprisoned briefly. They were imprisoned not for any radical statement reassigning sovereignty or enlarging basic liberties, but for the intemperance of their language, which too blatantly insulted powerful interests, especially the financiers and tax farmers. Even so, we can begin with them, looking for an enumeration of the liberties of the French, some of which have been mentioned in earlier sections of this book.

Mirabeau opened his attempt to create a *Théorie de l'impôt* by asserting the responsibilities of ruler to subject. "L'objet de la finance dans la recette est le service du public; dans la dépense il est le maintien & la sûreté des particuliers." [70] Basic to this theory was the proposition that monarchy is the union of the self-interested particularism of the king's subjects, which may be in harmony or disharmony.

[69] *Arrêt du parlement* (Rouen, 1763), p. 2, of which a copy appears in Bibliothèque Nationale, Joly de Fleury, 577, folios 166-67.
[70] P. 13.

Harmony depends on the observation of certain basic rights and on the security of property and the enjoyment of its fruits. The sovereign must provide order without hindering the pursuit of private interests. To Mirabeau, the emerging physiocrat, the liberties of the French begin and end here, and all prescriptions for reform depart from these premises. Thus Mirabeau iterated Montesquieu's argument about political liberty, which consists of security and more specifically of taxes from the portion of his property that each subject gives "in order to secure or enjoy the remainder."[71]

Darigrand opened *L'Anti-financier* with a call to patriotism: "Je suis Français, c'est-à-dire, rempli du plus respectueux amour pour mon Roi, soumis aux loix, aimant plus que la vie les droits sacrés de ma liberté, aimant mes Concitoyens, & compatissant aux maux que leur font éprouver, moins encore les impôts excessifs qu'ils supportent, que les déprédations des Traitans." "Puisse l'heureuse révolution qui purgera la France du fléau des Financiers, être une des glorieuses époques du règne de Louis le Bien-aimé."[72] For both Mirabeau and Darigrand, stepping beyond Montesquieu, the people with a role to play in the collection and management of the taxes (and therefore not just the *traitants*) compromised the basic liberties of the French. The present regime had two ills—fanaticism (in religion) and its tax system, which violated liberty. Specifically, Darigrand objected to the right of tax agents to search person and property.[73] For Darigrand as for Mirabeau and the physiocrats, the great compromiser of French liberties was the despotism of the tax collector.

Here are restated, in the language of the early 1760s, conceptions about liberties basic to the French which did not arise in the 1760s, but at some unknown time many decades earlier. They are not liberties of the Enlightenment or of a regime like Britain's, which Montesquieu admired, but time-honored claims of personal rather than philosophic rights. Foremost among these is the principle that lay behind the French loathing of their taxes: that the individual possesses the right to maintain the secrecy of his own finances. The searches to which Darigrand objected—like much of the program of

---

[71] Charles Secondat de Montesquieu, *The Spirit of the Laws*, trans. by Thomas Nugent (New York, 1949), 183 and 207 (quote from p. 207).

[72] Respectively, pp. 1-2 and p. 2.

[73] [Darigrand], *L'Anti-financier*, 42-56.

tax reform articulated by the debaters and the parlementaires of 1763—threatened this right of the household to the secrecy of its affairs. This right militated against the enumeration of the population, against the recurrent royal effort to measure the wealth and taxability of the realm, against infringement of the father's authority over wife and children, and against the surveillance of income and assets. The second basic liberty that was articulated—in current form by Mirabeau, again restating an older notion—was that taxes could not be so large as to compromise economic activity. The king could take part, or even all, of the surplus that his subjects produced individually and collectively. But he should not take anything beyond this surplus, which itself of course defies definition or identification.

This is not therefore a discussion about French liberties articulated merely from a sense of the desirability of adopting English modes and English liberties. For all the familiarity in mid-eighteenth-century France with the phrase "the liberties of the English," we are not dealing with reformers who knew conditions in England and wished to install them in France. The unfamiliarity with English modes is evident from the attorney Darigrand's incredible cry that France should adopt the English law which punished with death anyone who proposed that the taxes be farmed for collection.[74] These instead were conceived to be fundamental and ancient French liberties.

The key words and ideas in this discussion—liberty, arbitrariness, oppression, privilege, property—join with and enlarge the circle of, in Keith Baker's phrase, "ideological claims that Jansenists hurled against oppressive clergy; that parlementary magistrates elaborated in exile and circulated in clandestinely published remonstrances; that provincial Estates mobilized against ministerial enemies."[75] In 1763, however, these words and ideas were part of public debate— they were not only circulated in "clandestinely published remonstrances" and in the provinces but openly in Paris itself. And they were not limited to magistrate circles. From May 1763 until March

[74] *Ibid.*, 27.

[75] Keith Michael Baker, "On the Problem of the Ideological Origins of the French Revolution," in Dominick LaCapra and Steven L. Kaplan, eds., *Modern European Intellectual History* (Ithaca, 1982), 208-209. Baker identifies liberty, despotism, property, and representation.

1764 the royal authorities allowed an open and sometimes insolent discussion of defects in the finances.[76] That it was a public debate was remarked upon by the author of *Réflexions sur les ressources actuelles*.[77] No longer did England alone enjoy the freedom of the press.

This was a discussion with a history. Baker calls attention to the marquis d'Argenson's attentiveness in 1751 to what seemed to him to be "a philosophical wind blowing toward us from England in favor of free, anti-monarchical government."[78] Argenson expected a revolution, acting out changes that had already occurred in people's minds, a revolution to install the insights and modes of thought of the Enlightenment. Surely this is the most long awaited of all revolutions.

Bringing together these two strands—the Enlightenment concern with despotism, privilege and equality before the tax law, and the more ancient preoccupation with freedom from surveillance and the security of property—we recognize the irreconcilability of the principles at stake in 1763. It is not only that some of those who would reform the old regime believed, like Mirabeau and the physiocrats, that the most adept reformer would be an enlightened king, and that others, such as Darigrand, preferred to rely on the parlements and their claim to share sovereignty with the king. The irreconcilability lies also in the principles most dear both to those who would reform and to those who would not. It lies in the sheer impossibility of finding a path of reform consonant with the preservation of ancient liberties, especially freedom from surveillance.

CONCLUSION

At first glance these proposals for tax reform seem to have offered an opportunity for the monarchy to be strengthened and reformed. The number of promising ideas is abundant, the realization of the

[76] The foreign press followed both the debate and the confrontation. See., e.g., *Gazette van Antwerpen*, Jun. 7, Jun. 10, Jun. 14, Jun. 24, Jul. 5, Jul. 19, Sept. 6, and Dec. 6, 1763; and *The Annual Register, or a View of the History, Politics, and Literature . . .*, 1764, pt. 1, pp. 7-8. Also Félix Rocquain, *L'Esprit révolutionnaire avant la Révolution, 1715-1789* (Geneva, 1971 reprint).

[77] (N.p., [1763]), 1.

[78] Baker, "Ideological Origins," 208, quoting Argenson's *Journal*, VI, 464. Also Egret, *Louis XV et l'opposition parlementaire*, 230-31.

costs of privilege and inefficiency and peculation clear, the will to adopt reforms impressive. But the significant reforms—those that would have delivered large enough returns to make a material difference toward repaying the debt and putting the finances in order—were contrary to principles and characteristics fundamental to the old regime. To adopt the cash form of equality before the tax law, to require therefore that everyone pay taxes in proportion to assets and income, was to destroy the motor of the old regime social and political system, which was that privilege most usefully expressed in tax advantages. To survey the quality and quantity of land in the realm, or to undertake any of a number of steps designed to end arbitrariness in the taxation of incomes, was to violate a liberty that the French judged to be basic. To reform the old regime in the ways suggested in 1763 was to abolish it.

Why was the abolition conceived but not enacted? The problem that the king and his ministers, the magistrates of the parlements and cours, and the reformers faced is apparent. For all the discussion of public opinion, especially by the magistrates, there is no evidence that the general public—merchants, artisans, stevedores, domestic servants, notaries, mechanics, peasants, clerics, and so many others—became engaged in this debate. The parlements' claim to speak for the people was not yet to be taken seriously; that would come only later.[79] Only the naive Du Pont de Nemours consulted a few of the "people," his father's cook and "quelques Chartiers qui labouraient le long du chemin," and then to confirm opinions already reached through abstract thought.[80] A revolution impended in 1763, but it was a revolution from above. It was born out of the joining together of old convictions—the parlements' and the king's beliefs about their powers in basic law and the articulate and perhaps also the inarticulate public's beliefs about its liberties—with the Enlightenment conviction that disharmony between man and his milieu might be ended, and happiness—meaning contentment in prosperity and civility—might be inaugurated.

Briefly everyone within the articulate public was enlightened; everyone in this circle possessed the rising expectations of an improvement in the human condition. Even the king believed that jus-

[79] François Furet, *Interpreting the French Revolution*, trans. by Elborg Forster (Cambridge, 1981), 36.
[80] Eleutherian-Mills Historical Library, Du Pont Papers, Autobiography, p. 27.

tice might be advanced by a reconsideration of the Calas case, public health served by better burial practices in Paris, and economic productivity enhanced by freeing the grain trade. But how far might the Enlightenment doctrine of improvements extend? In taxation and finance the number of remedies was too great rather than too small, and many of them came into conflict with principles and institutions basic to the old regime. The limits of the doctrine had been exceeded by the problems posed by finance and taxation, with the result that the public debate and the confrontation between parlements and king could not identify what was to be done. They only articulated an impasse, ideals that could not be achieved at all or that could be reached only at the expense of the old regime itself. But the revolutionaries of 1763 were the old regime.

CONCLUSION

In 1755 France embarked on another war. It was an uncommon example of a commonplace activity, for in the terms counted most dear in the old regime, the Seven Years War cost the monarchy much. France lost large blocks of territory and even more prestige. Its armies in Germany, in alliance with Austria and Russia and with a combined population of some 70 million behind them, failed to defeat the armies of Prussia, which drew sustenance from a populace of some 3.5 million. Its navy failed to slip away from the British in order to assist in the first of a series of grand designs for an invasion of England. Instead British units forced battle, and the French lost. In Africa France sacrificed a small west coast colony; in India it traded conquests with the British; and in the Americas France lost Canada and, only temporarily, some important sugar islands in the Caribbean. At the end of the war, to compensate Spain for the loss of Florida, France ceded the Louisiana territory. The risks posed by old regime war were attractive enough to European kings and oligarchs to induce them to fight often. For France, taking these risks in 1755 led to humiliation: France lost the most in the very areas—territory and prestige—that bulked largest in justifying the inordinate expenditures on war with which old regime rulers indulged themselves.

The French felt this humiliation more keenly than did their enemies and allies, who understood that France still commanded vast resources in manpower and money and that France remained the single most powerful state in Europe. Thus the effects of the war were played out in France itself rather than in international affairs, where France's enemies might, except for their sense of how strong France remained, be expected to have continued to press their advantage. And in France it was not the king who was most deeply humiliated, but a broad spectrum of people who wished to introduce reforms. Louis XV sensed the humiliation so little that he allowed the completion and unveiling of an equestrian statue of himself to proceed in June 1763, at the risk of public smirking about unveiling a martial statue after the greatest French defeat in many decades. Those who felt this humiliation, or who professed to feel it, were instead the magistrates of the parlements, the physiocrats, the enemies of the tax farmers and financiers, and a host of other still smaller groups and individuals who shared with the king a sense of the timeliness of reform, but who disagreed among themselves about the reforms that were needed.

The conventional wisdom of the old regime seems to have been accurate, to a certain extent. The risks in going to war were political more than economic. Searching in the way followed here, using existing evidence about the economy, it is difficult to find any area of the economy in which the Seven Years War involved substantial costs. In neither the visible areas of economic impact about which the authorities worried—especially the money supply—nor the invisible areas—the scale and trend of economic resources construed more broadly than money—has this investigation uncovered evidence of large and immediate costs. It is true that this war, like other old regime wars, temporarily reversed the flow of specie and changed the composition of the money stock, enlarging the portion in paper and cutting the part in specie. After the war, however, the specie stock quickly regained its prewar level. And in this instance much of the paper put into circulation during the war remained in circulation, without the larger overall money supply leading to immediate inflation. Only in 1766 did prices begin to rise, and then the cause seems real—harvest shortfalls—rather than monetary.

It is true also that this war, like every other eighteenth-century conflict, cost the French much in the capital equipment of trade: ships. Hundreds of coasting, fishing, oceanic, and naval vessels were lost, requiring a large rebuilding effort that began in the last years of the war. But French trade suffered much less than these losses, or the conventional judgments of historians, would lead us to expect. Merchants both compensated for the wartime curtailment of exchanges by heavy postwar trading—presumably in many new vessels built toward the end of the war—and anticipated wars, by watching international news, gunpowder and saltpeter prices, and munitions orders. They watched these signs so closely that French merchants laid in stocks of colonial goods before the Seven Years War; and sugar, which by itself accounted for more than half of imports from the colonies, did not increase in price until 1758 or 1759, even though trade routes along which sugar was carried had begun to suffer British interference in 1755. And these merchants foresaw war so effectively that the number of bankruptcies in one city, Marseilles, actually declined during the war even while the number of ships taken by the enemy rose. Furthermore, French merchants compensated for the closure of peacetime trade routes by expanding trade with Germany and Spain. As a result, the volume of goods that might have been carried in the counterfactual case of trade unimpeded by war does not seem to have been much greater than the volume of goods actually carried in a world repeatedly facing war. War certainly added costs to international trade, requiring more extensive storage facilities and setting a premium on the flow of information, especially information about certain key signals. But its inroads fall far short of those implied by the dramatic language ordinarily used to assess the impact of the Seven Years War on French trade.

Behind the front lines of the economy exposed to war, it is more difficult still to detect effects. In the horn-shaped area demarcated by Charleville, Paris/Pontoise, and Tonnerre, which furnished grain and forage to the French army, wheat prices moved in a mild countercyclical manner during both mobilization and demobilization. Thus the conversion of the peacetime army of some 130,000 French soldiers into a wartime army of some 200,000 French soldiers, and the larger and in these terms more serious wartime staffing of militia and coast guard, seem to have been felt in wheat prices. Recruits, drawn especially from an unskilled pool of single men living in the countryside, became full-time consumers whereas they had previously made some contribution to production. But for most of the war the troops in Germany were fed from Germany rather than France. For the domestic economy, their departure takes the form of outdoor relief in which the countryside was temporarily relieved of men who would not, in any case, have produced as much as they consumed. For the rest, it is difficult to find more than a few industries—cotton and verdigris—whose output suffered in the war. French agriculture enjoyed an unusual run of good harvests, the result of course of good fortune rather than of the war. A benevolent Nature may have tempered the price effects of mobilization and demobilization. The available sources are not sensitive to this possibility.

A balance can be struck about the economic effects of this war in particular and of old regime war in general, insofar as French participation in the Seven Years War may stand for other wars and other countries, and under the important provision that this war stands at neither end of the extreme: it was neither as grave as the late wars of Louis XIV or the Thirty Years War, nor as mild as the War of Polish Succession or the early wars of Louis XIV. The evidence does not point toward either the profound or brutal effects asserted by those who would view old regime wars as having serious economic consequences, or the stimulative or even profitable consequences of those who would view these wars most generously. This war was not benign; it made itself felt in prices, in capital equipment, in interest rates, in trade overheads, and in other ways. But taken individually and together these effects do not amount to enough to have made war an economic event of profound and immediate importance. War brought some costs, but its aggregate economic effects were mild. The transactions costs that war added, and even the slight effect that war had on other indicators of economic activity, do not amount to enough to warrant a claim that it was this war that held the old regime back from long-run growth, although the iterative wastefulness of many wars, and the ravages of wars fought at home, must have been contributing factors to the absence of sustained growth in the era of the warring state.

Nor does this example of old regime wars sustain the still undeveloped suggestion from scholars such as Crouzet, Carrière, and Butel that these wars were able to obscure short-run and intermediate-run economic cycles, or, as Morineau argues, to dominate the waves or sequences of economic life. The evidence about cycles and sequences, which is based on price series limited to agricultural goods rather than on output series or even on prices covering most goods consumed in significant quantities, does not reveal regularly reoccurring waves except perhaps in very long-run form. But it also does not show that the onset of this war had any effect on the short and intermediate but irregular cycles that the price series reveal. If war shaped these cycles in some way, then the mechanism, which must have been indirect and lagged, remains obscure. As a result, old regime war resembles not that "fait essentiel de l'histoire économique du XVIIIᵉ siècle,"[1] but a much less important economic event. It had limited effects not because the economy was geared to war, which, except for merchants, it was not. The effects were limited because war was geared to the economy.

[1] Paul Butel, *Les négociants bordelais, l'Europe et les Iles au XVIIIᵉ siècle* (Paris, 1974), 382.

War's effect on the distribution of wealth and the mid-century trend in income distribution in France remain unsettled. Considering especially the last two decades of the old regime, the 1770s and 1780s, social historians detect a widening of the gap between rich and poor and tend to project that trend backward in time. A political scientist, Arthur Stein, attempting to theorize about the income effects of war in general, suggests a democratizing effect, that wars tend to augment employment and to bring price effects more harmful to the rich than the poor. But the evidence that speaks to these issues—primarily the failure of mobilization to produce higher wages, which failure indicates a large scale of prewar unemployment and underemployment—is weak. Specific manifestations of immiseration or democratization remain poorly articulated, both in the theory about what should be looked for and in our knowledge of French history in these years. Impressionistic sources stress a popular misery pervasive in time but run counter to persuasive evidence of aggregate economic growth. France went to war at a point close to the apogee of per capita incomes in the old regime, after several decades of vigorous growth in trade and some industries, and of agricultural output at least keeping pace with population growth. The evidence is not very sensitive to shifts in trend, but growth seems to have persisted through the war and until the second half of the 1760s. While there is a tilt toward Stein's case and good reason to suspect that the scale of poverty in the 1750s and 1760s has been exaggerated, these issues remain unresolved.

Hence the private rather than the public opinion of scholars about old regime war is upheld. In the large cluster of elements constituting the old regime economy, war did not disrupt. It was, if anything, one of the preservatives of the long-run immobility of this system, of the persistent equilibrium of the seventeenth and eighteenth centuries that has come to be called the old regime. But two qualifications are needed. The first is that this war had some effect on the series ordinarily used to detect trend in the old regime: some effect on the money stock, prices, and interest rates. These effects underscore the short- and medium-run variability of this regime, the fact that the equilibrium encompassed a constant rearrangement of elements, a high mobility behind immobility. The second qualification, a more important one, is that all these judgments refer to the immediate impact of this war. The long-run effect is another matter.

If the immediate economic effects of this war were not profound, the short- and long-run financial effects were. Because the public sector bulked large in the old regime economy, the financial effects had economic ramifications. And because financial issues and institutions cannot be separated from political issues and institutions, so too there were political effects. If old regime warfare was limited or controlled, in the way military historians ordinarily argue, and if France's part in this war was a limited military, political, and economic enterprise, as evidence surveyed here suggests, there are nevertheless ways in which this war was neither limited nor under control. Here we leave the territory in which French participation in the Seven Years War may stand for the effects of old regime war in general and enter a territory in which our attention is drawn almost entirely to French history. It is true that the financial issues in the Seven Years War are not unique. French borrowing between 1756 and 1762, for example, contributed to the further development of capital markets, as had happened in earlier wars also, and thus to the eventual development, in the nineteenth century, of markets primed to the mobilization of funds for investment in capital goods contributing to sustained economic growth. And this war revived the tensions that every occasion for increased taxation brought to the surface in the French polity and in every other old regime polity. The belief that taxes, or at least additional taxes, constituted a usurpation was not limited to France. But these issues are secondary in importance to the ways in which the Seven Years War was, for France, an event of transcendent long-run importance.

The story has another level of significance as well. An earlier remark—"governments tend to spend more than they take in"—reminds us that the account of French finances in the eighteenth century speaks also to the general problem of large deficits and debts. Unaccountably, historians have paid little sustained attention to this tendency, which, whenever it is present in serious form, undermines the possibility that a political status quo may persist. The way in which a government finances its operations is ordinarily a fundamental feature of its basic laws. This is so because people take paying for government very seriously. Large deficits and debts call the adequacy of existing fiscal practices into question, and thereby call into question elementary structures upon which a status quo rests. They provide an opportunity to rethink those structures, and in rethinking lies the potential for fundamental change. To say this is to recognize a built-in tendency toward undermining any regime and every regime, to identify one of the motors of history. To say this is also to recognize why, intuitively, those who are conservative in outlook loath deficits and debts, and why those who are progressive or revolutionary tolerate them.

In a certain dosage, radiation leaves the individual with a few immediate signs of illness, signs that gradually grow more pronounced and eventually take hold, robbing the organism of life. Here the organism is the old regime, the warring state that fought wars for territory and prestige, the monarchy in which the king professed to enjoy absolute but not despotic powers, the regime of social hierarchy conveyed most effectively in privilege taking the form of access to positions of political influence and opportunities for tax avoidance, the polity in which the idea of monarchy was so thoroughly habitual in public thought that the most radical calls for reform assumed an enlightened despot. The exposure came in the Seven Years War. Its effects began to reveal themselves immediately, and they were also deferred. The crisis came in 1789.

Like all organisms, the old regime in France blended a measure of sickness with a measure of health. Not everyone was content with the leading characteristics of this regime. But the criticisms of it that preyed on the minds of people in the 1740s and early 1750s were fragmented. To some the regime seemed to fall short of Britain in the basic liberties that it guaranteed or in the extent to which the despotic tendencies of royal authority were tempered by constitutional restraints or parlementary powers. To other critics this regime suffered from an ineffectual king, a man who hid his talents too well, or who had few to begin. For them, what was needed was not less but more royal authority, exercised in a certain manner thought to be enlightened, which is to say, exercised in a way that harmonized with some new ideas about basic patterns in Nature and humankind. An insider, Argenson, despaired because the court seemed utterly corrupt. An outsider, Rousseau, hoped for a redistribution of wealth from the rich to the poor. Louis XV was so little troubled by this growing barrage of ideas about change that he tolerated a censor who did not censor, Malesherbes; he allowed the publication of a unified collection of reformist ideas, in the *Encyclo-pédie*; and he let the parlements resist his will on matters religious, political, and financial at their pleasure. These are elements of a great mid-century sampling of remedies, which might have altered fundamental characteristics of the old regime in a peaceful way, so that the old regime could evolve. Many ideas for basic reforms were present. But something intervened. Something happened to stiffen resistance to reform. What? One answer has been offered by Dale Van Kley, who argues that an old religious dispute, inaugurated by the 1713 Bull Unigenitus, came to life in 1751 and was intensified in 1757 by the attempted assassination of Louis XV by a confused, and mad, domestic servant who believed himself to have lofty motives. For Van Kley the issues of fundamental importance were religious; they centered on the structure and theology of the Catholic church (Gallican or ultramontane, Jansenist or orthodox). The religious is-sues blended into politics so that the struggle between the Jansenist and Gallican parlements and the orthodox archbishop of Paris, sec-onded by the king, which worked itself out by 1765 in a victory for the parlements, was transformed into a political struggle in which the issue was the location of sovereignty. Having defeated the king in the religious struggle, the parlementaires took the king on in a battle for the right to make law.

Here another answer is given. What intervened was the Seven Years War, and more especially two decisions in policy. The first of these, rather hastily reached, constituted a decision in 1755 and 1756 to fund the war from credit rather than taxes. Even the small additions to the taxes adopted for 1756 provided an occasion for strenuous parlementary objections, an insolent expression of the French aversion toward taxation as understood by the parlemen-taires. The king and his ministers yielded, demanding the taxes they had asked for but declining to add enough more to pay for the war. The second policy decision, much more carefully planned, con-sisted of a resolution to preserve the sanctity of the French debt, to avoid any and all measures used in the past for scaling down the debt. The first decision fostered the growth of the debt so that by 1763 France owed a debt-in-securities as large as the overall debt left by the wars of Louis XIV. If other elements are added in—the value of venal offices chief among them—then the 1763 debt was larger even than the 1714 debt, in terms of its constant value magnitude and perhaps its part of national output. The second decision assured that this debt would be allowed a free rein in exercising its influence on the polity, the economy, and the finances. The most straightforward way to identify this novelty is to point to its budgetary character. Before the Seven Years War the French treasury spent about 30 percent of revenues on debt service, consisting mostly of interest payments. After the war the treasury had to spend more than 60 percent of revenues, still chiefly to pay interest.

This vast growth of the debt—which was the leading and specific cause of the financial and economic problems that France faced after 1763—occurred both because France elected to fight yet another war, funding it from credit rather than from taxes, and because the financial authorities led by Machault understood their charge so poorly that they failed to seize opportunities to reduce debt service charges, instead introducing policies that would increase those charges. The want of training among the financial authorities in finance led to blunders, of which the greatest was Machault's plan to convert the perpetual annuities into life annuities at a time when the yield on the debt, and thus the cost of debt service, might have been reduced significantly. The first five loans floated in the Seven Years War—for a total of 168 million l.t.—were all life annuity lotteries and loans. They reversed the effect of the Law system, which had reduced the interest rate on the royal debt, and they needlessly replaced low yields with high. Inefficiency and peculation undoubtedly contributed to the financial problem. But this search into fresh documents has not turned up evidence that the tax collection overhead was much higher in France than in Britain. The administrative monarchy does not seem to have been as corrupt as its critics said, or to be very precise, the scale of corruption that can be documented is not large enough to explain France's financial problems.

The central action that initiated the downfall of the old regime arose both within things characteristic of this regime and within things uncharacteristic of it. Among the first, it arose from the decision to go to war one more time and to avoid the tension associated with tax increases large enough to pay for the war. Among the second, it arose from a departure in policy, a shift away from the pragmatic and flexible attitude of prior French governments, and of other old regime states such as Britain and the Dutch Republic, toward a policy asserting the sanctity of the royal or public debt. Even though a write-down had been paid in advance, in the form of excessively generous interest rates, most especially in the life annuity loans, France would preserve the full value of the debt. An annulment was out of the question, but the authorities also rejected a tax on interest, a negotiated write-down, an induced inflation through the monetization of part of the debt, or any other measure that would have brought the bulk of this debt down to a level that could be tolerated in the long run.

Thus this debt too large became an issue of overweening importance to everyone in France, to the privileged elite threatened with losing a shrinking quantity of remaining tax benefits; to the king and his ministers who knew the scale of the problem and were loath to share that knowledge; to the parlementaires, who saw themselves as defenders of public interest and who doubted the king's vague but consistent claims about the gravity of the fiscal crisis; to taxpayers who resented the royal levies in any event and who believed, mistakenly, that the burden of taxation was rising. Fiscal issues had never been matters of merely secondary importance in the old regime. But in 1763 in France, fiscality in general and the debt in particular swept the central theater clear of rivals. For the next thirty years and more, no one would be able to think seriously about any major political reform without considering its costs. Moreover, the debt assured that the downward trend of interest rates, which France had enjoyed for a century and a half before 1750, would be reversed, to be replaced by rates pushed up by the government's compelling need to borrow. Each year the government would throw a large sum onto French capital markets by paying interest and amortization to its creditors—in 1769 to the tune of 196 million. But because the necessary expenses of government—defense, civil administration, the court—could not be forgone, and because the burden of debt service was so large, the treasury would also have to go to the capital markets each year to borrow large sums. The era of large peacetime deficits was at hand. The government's need to increase taxes in order to meet its expenses would also assure a constant tension in the polity. No longer were the ordinary revenues—or even the ordinary revenues supplemented by one, two, or three vingtièmes—sufficient to meet expenses. Now the government needed, but the people and the parlements were loath to give, new taxes to be assessed in war and peace.

These tensions over the scale of the debt and taxation came to the surface during the Seven Years War, in conflict between the parlements and the king and in a small cluster of anonymous books beginning with Mirabeau's *Théorie de l'impôt* and continuing through several responses to Mirabeau. Mirabeau felt a passionate hatred toward the tax farmers, wished to resolve the bitter disputes around taxation by replacing a variegated system with a single tax, and believed that from abstract logic he could articulate the natural laws of public finance so that policy might be altered to accord with them. The debate renewed itself with the publication in May 1763 of another plan for a single tax, Roussel de la Tour's version of the *capitation*, which would levy all taxes in cash rather than in service, and in more than forty pamphlets published in the months that followed. This part of the new tension over finance resembles the reformism of the 1740s and 1750s, which the king had tolerated. Again Louis XV and his censor allowed debate to take place and became annoyed only when Darigrand attacked the tax farmers in a particularly scurrilous manner, after which it seemed wise to restrict the discussion to a parlementary commission.

Like the earlier reformers, Roussel and his fellow debaters proposed a barrage of ideas about how the taxes should be modified. They were thinking still in the context of the 1740s and 1750s, when the issue at hand seemed to be to identify the reform promising the most, to single out the most appropriate panacea. They did not yet know the scale of the debt, and they did not fully understand its implications. Yet they did sense that the moment for some major transformation of the financial apparatus was at hand. Briefly everyone was a reformer, everyone agreed that the existing system could not stand unreformed. Even the king entertained proposals with far reaching implications: review of the Calas case, which raised issues of religious orthodoxy and of customary judicial practice, and freeing the grain trade, which risked, and in the event revived, the shortage of grain—or the apprehension of shortage—that would mobilize the people in bread riots. And the king also considered the possibility of fundamental reforms in the finances.

This debate overlapped a confrontation between king and parlement on an issue as old as the parlement, the claim that the edicts of the king were subject to review by the parlements to determine whether they harmonized with the basic law of the land. In the old regime the parlements' assertion of this right had been beaten back but not obliterated so that now and again they revived the claim. In 1756 and 1760 the reassertion occurred over fiscal and taxation issues—should the king be permitted to levy new or to increase old taxes?—and in 1763 over whether some of the taxes laid on for the war would be sustained and whether financial matters would remain secret and under royal control. The parlements, led still by Paris but now seconded vigorously by a few provincial assemblies and by courts with specialized responsibilities, claimed not merely the right to review royal edicts and declarations but also the right to review administrative procedures, even to initiate policy. The king resisted, wanting both to augment the ordinary revenues and to maintain secrecy about the things that remained unknown, such as the scale of the debt. This confrontation persisted until 1789. Its immediate and abiding legacy was to revivify the belief that the taxes were too heavy, when in fact they were reduced, by 1768, to a level as low as that at any other time in the eighteenth century.[2] The burden of taxes in force in 1768 was not great enough to sustain the regime, but the king found himself in a position where he had to fight merely to struggle back to the level of taxation that had prevailed earlier.

In the customary judgment, the first round of this struggle is said to have been won by the parlements, which beat back the plan formulated by Bertin and revised by Laverdy to raise taxes and to survey the lands of France. This interpretation is in error. In truth the king won more than the parlement in late 1763 and early 1764, for he won the extension of the two *vingtièmes*. And he preserved secrecy about the debt, the size of which was a problem fully as fraught with risk as Mirabeau had claimed in predicting that bankruptcy would bring a watershed, even the destruction of the state. Documents in the possession of foreign powers, which are copies of documents drafted by French officials but apparently destroyed by fires in the archives, and the collection of *états* published in 1788 by Mathon de la Cour, reveal that royal servants, and presumably the king himself, knew the scale of the debt. Thus the king may be presumed to have known what he could not afford to reveal, that the total debt was larger than it had been at Louis XIV's death. He successfully prevented the parlements from learning the amount of the debt, from learning the magnitude of a problem the king believed,

[2] James C. Riley, "French Finances, 1727-1768," forthcoming, *Journal of Modern History* (1987).

optimistically and mistakenly, that he could resolve. But if Louis XV won the first round, he lost the second, in which both the parlementary commission appointed to investigate reform and the cadastre came to nothing, so that no way was found to reform the finances or to reduce the debt to a manageable scale.

Both in the confrontation between parlement and king and in the debate inaugurated in one form by Mirabeau and another by Roussel de la Tour, the participants resorted to a new language of political discourse. They spoke openly in public exchanges of the nation and the state and the people rather than of the monarchy and the king's subjects. They identified and asserted liberties and made the claim of profound liberties able to withstand the royal will, even if they agreed more readily about the identity of old liberties—the secrecy of personal finance and the right not to have economic activity compromised by taxes—than of new. They spoke of patriotism, of cash equality before the tax law, of fundamental changes in the society and the polity. They spoke in what we have become accustomed to regard as the language of 1789. In using so many of the same words and phrases, they signal the advanced nature of political discourse in the 1760s.

The speakers—these putative revolutionaries of the 1760s—were both the personnel and the beneficiaries of the old regime. They might bandy about every possible reform, but the range of the reforms they might adopt was narrowed by the threat that so many of the reforms posed to the old regime. The king had been engaged in a campaign against privilege, a campaign too seldom noticed. It took the form both of a shift toward taxes incorporating fewer opportunities for privilege and legal avoidance and a squeezing of venal officeholders, who received lower yields in their *gages* than ordinary rentiers and who performed administrative services for returns smaller than obtained by entrepreneurs in trade or banking. Those with privilege wished to reassert its value, to limit access— which is part of a seigneurial reaction—and to augment their power at the expense of the king. Precious few of the proponents of reform occupied positions that would not be damaged by any major overhaul of the regime. And although the call to principle was common, passionate, and often sincere, it was also fragmented into nearly as many visions of reform as there were visionaries. In the end, the idea of reform was less powerful than was self-interest.

The debt too large, the debt of 1763, eliminated fiscal freedom of movement. Every effort by the king and his ministers, who alone in France knew the scale of the problem, to diminish it within the terms of their cautious approach to the sanctity of public credit guaranteed a confrontation with the parlementaires, who wished to defend that most fundamental of French liberties, the right not to pay more taxes, as well as to safeguard their own interests, tied up with privilege and venality. Thus the struggle occurred at the brink. The Seven Years War, which cost on an annual basis more than twice as much as the preceding war, transformed the perpetually worrisome fiscal problem of old regime France into a financial crisis with immediate and large political and economic implications. It exposed the old regime to radiation, which took the form not of enlightened ideas or of reformist insolence, but of a familiar problem in finance. The crowning irony is that the treatment and solution—a debt conversion or reduction on the British or Dutch model—was also familiar. But the guardians of the regime, who included the king, his ministers, the parlementaires, and many of their critics outside government, would not accept such measures. They appear to have believed that by preserving the sanctity of the debt they were securing the regime whose benefits they enjoyed, or that they were establishing a principle of heroic importance. In truth, however, their actions put the very regime at risk. When the financial crisis would finally come to a head, between 1787 and 1793, it would bring down not only the king and the parlements but also the political and social institutions with which they had surrounded and safeguarded themselves. In the meantime this huge debt would be allowed unrestricted influence over the economy, to foster inflation, to push interest rates up, to squeeze out investment, and therefore to help transform the economic growth of the decades up to the 1770s into recession, and finally economic crisis.

ESTIMATING THE PRICE TREND IN FRENCH TRADE

Price data on French imports and exports are in short supply. Even in the exceptionally dynamic sector of colonial trade, little is known about prices in French ports for such basic goods as sugar, coffee, and cocoa.[1] Because of the likelihood of shifts in relative prices, it is unsatisfactory to use another French price series as a proxy. The only series that might be used in this manner, which represent the trend of prices in wheat or a cluster of several grains, would fail to capture such shifts.

Since the problem lies in measuring goods in international trade, it is preferable to turn to another series intended to measure the movement of prices among such commodities. That index would weight grains at a much lower value, because of their lesser importance, and would bring into consideration some of the many items involved in international trade. Several indexes of this type are supplied by N. W. Posthumus for the Amsterdam entrepôt. Two are of particular interest: 1) the unweighted series of Amsterdam trade goods during 1620-1864, and 2) the weighted series of Amsterdam trade goods during the same period, in which the weights are determined by multiplying the quantities traded by price.[2] Posthumus suggests that the unweighted series would be preferable to the weighted series because it is more nearly a measure of the price trend, while the weighted series measures trade volume. Nevertheless, the curves drawn by the two series do not deviate in a significant manner during the eighteenth century.[3]

Of course, an unweighted series is not altogether devoid of weights. In this instance Posthumus selected forty-four items rep-

---

[1] Jean Tarrade, *Le commerce colonial de la France à la fin de l'ancien régime: L'évolution du régime de "l'Exclusif" de 1763 à 1789* (2 vols.; Paris, 1972), II, 771-72, supplies some prices for 1749-1769, but other data are scarce and fragmentary.

[2] N. W. Posthumus, *Inquiry into the History of Prices in Holland* (2 vols.; Leiden, 1946-1964), I, lxxxv-ci.

[3] *Ibid.*, I, ci, compare columns A and H.

resenting harvest and non-harvest goods from the range of goods for which price data were available during much of the long era he wished to survey. He did not introduce any weighting among the forty-four, but these items, from wheat to soap,[4] may be clustered by type to discover the relative weights that emerge from this selection and from the happenstance of price information survival. Presumably prices survived because these goods were of leading importance, and that presumption is supported by comparing Posthumus' list to general knowledge about goods in trade. These weights can be compared with the distribution of goods in French trade to discover whether the items most commonly found in Amsterdam trade are also the items most commonly found in French trade. Table A.1 places weights from Posthumus' unweighted and weighted series beside a breakdown of French trade by value in 1716 and 1787.[5]

TABLE A.1
Weights in French and Amsterdam Trade Compared
(in percentages)

	French trade		Amsterdam trade		weights implied in unweighted series
	1716	*1787*	*1700-1759*	*1760-1789*	
Raw materials	14.8	22.0	18.8	19.5	25.0
Manufactures	26.2	25.9	25.8	25.0	29.5
Food and drink	25.3	17.2	22.0	25.1	20.5
Colonial goods and tobacco	19.7	29.6	28.8	26.3	11.4
Miscellaneous	13.6	4.9	4.6	5.0	13.6
TOTALS	99.6	99.6	100.0	100.9	100.0

NOTE: Totals vary from 100 because of rounding.

4 *Ibid.*, I, xcv.
5 A. Foville, "Le commerce extérieur de la France depuis 1716," *Bulletin de statistique et de législation comparée*, 13 (1883), 48-71, provides these values for seventeen categories (each beginning with the following terms: 1. bois, 2. matières, 3. objets manufacturés, 4. autres articles d'industrie, 5. comestibles, 6. boissons, 7. bestiaux, 8. bêtes, 9. drogueries propres à la peinture, 10. drogueries médicinales, 11. épiceries, 12. tabacs, 13. marchandises diverses, 14. noirs, 15. marchandises provenant du commerce français en Asie, 16. marchandises des colonies françaises de l'Amérique, and

The relevant comparisons to be made are between the first and third columns, between the second and fourth, and between the last column and the first two. In the first comparison, early century trade weights were similar except that Amsterdam was more extensively involved in the colonial trade. By late century, as the second comparison reveals, France had caught up in the colonial trade, and Amsterdam had enlarged its movements of food and drink. Both these comparisons indicate a high degree of similarity in the distribution of trade goods between the French and the Amsterdam trade baskets. It is in the third comparison that some differences are revealed. The implied weights in Posthumus' forty-four goods deviate from actual weights in French trade especially for tobacco: a single entry undervalues the importance of this item in trade. In other areas Posthumus elected to list several items even when some of them (Leiden textiles) hardly figured in Amsterdam's trade. Drink in general and wine in particular are also underrepresented in these implied weights, but that is compensated for by the longer list of food items.

Since Posthumus' two curves follow each other in close order during the eighteenth century, we can conclude that the lesser similarity between the last column and the first two does not mask either relative price shifts or trade baskets with significantly different price histories. The close similarity between the two curves, and the close similarity between the French trade baskets and the weighted Amsterdam trade baskets establishes the value of using Posthumus' series to gauge the trend of prices in French trade. Since the match of the Amsterdam weighted prices is closer, that series is used here.

---

17. piastres). Posthumus numbers items from 1 through 44. Each series has been reorganized for Table A.1. See also Michel Morineau, "Trois contributions au colloque de Göttingen: II. 1750, 1787: Un changement important des structures de l'exportation française dans le monde saisi d'après les états de la balance du commerce," in Ernst Hinricks et al., eds., *Vom Ancien Régime zur Französischen Revolution* (Göttingen, 1978), 402, for a breakdown for 1750 in a somewhat different form.

CALCULATING THE PRINCIPAL OF LIFE ANNUITY LOANS

Lacking comprehensive records on life annuity and tontine loans, it is possible only to estimate. For life annuities the procedure used here assumes that all contracts were on one nominee (when in fact a small fraction of contracts was on more than one) and uses the average nominee age chosen by investors in the life annuity loan of 1771.[1] Both assumptions tend to underestimate the life annuity principal, the first because multiple-nominee contracts remained active longer, and the second because investors probably chose younger average nominees in most loans. To create a schedule of extinctions, I have adopted a table of life expectancy of a female population as modified by a two-year period of selection effects.[2] Treating the life expectancy at age seventeen as the initiation point, I built a curve of the annual decrement, taking eighty-five as the maximum age to which any nominee survived. That decrement, expressed as a percentage, has then been multiplied by the subscription total for each life annuity and known life annuity lottery.[3] Thus to estimate the unpaid principal of the life annuity loan of November 1761 as of 1764, I found the decrement after three years (5 percent) and multiplied its inverse (95 percent) by the subscription total, 43.5 million.[4] Results were then summed for 1753 and 1764. Both estimates exclude lotteries before 1755 with prizes paid in life annuities and life annuity debts contracted on behalf of the central government by provincial or local governments.

---

[1] See George Alter and James C. Riley, "How to Bet on Lives: A Guide to Life Contingent Contracts in Early Modern Europe," forthcoming, *Research in Economic History* (1986).

[2] That is, Table A7b in Alter and Riley, where the method of construction is explained. The appropriate column is that for no interest.

[3] From Marcel Marion, *Histoire financière de la France depuis 1715* (5 vols.; Paris, 1927-1928), I, 472-73. Some modifications in data used were adopted from the documents found in foreign archives discussed in Chapter 2.

[4] The decrements are interpolated from Alter and Riley, Table A7b.

Between 1696 and 1759 France drew 125.81 million in subscriptions from tontine loans.[5] In these, the principal remaining to be paid depends on the age distribution, which was arranged in each of the nine tontines in classes. In approximate terms, I estimate that the unpaid tontine balance amounted in 1753 to at least 50 million, and in 1764 (including the 4.6 million tontine of 1759) to at least 85 million.

[5] Marion, *Histoire financière*, I, 473.

LIST OF MANUSCRIPT SOURCES CITED

ALGEMEEN RIJKSARCHIEF, THE HAGUE

Archief Fagel

1565 Mémoires de ce qui s'est passé de particulier en France . . . (May-Dec. 1752)

1566 The same (Oct. 1753-Feb. 1754)

1567 Mémoires critiques de l'année 1752 concernant l'état présent des affaires du Roiaume en général

1571 French debt, 1750

1572 Memoir on the king's personal finances

Archief Pieter Steyn

17 Diplomatic correspondence 1750-1792

Legatiearchief, Eerste Afdeling, Frankrijk

776 French subsidies to foreign powers, 1730-1750

779 Mémoires concernant ce qui s'est passé de secret et de particulier en France . . . (Feb.-Sept. 1753)

783 Prospective *état* for 1751 and other *états* for 1751-1755

784 *Etat*, 1752

786 Observations et réflexions critiques et politiques sur les affaires des finances en 1750 et années suivantes

787 *Etats*, 1744-1746

788 *Etats*, 1747-1749

789 *Etat*, 1750

793 Memoir on French commerce, 1752

ARCHIVES NATIONALES, PARIS

P Series *Etats* for a number of *generalités* and *élections*, 1750-1763

2AQ9 Papiers des banquiers Laborde

BIBLIOTHÈQUE DE L'ARSENAL, PARIS

4062 Idée des finances, mostly 1745-1763 [Brunet]

4063 Secrets des finances du royaume pour l'année 1747

4066A *Etat*, 1756-1762
4066B Memoir on financial practices
4489   Memoirs on finances

BIBLIOTHÈQUE MAZARINE, PARIS

2767 Observations sur les opérations de finance, par le Sr. Dufort
 de Lagraulet, 1759
2825 *Etat*, 1755-1761

BIBLIOTHÈQUE NATIONALE

Joly de Fleury Papers 577, 1079, 1432, 1446
Ms. fr. 11162 Memoirs on taxation
Ms. fr. 14081 *Etat*, 1755-1762
Ms. fr. 14101 Plan de finance formé dès 1769 . . .

BRITISH LIBRARY, LONDON, MANUSCRIPT DEPARTMENT

Additional Manuscripts

6818   Despatches of Lord Holdernesse, 1760
25597 *Etat*, 1755-1762
35498 Trudaine's Etat des finances de la France
38331, folios 146-152 Summary of Trudaine's project and *état*
38335, folios 254-259 Debt repayment proposals
38339, folios 287-293 Notes on French finances, c. 1763
38468 *Etats*, 1756-1762
40759 *Etat*, 1756-1762

Egmont Manuscripts

3465 Intelligence reports from Michael Hatton, 1754-1760

Stowe Manuscripts

86 *Etat*, 1756-1762
87 Copy of Arsenal 4066B

ELEUTHERIAN-MILLS HISTORICAL LIBRARY,
WILMINGTON, DELAWARE

Papers of P. S. Du Pont de Nemours

Series A Correspondence
Series E Autobiography

HAUS-, HOF- UND STAATSARCHIV, VIENNA

Böhm-Supplement, Frankreich

960-w922 Mémoires rassemblés par le Comte Charles de Zinzendorf . . . , 1764, 1767, & 1769
961-w923 Memoir on the French navy, 1751
992-w939 Trudaine's manuscript, January 1751
991-B717 *Etats, 1741-1742, 1749*

Staatskanzlei.5.Notenwechsel mit der Hofkammer

252 Memoirs on French finances

HUNTINGTON LIBRARY, SAN MARINO, CALIFORNIA

Stowe Collection: Grenville Correspondence

STG Box 16 Correspondence

DET KONGELIGE BIBLIOTEK, COPENHAGEN,
MANUSCRIPT DEPARTMENT

Ny kgl. S.

495 (a)-(j) Mémoire[s] sur la France, in 10 volumes

KONINKLIJKE BIBLIOTHEEK, BRUSSELS, MANUSCRIPT
DEPARTMENT

3132 Memoir on financial administration in the seventeenth century
10744 *Etat, 1756-1762*
15723 Memoir on finances, c. 1779

MANUSCRIPT SOURCES CITED

KUNGLIGA BIBLIOTEKET, STOCKHOLM, MANUSCRIPT DEPARTMENT

Engeströmska Samling

C.XIV.1.24 *Etat*, 1755-1761

KRESS LIBRARY OF BUSINESS AND ECONOMICS, HARVARD BUSINESS SCHOOL, BOSTON

Taux des gros fruits commencé le 20 Juin 1753 et finis le 18 Xbre 1762 [*sic*]

MINUTIER CENTRAL DES NOTAIRES DE PARIS

Etude LXXXIV, various numbers, dealing with foreign acquisitions of French securities

NORTHAMPTONSHIRE RECORD OFFICE, NORTHAMPTON

Fitzwilliam Manuscripts (Milton) (Edmund Burke Papers)

A.xxxii.21 Summary of projected accounts for 1765
A.xxxii.22 Summary of *état*, 1759

PUBLIC RECORD OFFICE, LONDON, CHANCERY LANE

SP 9 86 *Etat*, 1756-1762

RIGSARKIVET, COPENHAGEN

Ges. Arkiv, Frankrig B

855 Diplomatic correspondence, 1763

RIKSARKIVET, STOCKHOLM

Skoklostersamling

E9027 Idée générale du commerce Etranger de la nation française ... en 1753

246

MANUSCRIPT SOURCES CITED

UNIVERSITY LIBRARY, LONDON, PALÆOGRAPHY ROOM

127(2) *Etats*, 1756-1763

INDEX

Affaires extraordinaires: explained, 55, 135, 138-41, 145; amount of, 146; mentioned, 136, 181

Agriculture: markets, 8, 12-13; output and performance, 15-18, 21-23; problems, 16-17; leases in and inflation, 35-36; effects of war on, 79-80; during war, 128-29, 130

Alter, George, historian, 175

Amsterdam: grain prices in, 7, 8, 9-12, 95-97

Archives: destruction of, xx

Argenson, René-Louis de Voyer d', 220, 229

Armançon River, xx, 95

Army: elements of, 76; in war, 76-80, 82; size, 77; recruitment and exemptions, 78; reforms of after war, 82

Bachaumont, Louis Petit de, memoirist, 197, 199, 207

Baehrel, René, historian, xvi, 4, 9

Bairoch, Paul, economic historian: estimates of French economic performance, 14-15, 18, 20, 22, 69n90

Baker, Keith, historian, xix, 219, 220

Balance du Commerce, 105n12, 107n13, 108, 121-26 *passim*

Balance of trade. *See* Trade

Bankruptcies, 117-18, 163. *See also* Debt

Barbier, E.-J.-F., memoirist, 194n9, 197, 199

Baudeau, Nicolas, economic writer, 173, 205

Baulant, Micheline, historian, 9

Beaujon, Goossens, bankers, 168

Beik, Paul, historian, 214

Beneficent war, 101. *See also* Stein, Arthur A.

Bertin, Henri, controller general: tax reform plan, 212, 213, 214, 234; dismissed, 215; mentioned, 66, 149, 158

Bien, David, historian, 181

Borrowing: effect of war on, 140-42, 148-61 *passim*; and output, 157; policies compared, 173. *See also* Debt; Loans; Short-term credit

Bosher, J. F., historian, 41

Boullongne, Jean Nicholas de, controller general, 149, 151, 158, 187

Braudel, Fernand, historian, 25

Bullion. *See* Money supply

Business cycle. *See* Economy, cycles

Butel, Paul, historian, xvi, 226

Cadastre. *See* Land survey

Calas case, 76, 192, 222, 233

Calonne, Charles Alexandre de, controller general, 41

Calsabigi, economic writer, 88

Canada, 105, 189

Cantillon, Richard, economic writer, 159

Capital markets, 156-57, 171, 188

Capitation: characterized, 47, 51, 195; collection costs, 60, 62; increase proposed, 212; mentioned, 52-55 *passim*, 59, 66-70 *passim*, 179

Carrière, Charles, historian, 24, 104, 112, 117, 121, 226

Cash balances, 34-35

Charleville: prices in, 95-99 *passim*, 225

Choiseul, Etienne François de, statesman, 81

Clamageran, Jean-Jules, historian: interpretation of finances, 40, 41, 51, 52; and accounts, 133; on revenues and expenditures, 138

Colardeau, poet, 102

Colbert, Jean-Baptiste, statesman, 41, 150

Cole, W. A., economist, 19, 20

Commercial services: and economy, 21; value of, 123, 125; during war, 126, 128

Compagnie des Indes, 57, 70, 76, 177, 178n40; debts of, 182-83

Compensatory trade: hypothesis of, 112-17, 224; tested, 117-21

Controllers general: public view of, 66; shortcomings, 158, 159, 161, 190-91. *See also* individual controllers general

Corvisier, André, historian, 76, 85, 103

Cour des aides, 211, 212, 214